CAMBRIDGE IBERIAN AND
LATIN AMERICAN STUDIES

GENERAL EDITOR

P. E. RUSSELL, F.B.A.

EMERITUS PROFESSOR OF SPANISH STUDIES,
UNIVERSITY OF OXFORD

Land and Society in Golden Age Castile

Land and Society in Golden Age Castile

DAVID E. VASSBERG

ASSOCIATE PROFESSOR,
PAN AMERICAN UNIVERSITY

WITHDRAWN

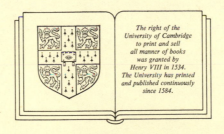

The right of the
University of Cambridge
to print and sell
all manner of books
was granted by
Henry VIII in 1534.
The University has printed
and published continuously
since 1584.

CAMBRIDGE UNIVERSITY PRESS

CAMBRIDGE
LONDON   NEW YORK   NEW ROCHELLE
MELBOURNE   SYDNEY

Published by the Press Syndicate of the University of Cambridge
The Pitt Building, Trumpington Street, Cambridge CB2 1RP
32 East 57th Street, New York, NY 10022, USA
296 Beaconsfield Parade, Middle Park, Melbourne 3206, Australia

First published 1984

Printed in Great Britain by
the University Press, Cambridge

Library of Congress catalogue card number: 83-2029

British Library cataloguing in publication data
Vassberg, David E.
Land and society in Golden Age Castile.
– (Cambridge Iberian and Latin American studies)
1. Real property – Castile (Kingdom) – History
2. Real property – Castile (Kingdom) – Social aspects
I. Title
333.3′2′094635   HD 771.5
ISBN 0 521 25470 1

Contents

Tables

Maps

Author's Foreword

Because of my background I have always had a special interest in agricultural history. I grew up on a farm, and at one point in my checkered career I dropped out of school to work for five years as a self-employed farmer before returning to the university to complete my doctoral studies in history. In school, my first-hand acquaintance with rural life caused me to ask many questions about the agricultural history of the lands I studied. It troubled me when I could not find answers to certain questions that I thought basic to understanding the agrarian economy. It often seemed to me that the scholars who wrote about agriculture and stockraising did not really understand the problems of the rural world.

I did my first serious reading on the history of Golden Age Spain in the summer of 1967, and I was shocked at the paucity of scholarly studies about the rural history of early modern Castile. Today, some fifteen years later, I would no longer be shocked, for a number of fine studies have been published in the interim. But there remain many questions to be answered. In this book I have tried to address some of the questions that have troubled me. Many other questions will have to be answered in subsequent studies. I hope that I can continue to work in the field for a long time to come, because I find it congenial, and, as the saying goes, the harvest is bounteous, but the laborers are few.

I am grateful for the financial support provided by Pan American University, by the National Endowment for the Humanities, and by the Comité Conjunto Hispano-Norteamericano para Asuntos Educativos y Culturales. I would also like to thank the many archivists and librarians who facilitated my research, both in Spain and in the US. And finally, I want to express my gratitude for the unfailing support of my family. My two young sons were thrust several times into Spanish primary schools for months at a time,

xi

while their father read documents in Spanish archives. It was not always easy for them, but they accepted the challenge with good grace. And my wife Liliane not only encouraged me with my work, she actually sat by my side as a co-researcher in Madrid, Granada, and Valladolid, thus greatly increasing my productivity, and making the long hours easier to bear. Some of the most pleasant memories of our marriage are related to our joint research activities. It is to Liliane that I dedicate this book.

Abbreviations

AAT	Archivo del Ayuntamiento de Trujillo
ACHGR	Archivo de la Chancillería de Granada
ACHVA	Archivo de la Chancillería de Valladolid
AGS	Archivo General de Simancas
AHN	Archivo Histórico Nacional (Madrid)
AM	Archivo de la Mesta (Madrid)
ant	antiguo
BN	Biblioteca Nacional (Madrid)
CG	Contadurías Generales
CJH	Consejo y Juntas de Hacienda
CMC	Contaduría Mayor de Cuentas
CR	Contaduría de la Razón
CSIC	Consejo Superior de Investigaciones Científicas
DC	Dirección de Cuentas
DGT	Dirección General del Tesoro
EH	Expedientes de Hacienda
FA (F)	Fernando Alonso (Fenecidos)
mod	moderno
mrs	maravedís
PC	Pleitos Civiles
pet	petición
SEVPEN	Service d'Édition et de Vente des Publications de l'Education Nationale

Glossary

abadengo: under ecclesiastical jurisdiction.

Actas: minutes of the Castilian Cortes.

alcaide: governor, warden.

alcalde: municipal official with certain administrative duties, but primarily functioning as a judge with civil and criminal jurisdiction.

almud: unit of area equal to half a *fanega*.

año y vez: biennial cropping.

aranzada: unit of area equal to 400 square *estadales*, or slightly over an acre.

arbitrista: reform writer of the sixteenth and seventeenth centuries.

arroba: unit of measure equal to 3.32 gallons of oil, or 4.26 gallons of wine.

asiento: written contract with the crown.

Audiencia: see Chancillería, below.

averiguación: inquiry, or report, for official purposes.

baldío: common, or crown property.

barbecho: fallow.

caballería: unit of area, originally the amount of land the crown usually granted a *caballero* (knight), normally 60 *fanegas* in Castile.

caballero: knight, member of the lesser nobility.

cadañeras, or *tierras cadañeras:* common lands requiring annual cultivation for continued possession.

cahiz: dry measure equal to 12 *fanegas*.

cañada: especially designated trail for transhumant herds and flocks.

carga: unit of area equal to 4 *fanegas*; dry measure equal to 3 or 4 *fanegas*.

carta de población: charter for the founding of a municipality.

cédula: royal order, or decree.

celemín: unit of area the twelfth part of a *fanega*, and equal to 48 square *estadales*; dry measure equal to one-twelfth of a *fanega*.

censo al quitar: redeemable mortgage.

censo enfitéutico: lease contract.

censo perpetuo: debt conversion, with a principal that could not be paid off.

Chancillería: Supreme Legal Tribunal. After 1505 there were two in Castile: one in Valladolid, and the other in Granada. Their jurisdictions were separated by the boundary line of the Tajo River.

comisión: commission, mandate, or charge.

complant: medieval contract conferring upon a peasant the ownership of half of a vineyard after he had planted and tended it for the proprietor for a certain number of years.

concejo: municipal council.

conversos: Jewish converts to Christianity, and their descendants.

corregidor: official of the crown placed at the head of a municipality, being president of the municipal council, and having extensive judicial, administrative, and financial powers.

Cortes: National Assembly of Castile, composed during the time of Philip II of delegates from eighteen major cities.

cortijo: farmstead.

coto: enclosed plot.

dehesa: enclosed plot (at least in theory), usually destined for pasture.

dehesa boyal: enclosed pasture reserved exclusively for draft animals, especially oxen.

derrota de mieses: custom of common stubble grazing.

ducado: unit of account, equal to 375 mrs.

ejido: multi-purpose common plot.

encomienda: grant of jurisdiction made by the crown to individuals and military orders, of lands conquered from the Moslems.

escribano: scrivener.

escudo: gold coin worth 350 mrs until 1566, and 400 mrs from then until the beginning of the seventeenth century.

estadal: unit of length equal to four *varas* (a *vara* varied in length, but was normally about 2.8 feet).

executoria: official dispatch; or sentence.

fanega: unit of dry measure equal to about an English bushel, or about a hundredweight of grain; unit of area originally equal to as much tilled ground as was necessary to sow a *fanega* of wheat, but usually standardized as 12 *celemines* or 576 square *estadales*, equal to about 1.59 acres.

fuero: law code; privilege or exemption granted to a certain province.

hidalgo: member of the lesser nobility.

huerta: land for garden or orchard crops; or irrigated land regardless of the crop.

jornalero: day laborer.

juez: magistrate.

labrador: independent peasant farmer.

maravedí (mr): unit of account, of depreciating value, used for calculating prices in sixteenth-century Castile.

marjal: unit of area equal to 100 square *estadales*, or 0.47 *tahullas*.

mayorazgo: entailed estate, or trust, a device used by the nobility to pass their property intact to succeeding generations of heirs.

mayordomo: chief steward, or majordomo.

Mesta: stock owners' association, notorious for the privileges it had obtained for its migratory flocks and herds.

millones, or *servicio de millones:* tax for rebuilding the Armada after the debacle of 1588.

monte: forest woodland.

Moriscos: Spaniards of Moorish ancestry.

Novísima recopilación: published Castilian law code.

obrada: as much ground as a pair of mules or oxen can plow in a day, usually standardized to an area of about 1.3 acres.

pago: well-defined, possibly even fenced, planting district.

peonada: unit of area equal to 0.65 *fanegas*.

pobre: poor.

pósito: public granary.

prado: meadow.

presura: squatter's right to use unoccupied land.

privilegio: royal grant, or privilege.

rastrojo: stubble remaining after grain harvest.

real: silver coin equal in value to 34 mrs.

realengo: under the direct authority of the crown.

regidor: municipal administrative official, or councilman.

Relaciones: answers to questionnaires sent by the royal government to all towns in Castile in the late 1570s.

repartimiento: apportionment of lands among settlers; or an assessment of taxes.

Repoblación: resettlement of Christian settlers on land conquered from the Moslems.

roza: fire clearing for slash-and-burn agriculture.

señorío: under seigneurial jurisdiction.

servicio: subsidy for the crown voted by the Cortes.

Siete partidas, or *Código de las partidas:* codification of law under the late thirteenth-century king Alfonso X.

solariego: village where the seigneur was also the landowner.

sorteo periódico: periodic allotment of common lands.

tahulla: unit of area equal to 1,600 square *varas*, or about 0.173 *fanegas*.

tasa: legal maximum price for grain.

término: territory under the jurisdiction of a municipality.

terrazgo: tribute of one-twelfth of the grain harvest paid by peasants to the seigneur, in recognition of his authority.

Tierra: territory of an intermunicipal union; also called a *comunidad de villa* [or *ciudad*] *y Tierra,* but usually referred to as a *mancomunidad* by modern historians.

tierras baldías: common lands, or crown lands.

tierras realengas: crown lands.

venta: sale, or bill of sale.

villa: municipality possessing juridical independence.

villazgo: attainment of *villa* status for a subject town or village.

yugada: as much ground as a yoke of oxen can plow in a day, the same as an *obrada*; in some places, the amount of land one could conveniently work with a yoke of oxen, usually standardized to 50 *fanegas*, or about 79½ acres.

yunta: meaning yoke; as a standard of measurement, it was the same as a *yugada*.

Introduction

In the sixteenth century Spain was the greatest power on earth. She enjoyed a preeminent position in Europe, and ruled over a vast overseas empire with immense resources. The Habsburg world hegemony during this period was supported primarily by a twofold economic base: taxation in Castile, and mining in America; the former far outranking the latter as a source of revenue. And in Castile it was agriculture that bore the brunt of the burden of supporting the Habsburg empire, for Castile was a rural society, with land the source of her wealth. Over 80 percent of her population lived in villages or small towns, and owed their livelihood to the growing of crops or the herding of animals. Even the great cities of Castile were parasites on the agropastoral economy, for there was little industry, and most industries that did exist (textiles, for example) were related to rural production. It was the toil of the peasant that produced the wealth of Golden Age Castile, and that supported her powerful and extravagant institutions.

Yet, we know comparatively little about the world of this all-important peasant, who constituted the foundation and the mass of Castilian society. Specialists in Spanish history have long deplored the paucity of information about early modern rural Spain. And despite the recent publication of a number of important studies on the subject, there are a host of questions remaining to be answered (Vassberg 1977).

One of the problems faced by scholars who deal with the subject is that the overwhelming majority of sixteenth-century Castilian peasants were illiterate, and illiterates tend not to leave records for posterity. Even if a peasant happened to be able to write, it was not normal for him to keep a record of his day-to-day activities. Ordinary people simply do not write things down unless special circumstances require them to do so. Of course there were chroniclers and other observers who kept records during this period, but most of them did not think that the activities of peasants deserved their attention. The peasant did not go completely unnoticed, though. We can learn about the life of rural inhabitants from certain governmental records and various other documents such as censuses, notorial records, and transcriptions of lawsuits. But nearly all of these relate to extraordinary circumstances, rather than to everyday activities, and we can never be sure how closely they reflect the reality of the peasant's life. Our documentary evidence could be likened to the tip of an iceberg; the iceberg itself a mass whose shape we cannot know from the shape of its tip alone (Freeman 1981).

This book is primarily about land and landownership. I think the importance of landownership to the life of the peasant is perfectly obvious. Land is the basis of agropastoral production. It is the medium in which crops are grown, and it provides the vegetation for grazing animals. It would be impossible to understand the society of early modern Castile without asking about landownership, for land was the means to agricultural and pastoral wealth, and to social prestige, as well. It is important, then, to ask: who owned the land? Who was the legal possessor, or the de facto possessor? And who enjoyed the fruits of the soil?

It is traditional to classify landowners according to their status as ecclesiastics, nobles, urban middle-class investors (the bourgeoisie), or peasants. But this classification is not complete: where does one put crown lands, for example? In some respects crown lands can be treated as the private property of a reigning member of the nobility; but in other respects they have the characteristics of publicly owned property, particularly in Castile, as we shall see. And where does one put municipally owned property, which was treated sometimes as the private property of the towns, and sometimes as commons? As one studies the landowning system of early modern Castile, it becomes clear that public, or common, ownership of rural property is important enough to merit a category of its own. Thus, it seems that a more suitable classification is one embracing five categories of rural property ownership: (1) public; (2) ecclesiastical; (3) noble; (4) urban middle-class; and (5) peasant (Cárdenas 1873). But because of the complexities of Castilian society, there is considerable overlapping between them. In this book I am devoting five chapters to the various forms of property ownership. But since the first category (public) is much less known than the other four, I am spending three

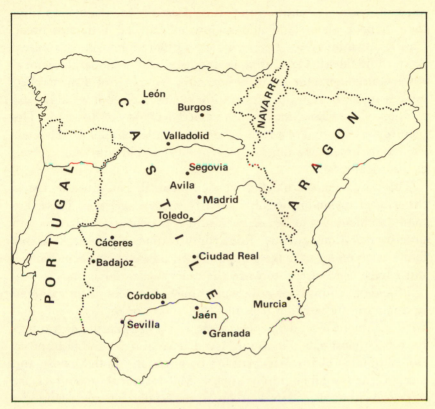

1. The Iberian peninsula in the 1500s

chapters on public ownership, followed by two chapters on private property. The final two chapters will deal with changes in ownership and production, and with the question of who enjoyed the fruits of the soil.

This book deals with Castile. In the sixteenth century 'Castile' in an administrative sense included all of peninsular Spain except for the kingdoms of Aragon and Navarre. But I have decided to exclude from my study the Basque provinces, Asturias, and Galicia, because the geography of these northern provinces has caused their rural institutions to develop along distinct lines. It should not be thought, however, that conditions in the rest of Castile were everywhere the same, for they were most certainly not. In fact, the different regions of Castile varied widely, and even within a given region the way of life of one community was often strikingly different from that of its neighbors. Throughout this book I have tried to stress the diversity

3

of conditions in sixteenth-century rural Castile. One might ask: why, then, a book about land and society in Castile? Why not break Castile down into more manageable and more homogeneous units? A splendid idea! There is a crying need for regional and local studies, although some excellent ones already exist, and I have relied heavily upon them in the preparation of this book. But we also need a vision of the whole, and that is what I have attempted here. The picture we see is that of a heterogeneous Castile, but one which lends itself to treatment as a unit, in geographical and institutional, as well as historical terms.

This is by no means a definitive treatment. It is an introduction to the subject of landownership in early modern Castile. There are many problems yet to be resolved, and many questions that remain unanswered. Consequently, from time to time in my work I have found it necessary to make guesses, based on fragmentary evidence, but I have been careful to warn the reader when doing so.

I have based this book on a wide range of sources, most gathered in Spain during research trips in 1968, 1969–70, 1974–5, 1976, and 1978–9. Among secondary sources, the works of Spanish geographers have been most valuable to me, but I have also been able to profit from a number of fine recent studies by historians (both Spanish and foreign), as my bibliography attests. My documentary sources are primarily from the central archives, especially Simancas and the Chancillerías of Valladolid and Granada. I have preferred to use these central archives rather than local archives, because my goal was to gain a vision of the Castilian situation as a whole, rather than of some isolated locality in Castile. Furthermore, it would have been impossible for me to spend the time necessary to exploit all the fine local archives in Spain, except through the works of other scholars, which I have done.

For the convenience of the reader, I have placed in parentheses the name of the province (using present boundaries) following my textual references to names of places, many of which are obscure villages. I did not do so when referring to provincial capitals, because in those the name of the province is the same.

I

The communitarian tradition

Few historians have recognized the importance of the communitarian tradition in early modern rural Castile. This is unfortunate, because the Castilian economy and society were profoundly influenced by a complex system of public ownership of the soil and its fruits. Both arable agriculture and animal husbandry were affected, and the communitarian system played an important role in preserving the relatively open society that characterized late medieval and early modern Castile (Vassberg 1974).

One explanation for the short shrift that historians have given the communitarian tradition (e.g. Smith 1966: 432–8; Weisser 1976: 48) is that the tradition has not generated much readily accessible evidence of its existence. It is characteristic of usages (including communal practices) that they do not normally need to be written down. This was particularly true in the traditional rural setting, where life revolved around the oral rather than the written word. There was no necessity to set to writing the local communitarian customs unless they were seriously challenged. By contrast, the institution of private ownership has provided historians with an abundance of documentation in the form of contracts and other documents – essential for the protection of legal ownership – regarding rentals, sales, inheritances, and other transfers of possession or of ownership. This type of documentation was not normally necessary in most forms of common ownership, particularly in a village setting. Consequently, the weight of evidence has suggested that private property ownership was far more important than public ownership. It is the dearth of written evidence that has masked the existence of many communitarian practices, and that has obscured the fact of their significance in the rural world.

5

THE PRINCIPLE AND ORIGIN OF PUBLIC OWNERSHIP

The principle that serves as the starting point for public property ownership is that no individual has the right to take for himself and monopolize those resources of Nature that are produced without the intervention of man. According to this idea, the only thing that an individual has the right to call his own is that which he has wrought from Nature through his personal efforts in the form of crops, flocks, or manufactured goods. Land, therefore, cannot be privately owned, but must remain permanently at the disposition of anyone who wishes to benefit from it (Costa 1944: 370). In the purest and most primitive application of this principle, an individual could use a piece of land simply by occupying it – no external authority would be needed. The use might be for pasture or for cultivation, but possession would be dependent solely upon use. When the individual no longer wished to use the piece of land, he simply abandoned it, upon which all of his claim would cease, and the land would be available for the next person who wished to use it. But it was rare to find public ownership in such a pure form. Usually the institutions of public ownership represented some form of accommodation with local conditions.

Historians do not agree on the origin of Castilian public ownership. It has been variously attributed to pre-Roman, Roman, and Visigothic civilizations (Costa 1944: 310; Hoyos 1947; Beneyto 1932; Salomon 1964: 137, n. 2; Nieto 1964: 27–54). But none of these suggested origins is entirely satisfactory, because examples can be given to refute each one. It is probably best to conclude that public ownership had not just one, but several origins, and that different communal practices were developed during the pre-Roman, Roman, and Visigothic periods. But whatever the origin, or origins, of public ownership, it is clear that the Reconquest of Castile from the Moslems (Salomon 1964: 150, n. 2), and the Repoblación (resettlement by Christian Spaniards) had the effect of strengthening it and of giving it important legal sanctions.

Throughout medieval Europe, the monarchs enjoyed the theoretical right of eminent domain over all the property in their kingdoms. In most places this right was limited, in practice, to certain types of property. But in Castile, the pretensions of the monarch were amplified because of the Reconquest, the success of which was in large part attributed to the efforts of the royal army. In principle, and according to the *Siete partidas* (codification of law under the late thirteenth-century king Alfonso X), all property won from the enemy was at the disposition of the king, who could grant it at his will. Furthermore, the Castilian monarch could invoke the ancient Germanic tradition according to which any ownerless property belonged to the crown; or the Roman principle according to which any ownerless property (*bona vacatia*) belonged to the state (Concha 1951; Valdeavellano 1968: 239–40; Higueras 1961: 112–13).

CROWN LANDS AND *BALDÍOS*

During the Reconquest of territory from the Moslems, the Castilian monarchs tried to attract settlers to the newly conquered areas by offering generous grants of land to their chief military supporters, and to settlers who would move in and colonize the new lands. All the lands in the realm that had not been apportioned through royal grants remained theoretically the property of the crown. Therefore, these ungranted lands were known as crown lands (*tierras realengas*). The monarchs were anxious to promote the colonization of their newly won territories, and for that reason they were generous in allowing the public use of crown lands. Furthermore, there was a pragmatic reason for generosity: the crown lands were usually so extensive that it would have been virtually impossible to keep people from using them. Crown lands tended to be lands of inferior quality, because the best lands were normally the first to be disposed of in royal grants. These tracts of inferior, largely unworked and idle crown lands were also known as *tierras baldías*, or *baldíos* (Vassberg 1974: 385–6).

The word *baldío* had several meanings in sixteenth-century Castile. Crown lands were called *baldíos* not only when they were ungranted and unused, but also when they had been appropriated for private use without a specific royal grant, even if that appropriation had taken place generations before, and the land was currently being treated as private property. In other words, *baldíos* were considered to be crown lands, but they could also be crown lands that had been usurped into the private domain. Because of the free-use privileges associated with crown lands, the *baldíos* were considered to be in the public domain, although under royal control. There was a strong identification of the concept of public land ownership with the word *baldío*. For that reason, lands belonging as community property to

7

municipalities were also called *tierras baldías*, even though they were in continuous use and had been given to the municipalities by royal grant. It would confuse the reader to use the word *baldío* in the loosely constructed Castilian fashion of the sixteenth century. Therefore, in this work, *baldíos* or *tierras baldías* will be used to mean crown lands not having been given in grants, and therefore theoretically available for public use.

In the first stages of the resettlement of formerly Moslem territories, a large proportion of the lands were *tierras baldías*. The first grants of new lands were to groups of colonists who formed towns either directly under royal jurisdiction (*realengos*) or under seigneurial jurisdiction. In either case, the colonists used the lands individually so far as was necessary for growing crops, but the rest of the land remained free for the common benefit. As more and more royal grants were made, the *baldíos* were quantitatively reduced, because the grants were made from the *baldíos*. But large tracts of *baldíos* were included in the newly formed municipal and seigneurial jurisdictions. Most of the *baldíos* remained uncultivated, and had no express owner, but were available for the common use.

The ownership of the *tierras baldías* was problematical, from the very beginning. Nobody held legal title to them, but they were claimed by the monarch, by the municipalities, and even by some seigneurial lords. Normally, however, it was recognized that the *baldíos* were at the disposition of the monarch. Proof of this can be seen in the fact that other parties who made claims to parts of the *baldíos* usually based their claims on some real, or alleged, royal concession. The question of ownership, of course, was confused by the imprecise use of the term *baldío* in the early modern period. But the crown could always find jurists able to uphold the royal claim to the *baldíos* as crown lands. And when legal arguments failed, and the question was reduced to the use of brute force, the crown had an obvious advantage over other claimants. Yet, even the crown tacitly admitted that the *baldíos* were public property (Nieto 1964: 147; Vassberg 1975: 629–54). In any case, in practice, during most of the sixteenth century the Castilian monarchs allowed the *tierras baldías*, or crown lands, to be used by the public and by the municipalities, with little interference.

It has often been assumed that the *baldíos* were of scant economic value (Nieto 1964: 138; Klein 1920: 92). And it is true that their value per unit area was normally much less than that of privately owned lands. But one should not underestimate the role played by the *baldíos* in the rural economy. In the first place, it must be stressed that they were of uneven quality, ranging from rocky mountain slopes where nothing would grow, to rich valley soils that remained ownerless merely because of a low local population density, or because of physical isolation. The *baldíos* were typically woodlands (*monte*) of varying density, and had a variety of uses. For example, around 1520 the town of Salvaleón (Badajoz) reported that the *baldíos* in its jurisdiction were used for pasture, firewood, lumber, hunting, water, acorns, and even arable agriculture.[1]

The most typical *baldío* use, however, was for pasture. A term used in some regions for *baldío* pastures was *alijar* (from an Arabic root meaning pastureland). Far more widespread was *llecos* or *tierras llecas* (from *froccus*, the Latin for uncultivated land), used to describe virgin land that had never been plowed. According to the Castilian Cortes (national assembly) of 1586–8 the public lands and *baldíos* of the towns and villages of the realm were 'their principal source of livelihood', as pasture for their various livestock (*Actas*: IX, 396–7; Salomon 1964: 141, n. 2). Some parts of Castile had *baldíos* with splendid natural pasture resources. For example, the *baldíos* of the Campo de Calatrava region of the province of Ciudad Real were used as commons by the livestock of local residents, and there was such a surplus of pasture that the animals of outsiders were also accommodated, for the payment of a fee (Quirós 1965: 228–9).

It is obvious that the cultivation of portions of the *baldíos* would have reduced the total amount of available *baldío* pasture. Therefore, in many areas it was forbidden to plant crops on crown lands, unless special permission had been obtained. Normally such permission was sought locally, from the town government. In 1560, for example, a certain Juan Muñoz received from the town of Segura de la Sierra (Jaén) permission to cultivate a certain portion of the local *tierras baldías*. It is significant that a dozen years later the municipal authorities took legal action against Muñoz, on the grounds that he had exceeded the limits of his license for cultivation, and was thereby damaging the *baldíos*.[2] In places such as the valley of the Andarax River (Almería) there was a general authorization to plant grain on the *baldíos* (this was in 1490, when population was sparse), but it was specified that these cultivated plots were never to be considered as private property (Sáenz 1974: 338).

In some places, the *baldíos* used for cultivation were of marginal quality, either because of the nature of the soil, or because of misuse. This was true of the village of Piedras Albas (Cáceres), a poverty-stricken place of eighty families near the Portuguese border. In 1575 the villagers reported that the soil of their *baldíos* was exhausted, and incapable of yielding enough grain to sustain the populace. Nevertheless, the villagers continued to plant them, at great effort, and little profit, because they had no other arable lands at their disposition.[3] On the other hand, there were places with unusually fertile *baldíos*. One of these fortunate towns was Castro del Río (Córdoba), which had 'a great quantity of *tierras baldías* that were very good for sowing grain, and a large portion of them were sown'. In certain areas, the *baldíos* represented the principal source of arable land. One example is the village of Tejeda de Tiétar (Cáceres), a place of 236 *vecinos* in 1531. It was reported that most of the residents of Tejeda lived fairly well (*medianamente*) in an economy based principally on agriculture and animal husbandry. They farmed 'some' rented lands, but their grain fields were mainly (*la mayor parte*) in the *baldíos*.[4]

PRESURA

One of the most interesting and basic institutions of the communitarian tradition in Spain was the squatter's right practice known as *presura* (also spelled *pressura*). This custom had its origin during the Reconquest, when Moslem lands were seized and occupied by armed might. The Castilian word for 'seized' or 'captured' is *presa*, which seems to be the origin of *presura*, although it may also have been derived from *jus adprisionis*, the Latin name for the practice. The right of *presura*, which was also observed by the neighboring Franks, was universally recognized in the regional *fueros* (law codes) of medieval Spain (Nieto 1964: 124–32; Pérez 1951). It also appeared in the municipal *fueros* granted from the eleventh to the fourteenth centuries to newly founded towns in Castile. The formula generally used was that of the *fueros* of Logroño (1095) and Hinestrosa (1287):

. . . and wherever these colonists find deserted and uncultivated lands within the limits [of the new settlement], they may cultivate them; and wherever they find pastures, they may use them, and they may even enclose them to make hay and so their cattle can pasture; and wherever they find water to irrigate orchards or vineyards, or for their mills, or for their gardens, or for other things that they might need, they may take them; and wherever they find firewood, and forests, and trees to burn or

the local *tierras baldías*.[6] And Joaquín Costa (1944: 250–2) found the practice to have survived in several parts of Spain as late as the last decade of the nineteenth century. Of course, the importance of the right of *presura* was continuously decreasing in any given locality, as the quantity of crown lands available for such exploitation was gradually reduced through royal grants.

Did the occupation of land through *presura* convey ownership along with the right of possession? That is a question which can not be answered easily. Certainly when the *presura* occurred with the express license of the king, there was a conveyance of ownership, as in a royal grant. But it is not clear whether the spontaneous *presuras* by peasants really resulted in legal ownership, even though they were made through the general authorization of the crown. Joaquín Costa (1898: 249–50; 1944: 332, 346) did not think so. He insisted that the inalienable property of the medieval Castilian peasant included only his house and adjoining yard and garden. Grain fields and pasture were not included, because there were ample public lands for those purposes. Therefore, when the possessor of a field taken in *presura* ceased cultivating it, his right to the field was extinguished.[7]

But there are also indications that *presura* was indeed associated with property ownership. In his study of viticulture in northwestern Spain, Alain Huetz de Lemps concluded that the system of *presura* favored the development of small property ownership in the ninth and tenth centuries, but he did not insist that ownership was necessarily conveyed directly through *presura*. In other parts of Castile, however, it is clear that proprietary rights were involved (Costa 1898: 261–2; Huetz 1967: 171). For example, the Fuero of Cuenca (late twelfth century) extended property rights to those who cleared and cultivated lands in the *tierras baldías*. Several different parts of Castile followed the example of Cuenca: in the Campo de Montiel (Ciudad Real and Albacete) the Order of Santiago stimulated the Repoblación according to the Cuenca principle (Planchuelo 1954: 131). And in 1569 the people of Quesada (Jaén) claimed to hold part of their lands according to the Fuero of Cuenca, explaining that 'whoever plows the [*baldío*] woodlands for the first time, or digs a ditch to irrigate [*baldío*] lands, shall have both the one and the other in possession and in property'.[8]

In conclusion, it is clear that the meaning of *presura* varied, depending upon the place and the time. The one constant behind the institution was the principle of the right of possession through use. Sometimes possession through *presura* was tantamount to proprietorship, and sometimes it was not. Insofar as it did convey property ownership, that ownership diminished the total available amount of publicly owned land, but it should be remembered that *presura* could also be applied to the unexploited lands of an absentee owner. Public rights were thus still maintained.

THE *DERROTA DE MIESES*

There was a far more important way in which privately owned fields were subject to public use. This was the custom of stubble grazing, called the *derrota de mieses*, or simply the *derrota*. It was by no means peculiar to Spain – it existed contemporaneously in most of the rest of Europe (Blum 1971; Salomon 1964: 141). The *derrota de mieses* was a mixed system of communal and private rights that was well suited to the complementary relationship of the pastoral and arable agriculture of the medieval and early modern periods. According to this custom, private rights to a field were limited to the period between planting and harvest. After harvest, every possessor of a grain field or meadow was obliged to open his lands to the animals of the general public. The entire territory of a town – fields and pastures – then became a continuous commons open to all the local livestock, and perhaps to those of neighboring towns as well, until the next sowing time, when individual rights to the cultivated plots were re-established.

Joaquín Costa (1944: 374–5) considered the *derrota de mieses* to be a semi-collectivistic remnant of a previous totally collectivistic state of agriculture. He shows that there was a perfectly clear juridical system in which a 'privately owned' plot of land had not one owner, but two: one was individual, limited to the period when the plot was planted; and the other was collective, covering the stubble and spontaneous vegetation on the plot between harvest and the next sowing. According to Costa, the community had been originally the sole owner of the soil, but over the years it had lost one of its two uses (cultivation), and retained only the other (pasture). Costa's theory of the origin of the *derrota* is borne out by the agreements through which the towns rented, sold, or gave cultivation rights to the local inhabitants (García Fernández 1965: 709–15). The agreements stipulated that when crops were not growing, the fields, whether in stubble or in fallow, would be treated as common pasture – in other words, the *derrota de mieses* was to be observed.

The *derrota*, of course, was not created by jurists rationally manipulating legal principles of ownership. Rather, it had its origins in the needs of the rural community at a certain time in history. There were several broad economic factors explaining the adoption of the custom. The basic justification for the *derrota* was the need to maintain an adequate supply of accessible pasture resources for the important pastoral sector of the rural economy. The celebrated development of transhumant herding was one solution to the problem. But it was not possible to send all animals on seasonal migrations across the peninsula in search of green pastures. Most of Spain's animals, in fact, did *not* participate in the periodic trans-peninsular migrations, but instead remained near the villages of their owners. It was essential to devise a way to feed them.

During part of the year the *baldíos* and common municipal pastures could provide for the local herds and flocks. But from the outset of summer there was normally a problem. The harsh Mediterranean sun parched the natural pastures in most parts of Spain, causing them to be of little value for grazing. It was then that the fresh stubble (*rastrojos*) and fallow (*barbechos*) of grain fields became a valuable resource. The stubble contained not only the residues of harvest, but also an abundance of spontaneous vegetation (weeds) that served as pasture until winter was well along. After the rains of autumn had greened the uncultivated lands again, the animals could move there for a while, then return to the stubble to graze on the new sprouts brought up by the rains. In this way the stubble maintained its value as pasture, though very diminished, until the following spring. The system of stubble grazing just described could not have functioned in an area where annual cropping was practiced. The prevalent system in early modern Castile was biennial cropping (*año y vez*), with half the land always left fallow. And to gain the full benefit of the *derrota*, Castilian peasants postponed plowing their stubble until March of the post-harvest year. Such a delay would have been totally irrational in the absence of stubble grazing, because it reduced to a bare minimum the time needed for soil recuperation and absorption of moisture before the next planting (García Fernández 1964).

The *derrota de mieses* freed cattle owners from the expense of having to maintain their animals in the stable during several months of the year. But it should not be thought that the *derrota* provided a benefit for cattle growers at the expense of the arable farmer. The nineteenth-century writer Francisco de Cárdenas (1873: II, 276–94) denounced the practice as such, referring to it as 'the ancient servitude of rural property for the benefit of the stock industry'. Cárdenas was thinking specifically of the Mesta (cattlemen's association), which was the *bête noire* of defenders of unrestricted property rights. But actually, there was no clearcut dichotomy between cattle growers and arable farmers. Grain farmers could not work their fields without draft animals – mules or oxen. Furthermore, most peasants found it expedient to combine crop growing with the raising of a few other animals such as sheep, goats, or pigs. All these animals had to be fed. But in most parts of Castile it was too arid for the kind of large-scale forage cropping that would properly provide for them. Therefore, the sparse weeds and stubble left after harvest were a pasture resource that could not be disparaged.

Even granting the above, one might well ask why the *derrota* was needed. Why did not each peasant graze his animals on his own stubble? The answer lies partly in the extreme subdivision of farmland. The plots of cultivated land belonging to each peasant were scattered around the territory of the town, and it would have been a great inconvenience to take one's animals to graze exclusively on one's own land. Moreover, the value of the stubble pasture was probably not sufficient to justify putting out guards to keep out intruders. And finally, it was the usual practice for each village to form a municipal herd made up of the few head of animals owned by each individual. The collective herd was watched over by special guards named by the village fathers. Thus animal care was made more efficient, and, since the village herd contained animals owned by possessors of fields dispersed throughout the village territory, it was sensible to allow the herd to graze on all the stubble lands of the village, without exclusion. So the custom of the *derrota* was by no means illogical. It was clearly of benefit not only to cattlemen with large herds, but to everyone owning animals. The custom was so strongly infused in Castilian life that it was defended even by the jurists most hostile towards communal practices. It was recognized as one of the irrevocable rights of the Castilian peasant. According to one sixteenth-century authority, 'neither the lords of vassals, nor even the King, could enclose their fields, to keep them from becoming common pasture after the harvest'. Even 'enclosed' fields were subject to the *derrota*, as were vineyards after the grapes had been picked. Naturally, when the kingdom of Granada was added to the crown of Castile in 1492, the *derrota* was extended to the new lands, as it was also to the American colonies.[9]

In addition to the pragmatic justification for the practice, there existed also a theoretical justification for the *derrota*, based on the medieval Castilian concept of property. According to the principle of public ownership, the only criterion for the individualization of the soil – apart from royal grants – was its cultivation. From this viewpoint, the growth of spontaneous vegetation in the stubble of harvested fields was not the result of the peasants' work, and thus had to be common like the *baldío* pastures (García Fernández 1964: 142).

The rules for the *derrota* varied slightly from place to place. In all parts of Castile there were towns that shared their stubble grazing rights with neighboring towns in communities of pasture. For example, there were reciprocal stubble grazing rights between the citizens of Andújar and Arjona (both in the province of Jaén) and of a number of other towns in the vicinity. And in the early 1500s in the jurisdiction of Arévalo (Avila and Segovia provinces), the inhabitants of one village could pasture freely in the stubble of another village. But the reciprocity of *derrota* rights could cause hard feelings, if the residents of one town had significantly more livestock, or less land than the residents of neighboring villages. This often led to local ordinances to deny stubble grazing rights to the animals of nonresidents. Inevitably, the restrictive ordinances led to fines, arrests, and to lawsuits initiated by one side or the other. Documents in the archives of the Chancillerías (Supreme Tribunals) of Granada and Valladolid attest to the frequent litigation about the denial of reciprocal pasture rights in all parts of Castile. For example, in 1573–4 there was such a suit lodged against the city of Córdoba; in 1548–9 the villages of Valdetorres and Guareña (Badajoz) went to court for the same reason; and in the 1520s the villages of Repariegos and Donhierro (in the jurisdiction of Arévalo) began a suit over the denial of *derrota* rights.[10] It should be said that it is often difficult, or even impossible, to distinguish suits involving *derrota* rights from suits involving other common pastures, because stubble was frequently described merely as 'common pasture'.

A troublesome feature of the *derrota de mieses* was that not all fields were harvested at the same time, and when pasturing animals on the stubble of one field, it was nearly impossible to keep them from straying into adjacent fields of unharvested grain. A related problem was the question of exactly when the *derrota* began on any given field, because some peasants wished to maintain possession of their fields for a few days after the gathering of the sheaves, to take advantage of grain lost through sloppy reaping, sheaving, or gathering. The town of Horche (Guadalajara) dealt with this question by delaying the *derrota* for a few days after harvest, to allow for the gleaning of fallen grain (García Fernández 1953: 214–16). In some places, the problem of the starting date was solved by fixing the date at which the *derrota* would begin. For example, the city of Loja (Granada) had an ordinance that permitted landholders to maintain exclusive rights to their stubble until mid-September – an ordinance which provoked a suit by cattle owners who maintained that such a delay was illegal.[11] And the towns in the jurisdiction of the City of Málaga established the day of St Mary (15 August) for the initiation of the *derrota*. The Málaga ordinance also established a regimen for the types of animals who successively would have the right to pasture on the stubble. In the village of La Rinconada (Seville) there was a lawsuit from 1543 to 1546 when two landowners from the city of Seville tried to monopolize the stubble on their lands until mid-August. The village council declared that although it had denied *derrota* rights to animals from Extremadura, there had never been any such restriction for local animals. According to the council, the local rule had always been that after the sheaves had been gathered, the oxen and other local work animals of all the residents of the village had the right to pasture freely on the stubble of any land-owner's fields. It is interesting that the La Rinconada custom was to keep out 'foreign' animals from Extremadura. Perhaps the Extremaduran animals were primarily sheep, and the local residents, having no sheep of their own, resented the incursions of the sheep. Perhaps it was merely because they belonged to outsiders, and perhaps it was because sheep, who graze much more closely than bovines, posed a real menace to the local pasture resources.[12]

Theoretically, *derrota* rights applied not just to local animals, but also to outside animals, including the migratory Mesta herds, which consisted primarily of sheep. But many communities, like La Rinconada, resented the migratory animals and attempted to curtail their rights. The consequence was a large number of suits between the Mesta and local governments. The outcome of these suits was mixed, but in the sixteenth century the Mesta tended to lose its legal battles, because the royal government no longer favored the cattle-men's association as it had in earlier times.[13]

The *derrota* represented a compromise between the two extremes of completely individualized and of completely collectivized exploitation of the soil. It was also a compromise between completely enclosed fields and the open range. In historical perspective, it can be seen as a rational utilization of the available pasture resources, both natural and cultivated, while maintaining the integrity of planted fields. Through the *derrota*, the livestock of a village, or group of villages, could move through an extensive and almost uninterrupted expanse of land in search of pasture. While pasturing on the stubble and fallow lands of cultivated fields, they enriched them with their manure, thus in a sense paying for the vegetation they were able to find there. In many places, the pasture accorded by the *derrota* was probably superior to the natural pasture of the local *montes*, which were frequently overgrown with a tangle of scrub brush of scant value. In conclusion, it should be said that the *derrota* is not merely a historical curiosity belonging to centuries past. It still existed in Spain in the second half of the twentieth century, showing that in many places it was still considered to be an essential custom.[14]

2

Municipal property

Virtually every Castilian city, town, and village had property of its own that was reserved for the use or benefit of the community as a whole. Much of this property had its origin during the Reconquest, when lands were assigned to the colonists of a newly founded town. Other community-owned lands were established much later by royal grants or *privilegios*, perhaps in exchange for some favor. In most cases these royal grants simply authorized the municipality to appropriate a certain portion of the *tierras baldías* within its jurisdiction for use as arable land or as pasture for the common benefit. But not all municipal property originated through royal grants. Some town councils, apparently confusing seigneurial jurisdiction with landownership, would get the lord of the area to give his permission for a quantity of land to be reserved for community use. The nobility in this way was sometimes able illegally to control the local *tierras baldías*. But the most common procedure used by municipalities to secure additional lands for community use was simply to appropriate what they wanted from the *tierras baldías*, using no authority other than their own (Vassberg 1974: 388; Nieto 1964: 54–7).

Probably because of the frequency with which the *tierras baldías* were used as the source of municipal property, in the sixteenth century there was only a vague distinction between *tierras baldías* and *tierras concegiles* (lands of the town council). In fact, the phrase *tierras baldías concegiles* was often used to describe property possessed by the municipalities, despite the fact that the juxtaposition of *baldías* and *concegiles* represented a contradiction of terms. Historians have used several different terms for municipal property ownership. Joaquín Costa called it 'agrarian collectivism' and Rafael Altamira used 'communal ownership'. But these terms are not appropriate for all the types of property involved. Noël Salomon's 'community property' would be far better (1964: 134–5) because it embraces the two basic forms of municipal property: commons and *propios*. However, 'community property' is too inclusive for clarity, because it can also be applied to the *tierras baldías*. That is why this chapter is entitled 'Municipal property', embracing the holdings of the local community and administered by the municipal council.

The juridical origin of the property of the Castilian municipalities was complex. As indicated above, some was acquired through royal or seigneurial grant. But the origin of many municipal holdings was unknown, even at an early date, because of the loss or destruction of records. Hence, many towns based the ownership of their property on 'possession from time immemorial' (*posesión de tiempo inmemorial*, or some similar formula), which was usually accepted by Castilian courts. Some towns had acquired their property through purchase, or through the arbitration of some dispute; others through court decisions resolving lawsuits. In early modern Castile there was a strong feeling of the inviolability of municipal property (Nieto 1964: 58–60). In his *Política para corregidores y señores de vasallos, en tiempo de paz y de guerra* (Madrid, 1597), the noted authority Jerónimo Castillo de Bobadilla asserted that neither the king nor the lords (even in seigneurial towns) had any proprietary right to municipal lands.[1]

The process of the Reconquest encouraged the development of strong municipalities with large property holdings. The Castilian kings of the time continuously sought ways to strengthen their own authority. This brought them into a confrontation with the nobles. And in Spain (as in the rest of Europe) the kings courted the support of the townspeople, trying to gain their favor by strengthening the municipalities – both the older cities and the newly conquered or newly founded ones. To provide the towns with a strong financial position, the monarchs were magnanimous in grants of property and of prerogatives. The municipal councils were usually allowed to supervise the apportionment (*repartimiento*) of local lands among Christian settlers who came to live there. And the towns were also granted extensive lands of their own. The municipalities founded in the first centuries of the Reconquest got their property by virtue of their charters (*cartas de población*). Sometimes the charters granted only the right to *use* certain types of property (which included not only land, but also markets, slaughterhouses, and other public facilities) but gradually the right of usage was transformed into full ownership. Christian settlers moving into newly reconquered areas liked to go where there was a rich municipal government, because that promised economic benefits and more freedom. And the crown tended to think it easier to deal with strong cities than with strong nobles. Thus, from the very beginning Castile had strong municipal governments that controlled large amounts of property (Nieto 1964: 103–13; Higueras 1961: 112–13; Alvarez 1963: 8–18).

PROPIOS

The property owned by the Castilian municipalities fell into two distinct juridical categories. On the one hand was common property, set aside for the free use of the residents of the place. On the other hand there were the *propios*, also called *propios de los pueblos, propios de los concejos*, or *bienes de propios*. The *propios* were lands or any other kind of property owned by the municipality as a juridical entity. Legally, the *propios* were treated as private property owned by the town government. They were usually rented out by the town council, with the proceeds going to defray the costs of public works or toward lightening local tax assessments. Municipal property of the *propio* type had existed in Spain as far back as Roman times. The *ager colonicus* of the Roman cities were usually rented out for short terms, and could not legally be leased for periods exceeding five years. During the Middle Ages, the Spanish monarchs tried to provide their newly founded (or newly conquered) municipalities with a strong financial position by granting them extensive *propios* (Vassberg 1974: 389–90). Usually the *propios* were in the form of land to rent out for income, but the kings often also turned over to the municipalities certain taxes and other royal perquisites. Because of the need for defense in areas bordering on Moslem states, the Reconquest monarchs were especially generous to frontier cities such as Toledo, and later, Seville and Murcia. The need for defense against the Moslems continued even after the taking of the kingdom of Granada in 1492. In recognition of this, Queen Isabella gave the cities of Granada, Málaga, and Almería a number of Islamic sources of revenue (the *tiguales* and *haguela*, and the office of *gelices*) to add to their *propios* to aid them in funding coastal defense against Moslem pirates (Alvarez 1963: 8–18).

Despite royal largesse, municipal treasuries tended to be perpetually short of funds. Cities with the greatest incomes also had the greatest expenses. To improve their financial position, the municipalities were constantly on the watch for opportunities to add to their *propios*. Sometimes this was effected through purchase. For example, in 1284 the city of Toledo bought from Fernando III the 2,500 square kilometer area known as the Montes de Toledo for the sum of 45,000 gold *alfonsís*. The Montes then became a *propio* of the city, which profited from its investment by charging fees for the use of the land and the other resources of the area (Weisser 1976: 24–5). Another way of getting additional *propios* was to take lands at a perpetual rent (*enfiteusis*, or *censo perpetuo*), as the town of Villarramiel de Campos (Palencia) did in 1466 (Fernández Martín 1955: 61–3, 92–5). More *propios* could also be obtained by encroaching on the local *tierras baldías*. Sometimes this was done with the connivance of the local lord. For example, the city of Arcos de la Frontera (Cádiz) got the permission of the duke of Arcos to plow 1,534 *fanegas* of *tierras baldías* for use as its *propios*. And some places, such as the village of Parada de Rubiales (Salamanca), secured title to new *propios* as the result of the arbitration of disputes with local landowners.[2]

In the thirteenth-century code of law, the *Código de las partidas* (partida III, título 28, ley 10) *propios* were thus defined:

The cities or towns can have fields, and vines, and orchards, and olive groves, and other property, and livestock, and slaves and other similar things that themselves produce fruit or that provide income, and although they belong in common to all the dwellers of the city or town to which they belong, nevertheless the people can not use such things as these for their individual benefit; rather, the fruits and income coming from them shall be used for the public welfare of the entire city or village . . . such as maintaining the walls or gates, or the fortresses, or holding the castles, or paying contributions, or in other similar things pertaining to the general welfare of all the city or town.[3]

Later laws were enacted to guarantee the integrity of the *propios* by protecting them from usurpation by unscrupulous municipal officials and other powerful local figures. A standardized procedure of renting *propios* was established, according to which they could only be rented publicly and to the highest bidder. And to prevent abuses, it was forbidden for officials of the local municipal council or 'powerful persons' to rent *propios*, either directly or indirectly. It was also provided that all *propios* that had been unjustly occupied without paying rent were to be returned to the municipalities. Other laws restricted the use of revenues from *propios* to projects of material benefit to the community. It was forbidden to use proceeds from *propios* for displays of mourning – even in the case of the death of the monarch. And it was specified that these funds were not to be spent for gratuities or gifts, nor for parties or celebrations or for food or drink or other things not necessary for the public welfare, nor were they to be given to officials of the court, except in the amount of legally prescribed fees (*Novísima recopilación*, libro VII, título XVI, leyes II, IV, and VI).

The character and the value of *propios* varied enormously from place to place. Most *propios* were in the form of land, which was rented out for cultivation or for pasture. But, as has already been established, *propios* could include any type of income-producer. And some towns came to acquire some unusual *propios*. For example: Cieza (Murcia) owned a tavern (*mesón*) and some salt works (*salinas*) (Salmerón 1777: 91, 99); Monteagudo (Cuenca) owned a half-interest in an oven, and a half-interest in a two-stone grain mill;[4] and Cazorla (Jaén) was the owner of a tile works (*tejar*) and a half-interest (the other half was owned by the nearby city of Ubeda) in a ferry crossing the Guadalquivir (Polaino 1967: 75–7). It was quite common for the revenue from certain *propios* to be earmarked for specific purposes. For instance, the city of Baeza (Jaén) owned as *propios* a large quantity of land, the proceeds from which were designated for the city's public granary (*pósito*). In some cases, the *propios* were created expressly for the purpose of funding a certain need. The city of Toro (Valladolid) is a good example: it needed funds to pay for hiring the carts that were used to help move the court of the Emperor Charles V from Valladolid to Madrid. Therefore it requested, and received royal approval to plow a certain piece of land, and to rent it out as a *propio* to help defray the moving costs.[5]

Some places had few *propios*, or even none. In 1586 residents of the town of Castilblanco (Badajoz) testified that the place had no *propios* at all.[6] On the other hand, cities like Toledo were rich in *propios*. Toledo had its Montes, from which it collected an annual tax called the *doçavo*, representing one-twelfth of the annual production of the area. This was a huge amount, yet it represented only one of Toledo's *propios* (Weisser 1976: 25). Another extraordinarily wealthy city was Trujillo (Cáceres), whose *propios* included not only land, granted at the establishment of the municipality after the Reconquest, but also houses, corrals, property mortgages, and income from various taxes and fines. The most important of Trujillo's *propios* were thirty-six *dehesas* (enclosed pastures) known as *caballerías*, so named probably because they had originally been granted to noble warriors of the

Reconquest. But at an early date the *caballerías* were listed among the *propios* of Trujillo, and the city rented them out, with the proceeds going into the municipal treasury to be used for various projects in the common interest. In 1485, for example, income from the *caballerías* was used to help pay the soldiers from the area who went to fight the Moors in Granada (Vassberg 1978: 53–4).

Despite laws designed to prevent such abuses, the councilmen of Trujillo fell into the practice of renting the *caballerías* almost exclusively to their noble friends and relatives. In 1502 Ferdinand and Isabella put an end to such favoritism by ordering that commoners living in the vicinity be given preference in the renting of the *caballerías*. However, these *dehesas* were so huge that the area and the expense were beyond the capabilities of most peasants. Consequently it became the practice for groups of peasants – as many as a dozen – to form partnerships in renting them. Some *caballerías* were rented by the councils of towns in the jurisdiction of Trujillo, who would then apportion them among local residents. Rental contracts for the *caballerías* were awarded by the city on the basis of competitive bidding. They were for periods as long as seven years, and could be for pasture, for cultivation, or for a combination of both. Payment was usually monetary, but occasionally was partly in grain. There were also seasonal leases for pasture, especially designed to accommodate the itinerant Mesta flocks (Vassberg 1978: 53–4).

The normal method of exploiting the *propios* was to rent them for short periods. Long leases were generally looked upon with disfavor, because they smacked of favoritism. For example, in the late 1400s the city of Cáceres, which (like Trujillo) possessed enormous *dehesas* as *propios*, was forced progressively to decrease the length of its rental contracts (Orti 1954: 243–4). The crown, sensitive to expressions of popular indignation from Cáceres, ordered the city to change from five-year to four-year contracts, and finally to contracts of one or two years.[7]

The *propios*, unlike common lands, were not legally inalienable goods as such. They were considered to be at the free disposition of their owners, and not different from private property in relation to the nature and extension of property rights. But in practice, the municipalities in Spain (as in the rest of Europe) did not sell their *propios* except in extraordinary circumstances. They tended, rather, to keep what they owned, and to increase their ownership of property whenever possible – quite understandable, because in many places the *propios* constituted the town's major source of income, and helped pay taxes to the crown. If a municipal council did sell part of its *propios*, it might be called to task in a lawsuit launched by some vigilant citizen or jealous official (Cárdenas 1873: II, 181–2; Ulloa 1963: 436). This, in fact, happened in the 1560s in the village of Sueros de Cepeda (León), when the council sold some questionable property. Therefore, it was prudent to secure royal approval before selling *propios*, as the council of Cazorla (Jaén) did in 1561 when it needed funds to pay certain debts.[8]

But if the towns did not normally sell their *propios*, they displayed no similar reluctance to mortgage them to provide ready cash for emergencies. *Propios* could not be mortgaged without specific royal license. But this was not difficult to obtain, particularly in those cases where the crown was to be the recipient of the borrowed money. For example, in 1585 the town of Ledanca (Guadalajara) purchased from the crown certain lands for a price of 1,978,375 mrs. The sale contract provided for the price to be paid in two equal installments in 1585 and 1586. But the town council was unable to raise the amount of the first payment. Nor could it even raise one-third of the money, after the crown had agreed to a three-payment schedule. In danger of losing the newly purchased land through foreclosure, the town council petitioned the crown to allow it to mortgage its *propios* for an amount equal to the first two installments. The crown approved the request, allowing the council to mortgage its *propios* for 1,318,917 mrs (the requested sum) at the best terms it could find, so long as the interest rate did not exceed 7.14 percent.[9]

The theoretical legal distinction between *propios* and common property was perfectly clear. In practice, however, the difference could be quite hazy. In some communities, for example, a pasture might be for common use insofar as grass was concerned, but the acorns and branches of trees on the land might be sold as *propios*. And there were cases where a piece of property was treated as commons during part of the year, but rented out as a *propio* for the remainder of the year. For example, the town of Priego (Córdoba) owned a pasture that was used as commons for eight months out of the year, during which it was reserved exclusively for draft animals. But from November through February of each year it was rented out as pasture to the highest bidder. There were also places where community property was used some years as commons and other years as *propios*, depending upon local needs as perceived by the municipal council (Vassberg 1974: 390).

The indistinct character of community property was accentuated by the fact that the *propios* had frequently been usurped from the commons, and both had frequently been usurped from the *baldíos*. Furthermore, it seems that in the early centuries of the Reconquest there had been no distinction between *propios* and common land – everything was for common use. But many towns possessed far more common land than they needed, and they rented part of the surplus to apply the proceeds to various expenses of the municipality, hence laying the basis for the differentiation between two types of community property (Cárdenas 1873: II, 181–2; Alvarez 1963: 8–11).

Sometimes, though apparently this was rare, municipalities were able to acquire temporary *propios* by getting royal permission to use a certain portion of *tierras baldías* as *propios* for a limited time. This privilege was extended to the towns in the jurisdiction of the city of Jaén in 1590 so the revenues thereby gained could be used to pay the *servicio de millones* (a tax for rebuilding the Armada). But it was far more prevalent for towns to appropriate lands from the *baldíos* for their *propios without* the proper royal authority – an illegal but much-used procedure. Some towns even usurped their own commons to add to their *propios*. One municipality that did so was Iscar (Valladolid), the council of which would take over a portion of commons at the death of its possessor and add it to the *propios* of the town, charging rent from the next occupier of the plot (Vassberg 1974: 390–1).

COMMONS

Whereas *propios* could be used only by paying rent, common property was (at least theoretically) for the free use of all the residents of the municipality. There existed several types of commons. The most prevalent were lands used for pasture or cultivation, but there were also other types of commons, all of which will be dealt with in the following sections.

COMMON PASTURES: THE *EJIDO*

Castilian municipalities possessed lands of several types that were used for pasture. The *ejido* (usually spelled *exido* in the sixteenth century) was a multi-purpose piece of land that could serve as pasture. The *ejido* (derived from the Latin *exitus*, meaning exit) was an area of land situated just outside the town, or at its exit. It was not planted or cultivated, because it was reserved for use as a threshing floor, as a garbage dump, for loafing, and as a keeping-place for stray animals. Virtually every little village and town seems to have had its *ejido*, which was considered to be a necessary part of municipal life (Salomon 1964: 140, n. 5). Some *ejidos* were established at the founding of a new settlement; others later, as the growing population demanded that type of property. For example, in 1353 the city of Trujillo designated *ejidos* for its most populous subject villages, because the villagers considered it an undue hardship to exist without that type of facility (Naranjo 1929: 187–8). The larger the municipality, the larger the *ejido* would have to be. Some cities, in fact, had several *ejidos*. The city of Andújar (Jaén) is an extreme example, boasting five *ejidos* in the mid-sixteenth century.[10] But in that particular case, we should suspect that the term *ejido* was used rather loosely.

The *ejido* was available for the free use of the *vecinos* of a place. But non-*vecinos* were normally excluded, and there were fines for violators. For example, in the 1540s the village of Valdetorres (Badajoz) levied a fine of 100 mrs per flock of outsiders' animals who entered its *ejido* by day, and 200 mrs by night. The fines in this case were mild, but the seizure of the transgressing animals to ensure payment of the fine represented a great nuisance to the animal owners. In fact, in the example at hand, there arose a lawsuit between Valdetorres and the neighboring village of Guareña, over the question of fines and the exact boundaries of the *ejido*.[11]

Because the use of certain communal pastures (as in the case of the *ejido* of Valdetorres) was contingent upon having *vecino* status, it became vital for an animal owner to secure official recognition as a *vecino*. This normally was not a problem, particularly for native-born residents of the place. But there could be difficulties for newcomers who moved in. People from other regions of Spain, and even from neighboring villages, were considered to be 'outsiders' (*forasteros*) by sixteenth-century Castilians. Yet, despite their prejudice against outsiders, a municipal council would not normally be reluctant to confer *vecino* status on anyone who moved to the place, so long as he had his household and livelihood there, particularly if he was a potential taxpayer. But at times the town council was dilatory in certifying new residents as *vecinos*, perhaps because of rural sluggishness, perhaps because of the inborn suspicion of the 'foreigner', or for building houses, or for all that they might need, they may take them without hindrance.[5]

The right of *presura* was accorded to colonists settling both north and south of the Duero River, although some historians have written that it was limited to the area north of the Duero. In fact, *presura* was not peculiar to Christian Spain, for similar incentives to colonizers had been offered in Islamic Spain during the Caliphate of Córdoba (Salomon 1964: 148).

It is noteworthy that in the *fuero* formula, the right to land was not differentiated from the right to the other benefits offered by Nature. Furthermore, the *fuero* guaranteed the right to use 'deserted and uncultivated lands' without distinguishing between privately owned and public lands. Hence an abstract and purely formal occupation of a plot of land by an absentee landowner would not exclude others from its use. According to the *Fuero Viejo* of Castile (general law code, dating from the late 1200s, and systematized in 1356) the right of *presura* could be effected on any plot that was *thought* to be unowned. If a landowner later showed up to demand a share of the crops, the occupier was to give him a third or a fourth of the harvest, depending upon the local custom. *Presura* was the right of possession through use. The institution, thus defined, was perfectly compatible with the pure principle of public land ownership discussed above. The use to which the land was being put might be for pasture, for planting trees, or for field crops. When it was the last, there existed a more precise term to distinguish that particular type of *presura*: the word *escalio* (from *squalidus*, the Latin for uncultivated) signified occupation qualified by cultivation (Costa 1944: 323–4; Nieto 1964: 124–32).

The occupation of new lands through *presura*, since it involved crown lands, was made either with the tacit or the express permission of the king. The *presura* could even be effected by the king himself, but usually the monarch delegated a noble or a clergyman (typically a bishop) to supervise it for him. There could also be spontaneous *presura*, either by the powerful or by the weak. The medieval Castilian right to *presura* could be described as a sort of 'homestead' law, providing free land for settlers in frontier areas. The principle of *presura* remained deeply imbedded in the Castilian consciousness. It did not by any means die out with the medieval period, but extended well into the modern period. For example, the ordinances of the city of Andújar (Jaén) of 1567 explicitly recognized the right of *presura* in

11

perhaps because of personality clashes or other factors. The council of Poveda de la Obispalía (Cuenca) acknowledged in 1578 that it did not wish to admit as a *vecino* a certain new resident who had lived in the village for eight months – perhaps because of the fact that he owned no property, and the council recognized that he would be a tax liability. The delay in granting *vecino* status, for whatever reason, could cause problems for the person involved, not only locally, but also in adjoining towns. Look what happened to Luis Alvarez, who moved to the town of Canillas de Aceituno (Málaga) in 1552: after he had lived in Canillas for around a year, with his wife and children, his herds of hundreds of goats, and his several servants and slaves, Alvarez was treated as a *vecino* in Canillas. But the local council never got around to officially certifying his status, and this got him in trouble with the government of nearby Vélez Málaga, which denied him certain pasture rights there on the grounds that he was not really a *vecino* of Canillas.[12]

The importance of the *ejido*, and the uses to which it was put, varied enormously from place to place. One local historian describes the *ejidos* of the villages in the jurisdiction of the city of Badajoz as 'gooseyards or duckyards' (*ejidos ansareros o patineros*) where domestic fowl and animals were left to wander about (Rodríguez Amaya 1951: 433). By contrast, in 1522 the council of Albánchez de Ubeda (Jaén) created a new *ejido* that was closed to all small animals and to full-grown mares and cows. It was to be a special place for colts, calves, and asses.[13]

DEHESAS

The *dehesa* (from the Latin *defensa*, meaning enclosed) was land that was enclosed, at least theoretically, and usually destined for pasture. The *dehesa* frequently had some trees growing on it, and was often partly under cultivation. The term *dehesa* did not automatically suggest common property. Whereas all *ejidos* were commons, *dehesas* could be common property, *propios*, or even privately owned. Virtually every Castilian municipality had at least one common *dehesa*. And if it had only one *dehesa*, that one would almost surely be a *dehesa boyal* – an enclosed pasture reserved exclusively for plow animals. *Dehesa boyal* literally means pasture for oxen, and these pastures were no doubt originally created exclusively for oxen. But in the sixteenth century mules gradually displaced oxen as the most prevalent draft

28

animals. Consequently, mules were allowed to share the use of the *dehesa boyal* (Vassberg 1974: 391). Although the most-often used name given to common pasture for draft animals was *dehesa boyal*, there were some interesting regional variations. In Chinchilla (Albacete) it was a *dehesa buyalaje* or *dehesa buyalage*,[14] and in Cieza (in neighboring Murcia province) it was a *dehesa boialage* (Salmerón 1777: 91). In Aliaguilla (Cuenca) the name was *dehesa boalaxe*,[15] and in certain mountainous areas of the province of León, these pastures were called *boirías* or *bueyerías* (Martín Galindo n. d.: 31–2; 1961: 177).

The ubiquitous existence of the *dehesa boyal* is significant, because it demonstrates the complementary relationship between stock-raising and agriculture in the early modern Castilian economy. According to tradition, this type of special pasture was founded by Alfonso X (1252–84, called The Wise), who granted from the *tierras realengas* the use of 3 *aranzadas* of land per pair of oxen, to be used for the benefit of poor peasants (Salomon 1964: 135, n. 3; 136–7). The tradition notwithstanding, the *dehesa boyal* surely had existed long before the 1200s. However, in the early Reconquest, when the population was small in relationship to the amount of locally available *tierras baldías*, there might have been little incentive to create a special *dehesa boyal*. But as the local pasture resources became strained, the desirability of a special ox pasture would be felt. The maturing of small settlements into municipalities, and the desire of town councils to enjoy the prerogatives of their neighbors would also explain the proliferation of *dehesas boyales*. In 1497 Ferdinand and Isabella ordered the *corregidor* of Soria to establish *dehesas boyales* for the villages in Soria's jurisdiction that lacked them. These newly established *dehesas* were probably adequate when they were founded, but in some places they soon became too small. In fifty years the population of the Sorian village of Pozalmuro trebled, growing from 25 or 30 *vecinos* to about 80, and the original *dehesa boyal* was too small for all the oxen of the place. Therefore, in 1556 the village council created a new and much larger *dehesa boyal* which was sufficient for local needs. It was imperative to provide adequate pastures for draft animals. This need was so acute that peasants were willing to make sacrifices to ensure that their oxen could be properly fed. For example, the villagers of Higuera de Calatrava (Jaén) voluntarily agreed to reduce the size of the local *fanega* of cultivated land from 12 *celemines* to 10, to enable them to add to their *dehesa boyal*. This altered standard of measurement not only reduced the size of their fields, but also raised their rent payments, which were based on the *fanega*.[16]

The size, the location, and the character of the *dehesa boyal* differed, according to local geographical and historical factors. The charter of the Mesta, an organization which was interested because its flocks could be excluded from these pastures, stipulated that the *dehesa boyal* should be limited in size to 3 *aranzadas* per pair of oxen in the town – the formula used by Alfonso X (Caxa 1631: 122). But some were much smaller, and others were far larger than that: whereas Hontova (Guadalajara), a town of 170 *vecinos*, had a small *dehesa boyal* of only about 20 *fanegas* (Salomon 1964: 32 137, n. 1), the town of Ajalvir (Madrid), with 124 *vecinos*, had one nearly eight times bigger, measuring a quarter league by an eighth of a league. The *dehesa boyal* of Ajalvir had some live oak trees (*encinas* and *coscojas*) growing on it (*Relaciones: Madrid*, p. 5). It was desirable to have a few trees in any pasture: they provided protection from sun, wind, and rain, and in a period of drought – all too frequent in most parts of the peninsula – the low-hanging branches could be used as emergency forage. The *dehesa boyal* would usually be located near the village, in a location where there was pasture, shade, and water. Large and wealthy cities, of course, had more than one *dehesa boyal*. The city of Andújar (Jaén) had five, dispersed in such a way that every peasant must have had one convenient to both field and home. Even some modest villages also possessed multiple *dehesas boyales*. The village of Aliaguilla (Cuenca), for instance, had three in the 1580s.[17]

The *dehesa boyal* was normally reserved for the exclusive use of animals of *vecinos* of the place. Fines were levied on outsiders' animals and on non-draft animals. But since the *dehesa boyal* was usually one of the best pastures of a locality, it was difficult to keep out the wrong kind of animals. The integrity of these *dehesas* was always being threatened. A law of 1438 had to be formulated to stop influential local figures from introducing illegal livestock into the *dehesa boyal* (*Novísima recopilación*, libro VII, título XXV, ley 1). The town of El Puente del Arzobispo (Toledo) was very specific in its Ordinances of 1547 about what animals were permitted in its large and inviting *dehesa boyal*. Specifically excluded were mares, horses, mules, sheep, goats, and hogs. And it was stipulated that only oxen that were broken (*domados*) and actually used for field work had the right to use the *dehesa*.[18]

30

In some places the *dehesa boyal* was only reserved for draft animals during a specified portion of the year. For example, for towns in the jurisdiction of Soria, the reserved period was from 1 March to Martinmas (11 November). In distant Priego (Córdoba) the reserved period was almost identical: from 1 March to 1 November. During the non-reserved portion of the year, some places – like the villages of Soria – opened their *dehesas boyales* to all types of animals. Others, such as Priego, treated the *dehesa boyal* as a *propio* during the non-reserved period, and rented it out to the highest bidder. During the rented period, it became a *dehesa acotada* (meaning enclosed) or *vedada* (meaning forbidden). And some towns, when pressed by financial necessity, occasionally rented parts of their *dehesas boyales*, even during the 'reserved' period, to provide emergency funds. The council of Aliaguilla (Cuenca) which had three *dehesas boyales*, did so from time to time in the late 1500s to help pay taxes.[19] Here was another example of the flexible character of municipal property, which unquestionably made it more valuable to the municipalities and to their citizens.

The *Relaciones* (answers to royal questionnaires sent out to all the towns of the realm in the late 1570s) show that the Castilian municipalities owned many common *dehesas* that were not specifically *boyales* (Salomon 1964: 136). Some of these were open to all animals without discrimination, while others were earmarked for the exclusive use of certain types of animals, the raising of which the municipal government wished to encourage. Throughout the sixteenth century there was uneasiness about the shortage of horses in Spain – a shortage caused by incessant war and by the production of mules (for agriculture and for transport) rather than horses. The Cortes (national assembly) of Castile regularly voiced its concern about the situation, and in 1573 asked the crown to allow the creation, out of the *baldíos*, of local *dehesas de yeguas* (for mares), reserved exclusively for broodmares and their young (*Actas*: IV, 471). Most Castilian municipalities possessed neither the space nor the funds to establish such broodmare pastures. The city of Trujillo (Cáceres), however, had both, and in 1574, with royal authorization, it began to establish a *dehesa de yeguas*, buying for that purpose a number of vineyards and orchards in addition to uncultivated lands.[20]

Another special-purpose pasture was the *dehesa carnicera* (fattening pasture). Technically, this was not a common pasture as such, but it was often selected from one of the common *dehesas*, sometimes on a

rotating basis. The *dehesa carnicera* was reserved for the herd of the
town butcher. To provide better and cheaper meat, town governments typically allowed the butcher's herd to have the free use of a
certain *dehesa*, or *dehesas*, or parts of certain *dehesas*. Sometimes the
butcher got other special privileges as well, particularly in small
towns where there were scanty profits in the meat business. The
council of Puebla del Príncipe (Cuenca), a town of only 93 *vecinos* in
1595, put it very well: 'Because it is a town with such a small population, and poor, and with such a small consumption of meat, no one
would want to take charge of the butcher shop, if we did not exempt
him from the sales tax [*alcabala*] and give him a portion of the town's
dehesa, which is called the butcher's quarter, and pasture rights in the
town's vineyards, and summer pasture rights in another *dehesa* . . .'
Notice that Puebla del Príncipe did not have a separate *dehesa
carnicera* but used parts of two *dehesas* for that purpose. Places with
even more limited resources might have to make a single *dehesa* serve
several ends. The town of Monroy (Cáceres), for instance, had a
dehesa which served as the *dehesa boyal*, as the *dehesa carnicera*, and
which also served as pasture for cattle (*ganado vacuno*).[21]

COTOS, PRADOS, AND ENTREPANES

A term that was often used interchangeably with *dehesa* was *coto* (from
the Latin *cautus*, meaning guarded). A *coto* was an enclosed piece of
land much like the *dehesa*. The theoretical difference between the two
seems to be that whereas the *dehesa* was normally partly in pasture,
the *coto* could be wholly cultivated. But, in practice, this difference
was usually not relevant, because most *cotos* were used partly for
pasture (Vassberg 1974: 391; Costa 1898: 284). Consequently,
sixteenth-century Castilians did not distinguish between the two. In
some places the *dehesa boyal* was a *coto boyal*, and in others the *dehesa
carnicera* was a *coto carnicero*.[22] Regardless of which term was used, the
basic principle was that the piece of land – *dehesa* or *coto* – was
'enclosed'. This was seldom true in a literal sense of being fenced,
but usually only in the sense that they were not merely *baldío* but had
distinct borders, and had some type of restriction, however minimal,
placed by the local government on their use (Caxa 1631: 142).

Another type of pasture was the *prado* (from the Latin *pratum*,
meaning meadow). The *prado* was an unusually high-quality pasture.
Typically it was a plot of humid land, along a river or in some well-

watered spot, or it was irrigated land. Grass was allowed to grow in the *prado*, or forage crops were planted there. In semi-arid Castile, not every place could have a *prado*. Even the well-watered mountain areas of the north could not have an unlimited number of *prados*, because the *prados* had to compete with the arable plots for terrain. And since croplands are more efficient food producers than pasture-lands, the *prados* were always menaced by the plow.[23]

In addition to the especially designated pasture areas, there was also common pasture in the spaces between cultivated fields. These were the *entrepanes*, literally the spaces between fields of grain – by far the most prevalent crop. The *entrepanes* were common pasture. How-ever, because of the difficulty of keeping animals from moving into the grain fields on both sides, the *entrepanes* were practically off-limits until after harvest. Some localities had ordinances prohibiting graz-ing in the *entrepanes* until mid-August, or until the harvest had been completed.[24] Thus, in practice, the *derrota de mieses* often applied to the *entrepanes* as well as to the stubble of the fields. It was mentioned earlier that the *derrota* applied to vineyards, after harvest. In Los Santos de Maimona (Badajoz), the municipal ordinances of 1583 also extended until the end of May the right to reap the spontaneous vegetation in unworked vineyards, so long as no animals were let in to damage the vines (Guerra 1952: 512).

THE QUESTION OF ELIGIBILITY

Theoretically, common lands were available for the free use of everyone. But in practice, as we have seen, the commons of a place were likely to be restricted to officially certified *vecinos*. For all *vecinos* the local commons were free, in theory, and usually also in practice. The chief beneficiaries of the system, seemingly, were the landless poor and the small landowners. But the upper-class-dominated municipal governments championed the integrity of the commons. Even the *hidalgos*, who tended to be upper-class landowners whom one would not think to be likely supporters of the communitarian system, at times staunchly defended it, even against wayward muni-cipalities. In 1515 a group of over a dozen *hidalgos* from the village of Santa Cruz de la Sierra (Cáceres) brought legal action against the village council for failing to respect the integrity of the local *ejido* and *dehesa boyal*. There were times when even the most principled municipal council had to put a temporary tax on the use of common property, because of financial exigencies. Such a tax would not excite much opposition if it was truly temporary, nominal, and fairly administered. Linking taxpaying with the use of common property, however, was contrary to the principle of common rights. And it could cause problems with the *hidalgos*, who claimed exemptions from most forms of taxation. In Fuente Obejuna (Córdoba) the town council insisted that no one could use the local *ejido* and *dehesa boyal* who did not pay taxes (*pechos*). And it insisted that even *hidalgos* had to pay taxes if they wished to enjoy the common rights of the ordinary citizens of the town.[25]

However, despite the principle of equality in the use of common property, not all people really received equal treatment. It is hard to believe, for example, that municipal officials and other powerful local figures did not get an extra-large share. According to Antonio Domínguez Ortiz (1971: 157), the lord of a place was considered to have a double share. The local lord might have other special privileges as well. In Monroy (Cáceres), he was allowed to pasture his sheep and goats in the town's *dehesa boyal*, whereas all such animals belonging to ordinary *vecinos* were excluded. And in the late 1580s there were some places still clinging to the medieval practice of assigning blocks of municipal property to *caballeros cuantiosos*, warriors who were obliged, in exchange, to maintain a horse and arms for defense against the Moors. In Cehegín (Murcia) these *caballeros* were granted lands called *caballerías* for life. But by 1583 the danger from the Moors seemed remote, and the town council was assigning the *caballerías* not to able-bodied warriors, but to the council members themselves, and even to children or to others who were unfit to bear arms in the event of war.[26]

One would not have to look far to find other examples of unequal treatment in the allocation of common resources. And certainly, the municipal councils were often to blame, since they controlled the system. But on the whole, the councils seem to have discharged their responsibilities regarding the property under their control – a most difficult task – with surprising equity. It is facile to assert, as does Angel García Sanz in his excellent work on Segovia (1977: 264–85), that the municipal government reflected the interests of the propertied classes. That assertion is correct. But in all fairness, it must be stated that the government also looked after the interests of the lower classes, who were the chief beneficiaries of many of the communitarian regulations enforced by the municipality.

The common lands were limited. Some could be expanded, and many were expanded several times, usually at the expense of adjoining *tierras baldías*. Where these were lacking, the councils of some villages, like Moya (Cuenca), went so far as to rent lands in neighboring places, in an effort to provide adequate pastures.[27] But somewhere there was a limit to the capacity of common pastures to accommodate the animals of the local population. Where there was no regulation of the use of common pasture other than the custom that each person tried to benefit as much as he could from it, there was a potential danger of overtaxing the local resources. Overgrazing could fatally disrupt the local ecology, and had to be avoided, for the benefit of everyone.

The city of Segovia and its subject villages – except in those mountainous zones where pasture was abundant – met this problem by limiting the number of livestock that each *vecino* could pasture in the local commons. The 1514 ordinances of Segovia and its Tierra (territory, including subject villages under its jurisdiction) specified that *vecino* status gave a village resident the right to graze in the common pastures a maximum of 100 head of sheep, 1 ram, 1 mare, 2 cows, and 2 goats. If, in addition to being a *vecino*, a person was also an important landowner (*heredero*, with 50 *obradas* of land, or 25 *obradas* of land plus 10 *aranzadas* of vineyard), then he was allowed twice as many animals in each category. The double-maximum for larger landowners was not necessarily unfair: after all, the landowners contributed to the amount of common pasture through the *derrota de mieses* (García Sanz 1977: 264–76).

There were other places that also established a maximum number of animals for their *vecinos*. For example, in Zaratán (Valladolid), the ordinances of 1539 limited each *vecino* to a maximum of 100 sheep. Villada (Palencia) had almost the same rule, except that lambs were not counted until St Peter's Day. But the 1524 ordinances of Aguilafuerte (Segovia) were more generous: they allowed 220 head per *vecino*. And in Valderas (León – ordinances of 1583 and 1585) the maximum was 300 sheep and goats, with the proviso that there be no more than 1 goat per 20 ewes; and no more than 12 cows and horses per *vecino*, not including draft animals. But the ordinances of Santa Fe (Granada) placed a limitation only in the number of hogs. The number there was 5 per *vecino* of the city, which was justified because there was a limited amount of space in the area, and too many hogs would have posed a danger to the local irrigation ditches.

There were also some places that limited the pasturage of animals only during a specified part of the year. For example, the town of Zaratán (Valladolid – ordinances of 1539) banned all sheep from its territory from 11 November until Easter. If the local guards found a flock there during this prohibited period, they could kill three animals from it, the slaughtered animals to be sold, with proceeds to be used for the maintenance of the town's walls. In nearby Fuensaldaña, by contrast, the ordinances of 1576 excluded animals only during December, January, and February. During the period of proscription, to be sure, all local animals were expected to be grazed outside the town's jurisdiction, in others areas with better pasture resources (Lapresa 1955: 609–24; Huetz 1967: 639–41).

MONTES

Much of the pastureland of early modern Castile was in *monte* (forest woodland). The *montes* varied greatly in character, ranging from great oak forests to scrub brush, depending upon the location. By the late Middle Ages the forests of Old Castile had already been reduced essentially to the mountainous or hilly areas. Hence, in the Castilian language 'mountain' and 'forest' have the same name – *monte*. The *montes* were considered to be common property, and both the crown and the municipalities watched carefully to ensure that everyone got an equitable share. The *montes* provided several types of pasture: not only were there grass and weeds growing between trees; there was also a valuable pasture resource in the leaves and small branches of certain trees and shrubs; and the acorns of the oaks and live oaks were a highly prized pasture, particularly for swine (Vassberg 1980: 480–1).

Many of the common pastures already described – *ejidos*, *dehesas*, and *cotos* – were partly or even wholly in *monte* of various thickness. In the rugged semi-arid parts of Castile these *montes* were often of marginal value as pasture. For example, the *monte* of the Sierra Morena near the city of Andújar (Jaén) was described as being dense with thickets and scrub brush (*monte malo y bajo*) – the vilest kind of pasture. Yet, one resident of the city insisted that there was no such thing as a 'useless' *monte*. Another, in 1567, confirmed this, testifying that 'all the livestock of the city . . . pasture in that Sierra . . . and especially goats and cows and mules and pigs and sheep, although wool-producing animals not so much, because the *monte* and Sierra are so dense that they strip the wool from the animals . . .'[28]

Acorns (*la bellota*) constituted one of the major benefits of the *monte*. Not all *montes* had oak trees, of course, but those that were rich in these trees were prized for their acorns. The city of Trujillo (Cáceres), for example, was surrounded by *montes* made up principally of live oaks. Because its *montes* supported a flourishing livestock industry, the city government closely supervised their use, to maintain the value of this valuable resource. One of the city's major concerns in regulating the use of its *montes* was to control the acorn harvest (*la montanera*), which was a matter of great importance because acorns constituted the final filling-out diet of Trujillo's great herds of swine. It was the city's goal to enable all pig owners to share equally in the acorn harvest. Toward that end, the harvest was strictly supervised by the municipal government. The first acorns were ripe around the beginning of October, and the season lasted until the end of the year, but the swineherds often hastened the harvest by flailing the branches (*el vareo*) to make the acorns fall within reach of their animals (Vassberg 1978: 50–3). In an effort to guarantee the maximum benefit from the fruit, it was necessary to prohibit early harvesting, before the acorns were fully mature. The date for beginning the harvest varied, depending on the location in the peninsula. In Ubeda and Baeza (Jaén) it was St Luke's Day (18 October), whereas in La Alberca (Salamanca) the season did not start until All Saints' Day (1 November). In some places, such as Ubeda and Baeza, flailing the trees was forbidden on the grounds that it damaged the branches and gave an unfair advantage to the flailer. But in other places, it was customary to use the flail. In 1592 a resident of San Sebastián (Madrid) testified that the people of that village flailed their common oak trees every year, and that as a consequence the harvest did not normally last more than three or four days, after which there would not be a single acorn left.[29]

The acorn harvest must have been an exciting and impressive time. According to the council of Montánchez (Cáceres), the local oak woodlands produced an 'infinity' of acorns which supported numerous herds of swine and other large and small animals.[30] And in the *Relaciones*, the council of Las Mesas (Cuenca) reported (Salomon 1964: 142–3) that in its acorn-rich common *monte* 'some *vecinos* gather as much as thirty *fanegas* [a *fanega* is about 1.6 bushels],

37

and others twenty, and others ten, and he who gathers the least gets over six *fanegas* . . .' And, waxing enthusiastic about its *monte*, the Las Mesas council concluded that 'This *monte* and *dehesa* is so good, and so beneficial, that the town would have become depopulated had it not been for the *monte*, and all the *vecinos* agree unanimously that the town is worth no more than the *monte*, and for that reason the *monte* deserves to be protected with walls and towers, like a castle.' Through the hyperbole, the message is clear: the *monte* was an exceedingly valuable resource. Acorns were not only used as food for animals, but in famine years they were also ground into a bitter flour from which acorn-bread was made for human consumption.

Since the *montes* were common, no fee was supposed to be charged for their use, including the gathering of acorns. But the temptation was great to assess a fee for the use of such a valuable crop. In 1543 the city of Cáceres, in the middle of the live oak forest area of Extremadura, suddenly began charging 2½ *reales* per head of swine using one of its common *dehesas* during the acorn season. The result of this abridgement of common rights was a lawsuit which terminated in 1547 with a ruling by the Audiencia (Supreme Tribunal) of Granada that the *dehesa* was common and that the city had no right to levy a fee for its use.[31]

The practice of *ramoneo* (cutting of small branches for use as animal food) was widespread in the *montes* of Castile. In some places the practice seems to have been the normal order of things. In areas where grass was sparse, or at times when the grass was too dry to be good pasture, livestock would spontaneously graze on the green leaves of shrubs and would stretch up to nibble on the low-lying branches of trees. It was normal for the herders to want to help their charges by cutting down a few branches to bring them within reach. A resident of Valle de Valdeporras (Burgos) described the *ramoneo* thus: 'They cut branches from the holly, oak, and beech trees [*acebos, cajigas*, and *hayas*], and from all the other trees that grow in the place, and at the foot of the trees they give these branches to their animals, who run loose there.' The danger of the *ramoneo* should be quite obvious: some overzealous herder might prune off so many branches that the trees would be stunted. For that reason, many places allowed the *ramoneo* only in droughty periods, and even then only with the license of the town council.[32] The 1583 ordinances of Los Santos de Maimona (Badajoz) prohibited the *ramoneo* of branches

thicker than a hoe handle. And here, as elsewhere in Castile, it was
absolutely forbidden to sever the trunk of a tree of any size (Guerra
1952: 507). The danger of excessive pruning was so great that some
places, like the city of Trujillo, which had a compelling need to
protect its *montes*, completely forbade the *ramoneo*.[33]

A widely used remedy for the forbidding tangle of scrub brush and
thickets of the *monte bajo* was clearing by fire. Stockherders learned
that fire clearings (*rozas*) would destroy most of the undesirable
underbrush, and that the fire would be followed, in a few weeks, by
a tender regrowth that provided an accessible and good pasture in
previously unsuitable areas. Caxa de Leruela (1631: 133) defended
the fires set by shepherds, saying that 'it is necessary to destroy the
underbrush that impedes pasture'. Ideally, some of the larger trees
would survive the flames, to provide shade or even acorns for the
grazing animals. Of course, many trees would die or would be
permanently stunted, but to the livestock owner with hungry flocks,
the advantages of fire far outweighed its disadvantages. The stock-
man meant to set small and controlled fires, but occasionally the
wind would whip the flames into a frightful inferno, menacing large
areas of woodland, and human and animal populations as well.

Fires were set regularly in the Sierra Morena of Andalucía, which
was largely in the kind of scrub brush that was so hated by sheep
growers. A resident of Andújar (Jaén) testified that sheep could not
pasture very well in the Sierra Morena, because they could not
manipulate the area except in the burned places that 'happened' to
appear in the *monte*. It was clear to everyone that these fires had been
deliberately set. In 1542 the city of Andújar adopted a new set of
ordinances designed to prevent deliberate damage to the *monte*. It
was forbidden to set fire to the *montes* or to order that such fires be set,
under penalty of 2,000 mrs. The authors of the new ordinances knew
that there would continue to be 'accidental' fires, and to remove the
temptation to instigate them, they made it illegal for cattle and sheep
to pasture in the newly burned parts of the *monte* until three years
after the setting of the fire. For goats, who were far more destructive
than cows and sheep, the waiting period was four years. These new
ordinances so alarmed the local livestock owners that they attempted
to have them revoked by the crown. Professing innocence, the stockmen blamed the fires on 'outsiders, beekeepers, hunters, and charcoal
makers'. This fooled no one, but it did succeed in retarding the

39

implementation of the new ordinances for several years. But even after the institution of the new regulations, there continued to be fires in the Sierra of Andújar.[34]

And the problem was by no means limited to Andújar. In 1536 a *vecino* of Córdoba reported that stockmen from that city and nearby towns 'set fire to the *montes* to expand pasture for their goats [and cows], to get the tender regrowth . . . in such a way that the *montes* and *baldíos* of Córdoba have been destroyed and leveled'. In 1555 the Cortes of Castile heard a complaint that in Extremadura, Andalucía, Toledo, and other parts of the kingdom, league after league of *monte* was being ravaged by the fires of livestock owners and herders. As the damage increased, penalties were made more severe. In Cáceres, for example, an ordinance of 1572 specified a hundred lashes and six years in the galleys (virtually a death sentence), in addition to damages, for anyone convicted of cutting down or burning trees in the local *montes*. Yet, despite all laws, ordinances, and penalties, there continued to be fires in the *montes* (Vassberg 1980: 481–4).

COMMON ARABLE

Common lands that were used for cultivation rather than for pasture required the formulation of more complex rules. The growing of crops not only demanded a far longer occupation of the soil than did grazing; it usually also demanded its exclusive use. A given area of pastureland could be used by a large number of animals belonging to several different people, whereas the same area of land planted to grain had to be monopolized by the sower until the crop was harvested. As long as population was small in relation to the amount of common arable, the rules – whether written or unwritten – governing its use could be few and simple. But the population expanded (the sixteenth century was a period of general demographic expansion), and there was a limit to the amount of land available for each community's use. The growing demand for common arable land ultimately brought about the formulation of strict rules guaranteeing each *vecino* an equal share in its benefits. The density of population of sixteenth-century Castile was extremely varied, ranging from areas with a population surplus to other areas whose lack of population demanded efforts of colonization. And the customs governing the use of common arable were as varied as the population density.

TIERRAS ENTRADIZAS

The most primitive and simple type of common land use was for a person to occupy whatever piece of land he wanted, to cultivate it for as long as he wished, and to abandon it whenever he saw fit. The sole authority for possession of the land was its use – the pure principle of public ownership. No governmental entity played any active part in the distribution of land, but local and national authorities gave their tacit approval to whatever apportionment of the land that resulted from the wishes of individuals. Common lands of this type were called *entradizas* (available for the entering or taking). In some places in Castile, where common land was plentiful or where there was no great demand for it, the occupier of a plot could enjoy the use of it for the rest of his life, or for the lives of himself and his spouse. At the death of the occupier, all his claim to the plot ceased, and the plot was considered to be available for the first person wishing to occupy it. Possession could not be passed on to one's minor descendants, because that would have implied a proprietary claim, whereas the only right to common land was that of possession through use (Vassberg 1974: 392–3).

A document from 1592 describes the *tierras entradizas* of Mohernando (Guadalajara) thus: 'Man and wife enjoy them and cultivate them and benefit from them only during their lifetime, and when one dies, the other retains possession, but if both die, although they have children, these cannot inherit the possession, which goes to the first person to go in and occupy, plow, and cultivate the lands.' A report from 1587 described the *entradizas* of Valdespina (Palencia) in somewhat different terms, but the principle remains the same. It said that there were around a thousand *obradas* of land, 'which are occupied and worked by any *vecinos* of the town who want to, and they leave them whenever they feel like it, and then others take them, having no ownership whatever to them'. In Malaguilla (Guadalajara) lands of this type were called *tierras halladas* (foundling lands), to emphasize the informal method of taking possession, and the lack of ownership. I have seen sixteenth-century documents with references to *tierras entradizas* in such widely scattered provinces as Badajoz, Burgos, Guadalajara, Málaga, Salamanca, Toledo, and Valladolid. And I think it highly likely that they existed in other provinces as well.[35]

Many common arable lands were actually *tierras baldías* that were being used as commons by the municipalities. In fact, since the town council did not play an active role in the allocation of the *tierras entradizas*, it could be argued that these lands were nothing but *baldíos* being exploited through *presura*. In many cases it is impossible to make a distinction between *tierras baldías* and municipal commons. The language used in the sixteenth century was vague, often the ownership of the lands in question was uncertain, and (as I have mentioned earlier) throughout most of the sixteenth century the crown acquiesced in municipal control over the *tierras baldías*.

CULTIVATION IN THE *MONTE*

Because many of the common arable lands were actually *baldíos*, like other *baldíos* they were often in *monte* and could not be cultivated without first doing away with the trees and shrubs. Agriculturalists normally accomplished this in the same way as did stockmen – through fire (*rozas*). In fact, the *monte* typically passed through a pastoral phase before being cultivated: the herdsmen would burn the *montes* to enlarge their pastures, and the farmers would grub out the stumps in the best locations for cultivation. Many agriculturalists, however, did not wait for the stock raisers' fires, but made *rozas* of their own. One reason for burning the *monte* was that the ashes served as fertilizer. But after the euphoria of the first year or two, crop yields usually dropped dramatically. The field was then abandoned to grow back in *monte*, and another *roza* was made in a different location. After a few years, when the *monte* had grown back again, the first plot could be burned anew, in a fresh *roza*, thus completing the cycle (Vassberg 1980: 482–4; Martín Galindo n.d.: 16–18; Méndez 1900: 17–25). In 1536 a resident of the city of Córdoba testified that there were many cultivated plots in the burned areas of the city's *montes baldíos*, but that the soil was so thin and weak (*débil, delgada y miserable*) that one could plant grain there only for one year, after which the field had to be abandoned to grow back into *monte*.[36]

The making of *rozas* for cultivation in the *monte* can be considered as an example of arable communitarianism. On the other hand, the *rozas* damaged the *monte* – a common resource. This placed the municipal governments on the horns of a dilemma: on the one hand, they were supposed to conserve and protect the *montes baldíos* and the tradition of common rights. On the other hand, the population explosion made it necessary to put new lands to the plow, and the people wanted to exploit the *montes* through *rozas*. In many places, the municipalities tried to effect a compromise by means of ordinances permitting a limited cultivation in the *montes*. For example, the city of Córdoba allowed its *vecinos* to burn and plant those portions of the *monte* that were in dead brambles (*jarales muertos*). But in practice, not only these, but also living trees were destroyed, so the Cordovan attempt at compromise was a failure.[37]

An interesting and extensively used scheme to allow cultivation in the *monte* while maintaining its communal character was inter-arboreal planting (*el cultivo en monte hueco*), in Spanish, literally 'cultivation in a hollow forest'. This scheme allowed the underbrush to be cleared out and burned, leaving only the large trees intact. Then the spaces between trees could be plowed and planted to grain. Naturally, however, the cultivators tried to grub out and remove as many trees as possible, to favor their crops. To counteract this tendency, the municipalities established regulations requiring that a certain minimum number of trees be conserved. For example, the ordinances of Salamanca of 1568 specified thirty trees per *fanega* (about 1.59 acres). Through inter-arboreal cultivation, the same plot had two distinct uses: one was individual, of the crops sown; the other was collective, of the *derrota de mieses*, and the acorns and other traditional common *monte* utilizations (Cabo 1956: 610; García Fernández 1964: 145–6).

TIERRAS CADAÑERAS

Most common arable lands that were occupied without the active approval of the local municipal council (*tierras entradizas*, in other words) were also *cadañeras* – having to be cultivated every year in order to maintain possession. Custom dictated that the occupier of a plot of land in this category could enjoy continuous possession for life on the condition that he plowed it each year to show that he still wanted it. These lands were also called *tierras de año y día* (lands of a year and a day), because if the occupier allowed a year and a day to pass without plowing a plot, he forfeited his claim to it, and it was considered to be abandoned and available for the use of the first person who wanted to plow it. Of course, as I have already indicated, many lands were of such poor quality that they could not be cultivated year after year, nor would anyone wish to move in and claim such lands after the passage of only a year and a day. But there were other lands that were sufficiently fertile to be used every year. I have seen references to *tierras cadañeras* in the provinces of Burgos, Ciudad Real, Córdoba, Cuenca, Guadalajara, Madrid, Seville, and Valladolid – a good sampling of provinces that indicates that commons of this type were not limited to one particular region or peculiar set of geographical conditions, but could exist anywhere in Castile where the soil was fertile enough to permit cultivation year after year.[38]

The documentary evidence is not clear on this point, but the yearly plowing that was required in the *tierras cadañeras* was not necessarily tantamount to annual cropping, because a field could be plowed to maintain continued possession, but left without planting (fallow) until the next year. Nevertheless, there are enough references to soil exhaustion (*tierra cansada*) to suggest that overcropping was in fact a serious problem in the *tierras cadañeras* (Vassberg 1974: 394).

As can be easily imagined, when succession to the possession of common land was based solely on a first-come, first-serve basis, there were frequent disagreements between individuals wanting to occupy the same plot of land. As a group of *vecinos* of Budia (Guadalajara) wrote in 1571, 'when someone dies, there are big disputes and lawsuits'. In Torres (Jaén) it was reported that the family of a deceased possessor of common land would conceal the fact of his death, even to the extent of denying him the sacraments, until a friend or relative could take possession of the land. These difficulties could have been avoided by allowing the possessor to designate a successor, but that would have been incompatible with the principle of common land ownership. Consequently, the right to designate a successor was rare. But it was by no means unknown: in Malaguilla (Guadalajara), for example, the possessor of common arable could transfer (*traspasar*) the possession of his plot, but if he died before having done so, the plot automatically reverted to common status, and was considered to be available for the first person to go in and occupy it. In Alcalá de Henares (Madrid), the children of a deceased possessor could inherit the possession (but not the ownership, which rested in the community) of the best one-third of the common land held by him. And in Belinchón (Cuenca) when a possessor of common arable died, his children could inherit the use of the father's plot if they plowed it within twelve days of the death. This inheritance right in Belinchón prompted a royal agent to write in 1569 that the common lands there were 'almost proprietary', because in practice they never fell vacant, but were passed down from one generation to the next.[39]

Most places, however, shrank from allowing users of common lands to choose who would succeed them. Instead, they adopted rules – albeit only by custom – governing the question of the length of tenure, which was crucial to the right of succession. In Belinchón (Cuenca) the plots of common arable had to be irrigated and plowed by 15 August of each year to maintain possession (Gómez Mendoza 1967: 524–5). In Torres (Jaén), the possessor of a plot just fallowed for a year had to show his intent to plow it by the end of April or risk losing possession. His intention could be indicated by opening a furrow around the plot's perimeter and plowing a few furrows down the middle. And in Talamanca de Jarama (Madrid) the possessor of a field of common arable could leave it lie fallow for over a year following his harvest, but by Martinmas (11 November) of the post-fallow year, he was required to plow a furrow around the field to demonstrate his intent to plow it, and he needed to have it entirely plowed by the end of the next March. Failure to abide by these rules would cause the field to revert back to unoccupied common status. In places where the soil was so weak that an extended fallow period was required, the rules governing tenure might be considerably relaxed. For example, in Manzanares, Valdepeñas, and Moral de Calatrava (all in Ciudad Real), possession was not lost until the passage of three years without cultivation. In San Román de Hornija (Valladolid), a *vecino* was allowed continuous possession for eight years, after which the plot became open commons again.[40] And in the *secano* (unirrigated lands) of Lorca (Murcia) possession was not lost until a plot had gone unworked for ten years, according to ordinance no. 142 of the year 1527 (Costa 1944: 262).

REGISTRATION

The question of succession to the possession of common lands caused so many problems that in many places the municipal council intervened in the mechanics of succession to introduce more order than that resulting solely from the free interaction of the wishes of the *vecinos*. It appears that it was population pressure, which caused a greater demand for the available commons, that prompted this change. For example, around 1579 the *vecinos* of San Román de

Hornija (Valladolid) made an effort to avoid some of the disorder and disputes arising over the question of succession in the use of the local common arable lands. It was agreed that no *vecino* could succeed in possession until he had showed the plot in question to municipal officials and registered a claim to it. This registration consisted merely of notifying the council of the location and the amount of land selected. There were many examples of this type of registration in various parts of Castile. In the Tierra of Alcalá de Henares (Madrid) the custom was to register common lands every two years before the local scrivener (*escribano*) in the presence of two witnesses. The would-be possessor, the scrivener, and the witnesses would all go out to the plot being registered, to ensure proper identification.[41]

In some towns, registration evolved into a quaint ceremony. In 1585 a resident of Montamarta (Zamora) described the local custom:

Around the first of January of every year, more or less, when it is time to work the [common] lands to plant them and to make use of them, the town council meets, and to the ringing of the [church] bell, everyone in town assembles [in front of the town hall], and when everybody is there, or those who want to be there, the council makes a public announcement that everyone – men, women, and widows – should go out immediately to choose for themselves and mark the common lands so they can plant them. And as soon as the announcement is made, they go right out to the common fields, and each person takes as much as he wishes and marks it [with a hoe, or in some other way], so no other person will take his plot, and the possessor can use the land he has marked for a year . . . and no longer.

In some places the registration of common arable also involved a limitation of the amount of land the registrant could possess. In Campo de Criptana and Socuéllamos (Ciudad Real), for instance, a *vecino* who wanted new lands would go to the local town council, which would appoint some official to go out and designate a certain amount of land, according to the number of draft animals owned by the applicant.[42]

Common arable lands were used not only for grain and other field crops, but also for vineyards and orchards, where the soil and other conditions were suitable. But because vines and trees required a far longer occupation of the soil than did grain – with a correspondingly greater reduction of the common rights of the community as a whole – the municipalities nearly always exercised control over this type of planting. The normal rule was that no one could plant trees or vines on common land without first securing the permission of the town council. For example, the city of Toro (Zamora) extended licenses for its *vecinos* to plant vines and fruit trees in the local common lands and *baldíos*. The planter had the right to maintain possession of his vineyard or orchard so long as it was growing, but if it became unproductive and he grubbed it out, or if he failed to cultivate it for two or three years, it then reverted back to common status, and could be used as pasture by all the livestock of the area, because the possessor of the vines and fruit trees had no ownership of the soil, but only the right to use it for a specific purpose. Lands of this type eventually developed into a disorderly patchwork of vineyards separated by abandoned vines overgrown with weeds and used as common pasture.[43]

The city of Badajoz extended similar licenses for planting vines and olive trees, with the condition that if the recipient of the license failed to make the plantings within a specified time, or if he failed to maintain them, the land would return to its original common status. Municipal governments also, and for the same reason, usually required a license to put up fences or buildings on common lands. But a license from municipal authorities did not always guarantee good order in the allocation of common lands for these more permanent purposes. The city of Trujillo (Cáceres), for instance, discovered that some of its councilmen (*regidores*) had been showing favoritism in the issuing of such permits. Consequently a new ordinance was adopted requiring that licenses be signed by *all* the councilmen present in the city hall on the day of issue. And it went on to provide for the nullification of the license if it proved to be prejudicial to the rights of any individual or of the community as a whole.[44]

PERIODIC ALLOTMENTS

The registration by the municipal government of the common lands selected by the *vecinos* of the place was but one step toward total municipal control of common rights. Many municipalities – perhaps most of them in sixteenth-century Castile – had already taken the next step, in which the selection of the plots of common arable was no longer left up to individuals, but was wholly controlled by the local town council. The arable lands of a town would be divided into lots of one or more parcels and distributed among the *vecinos* for a fixed period, or in some cases for life. This practice of a periodic allotment of common lands (*sorteo periódico de tierras comunes*) was widespread by the twelfth and thirteenth centuries in Old Castile and León. And it had existed in the Iberian peninsula at least since the tenth century (Vassberg 1974: 396–7; Costa 1944: 325; Salomon 1964: 150, n. 2).

The method of dividing the lands was often quite picturesque. Typically, a committee of town councilmen would meet in public session to divide the common arable land into lots (normally called *suertes*, but in some places *quiñones*, *cáñamas*, or *divisas*). A slip of paper representing each lot would then be placed in a jar (*cántaro*) and a child might be called forward to draw out the lots to be assigned to each *vecino*. The lot (which could consist of several parcels of land) given to each person would be recorded, of course, for the municipal records. In Jerez de la Frontera (Cádiz) the lots were drawn sometimes from a jar, and sometimes from a hat. Unfortunately, the documents from the period seldom state clearly what the method of division was, but often tell only that 'the council . . . divided the lands', or that 'the *vecinos* . . . [would] meet each year and divide all the lands into equal lots', or that 'the officials of the council . . . named dividers [*repartidores*] to divide the said lands among all, making equal lots'.[45] But though more often implied than specifically stated, it is clear that some form of random drawing was a widespread way (if not the prevalent way) of determining what parcels would go to whom in the periodic divisions of common lands (Vassberg 1974: 396–7; Hoyos 1947: 129–30).

Each municipality had its own customs about when the lands would be divided and who would be eligible to receive a share. Participation in the allotment was usually open to all the resident *vecinos* of a town, or occasionally to *vecinos* of a federation of neighboring towns. Documents from the period frequently emphasize the universality and impartiality of the lottery. For example, in 1587 an illiterate elderly *vecino* of Brincones (Salamanca) testified that 'they assign as good a lot to the little man as to the big, and to the poor as to the rich'. Some towns reserved their common lands for married *vecinos*, or, if the lands were assigned for life, for recently married *vecinos*. Although the normal custom was to allot equal shares to everyone, some towns gave larger lots to those who owned more draft animals, or who had the other resources necessary to exploit more land than their neighbors. The council of Montánchez (Cáceres) gave two lots (two was the maximum) to *vecinos* who had two yokes of oxen, one lot to those with one, and a half lot to those with no oxen. These last would have to borrow or rent animals to work the land they were assigned, because recipients of common lands in Montánchez were required to work them properly, with the appropriate number of animals, not only during the planting year, but also during the (two) fallow years, under pain of the uncompensated loss of the lot.[46]

In Alaejos (Valladolid) there was also an unequal distribution of lots, depending upon the net worth (*hacienda*) of each *vecino*: everyone worth over 80,000 mrs (a moderate sum) was placed in a single category and was given lots of a standard size, but those whose net worth was below 80,000 mrs would be given only one-half or one-third of a lot, depending upon their wealth. Alaejos also followed the practice of assigning a newly married person who asked for land following the regular division only one-half a lot, 'and no more, even though the person was very wealthy'. And in some areas, for instance in the territory of the city of Soria, participation in the lottery of common lands was available not only to *vecinos*. but also to outsiders living there, on an equal basis with the natives. The criterion here was residency, rather than *vecino* status. In fact, it seems that most places excluded from the lottery their own *vecinos* who were non-residents. This was sensible – after all, why assign a lot to someone who could not use it? Following the same logic, of course, one could justify an unequal distribution of commons, to favor the more affluent, or to exclude the destitute, who might not even be able to work their lands. In 1552 a royal agent was told that some lots in the village of Yemeda (Cuenca) were left unworked, because the persons to whom they had been assigned were too poor to exploit them.[47] This was a poor utilization of resources – a situation best to avoid.

In accordance with the principle that possession of common land was limited to the benefits received through personal use, most places required those who received allotments to use the plots themselves. In the lands under the jurisdiction of the city of Soria, for example, the *vecinos* 'could not sell or exchange them or use them for any gain other than the possession of them'. But the right to dispose of one's lot as one wished also existed. In Lumbrales (Salamanca) a *vecino* who did not care to (or who was unable to) work the land that fell to him could assign it to the person of his choice, or he could turn it back to the town council, which would rent it out. Some places even allowed the recipient of a lot to rent it out for whatever price he could get, but that was a rare privilege (Vassberg 1974: 398–9).

49

Tenure of possession of common lands allotted by periodic lottery varied from one year to life, depending upon local custom. There were many places that held annual lotteries of common land, which might have been preferred on the grounds that it would allow the maximum responsiveness to demographic changes. Although some places holding a yearly lottery practiced annual cropping, the soil and rainfall did not permit that in most parts of Castile. Therefore, although there might be annual allotments, the common land was typically divided into several *hojas* (strips), according to the local custom of rotation, and only the *hoja* to be planted was subdivided into lots and apportioned in any given year. The towns of Lumbrales and Vermellar (both in Salamanca province) both used the widespread three-*hoja* system of rotation in which one-third of the land was sown, and two-thirds was allowed to lie fallow. The soil there must have been poor. In 1588 it was reported that some *vecinos* of Vermellar did not even care to use these lands, because the soil was too 'light' (*ligera*).[48]

The binary (two-*hoja*) system was more efficient, and was more likely to be practiced in areas with better soils, but there were also places with even poorer soils, which required three or even more years of fallow. The common lands of Valencia de Alcántara (Cáceres), for example, were organized on a four-*hoja* schedule in which three of the *hojas* lay fallow. The quality of soils varied, even within the territory of a given municipality, depending upon natural and historical factors. And a town – Valencia de Alcántara is an example – might have several types of arable commons, to take advantage of the varying soil conditions or of the differing needs of the local population. As conditions or needs changed, the municipal government might alter the existing customs. In Jerez de la Frontera (Cádiz), for instance, common lands were originally allotted for only one year, but the tenure was later increased to four years. And in the territory of the city of Soria, lots of common arable were given sometimes for four years and sometimes for eight – the reason for the change is not clear. A longer tenure, however, might have been preferred on the theory that it would encourage better care of the land.[49]

The allocation of lots with long tenure was somewhat unusual, but was by no means rare, and was found in various parts of Castile. In Carbajosa (Zamora) common lands were distributed for periods of eight years; in Tarifa (Cádiz) it was for six years; in Almazul (Soria) it was eight; and in Alaejos (Valladolid) the lots were assigned for periods of ten years. I have not found much information about what would become of a lot after its possessor died. But in the village of Villalube (Zamora), which had lots given for six years, the spouse of a deceased possessor would complete the remainder of his tenure, and if both died, or if there was no spouse, that lot would be left to lie fallow until the next lottery. In Castrogonzalo (also in Zamora) if a lot became vacant through death or emigration, it would be assigned to a newly married or newly arrived *vecino* of the place. And in Villarramiel (Palencia) a plot of commons that fell vacant when its possessor and spouse died would be assigned by the town council to another married *vecino*, in order of seniority. When lands were allotted for the ultimate tenure (for life) as in the case of Villarramiel, there was obviously a far greater likelihood that the possessor would die. Perhaps that is one reason why life tenure in the periodic distribution of common lands was rare.[50]

There was a large variation in the size of the lots of common lands apportioned through the *sorteo periódico*. In Lumbrales (Salamanca) each *vecino*'s share amounted to only about 1 *fanega*, whereas in Huéneja (Granada) the typical lot was of 12 *fanegas* (Bosque 1971: 129). The difference reflects the fact that not all towns were equally endowed with common lands, nor did they all have the same number of *vecinos*, and the size of both common property and population was flexible. As the years passed, the number of *vecinos* tended to grow far faster than the amount of communal land used in the annual divisions. Therefore, with the passage of time, the size of the lots tended to grow smaller and smaller. The repeated subdivision of the common lands sometimes resulted in some oddly shaped or oddly proportioned lots, such as extremely long and narrow ones barely wide enough to accommodate a yoke of oxen. And it should be said that the arable commons of a place were not necessarily located all together in one continuous field. The *hojas* might be spread around the municipal territory, located between privately owned fields. As an example of the complicated structure of the common fields of sixteenth-century Castilian towns, take the town of Villarramiel (Palencia): here there were 1,338 *yugadas* of common arable – a large amount comprising about a quarter of the entire territory of the town. These commons were divided into some 69 *pagos* (well-defined districts, possibly even fenced). The *pagos* were in turn subdivided into a total of 1,354 parcels: one *pago* of 78 *yugadas*, for example, was broken up into 70 parcels (Fernández and Fernández 1955: 104–21).

Because of the extreme subdivision of the commons of Villarramiel, the share of each *vecino* of the place might include several parcels in different parts of the town's territory. This would be an advantage, because it would mean that each lot could include several types of soil in several locations.[51]

PAYMENT FOR THE USE OF COMMONS

Common lands were customarily allotted free of charge. After all, the ownership of these lands rested in the community of *vecinos*, and they would not normally charge themselves rent. The *vecinos* were proud of the fact that they could use these lands without payment. In Villalube (Zamora) they bragged that they enjoyed their common lands 'without paying rent or recognition to the council or to anyone'. But the municipal governments often found that they needed funds for extraordinary expenses that their ordinary revenues could not cover. And in many cases they considered that the least onerous method of raising additional money was to set a fee for the use of the common lands. Some councils used certain special circumstances as an excuse to charge a fee. In Brincones (Salamanca), for instance, the commons were normally allotted free, but if a newly married or newly arrived *vecino* wanted a lot after the normal division time, he would be charged a fee of 1 *real*. If the needs of the municipal government were truly pressing, there would probably not be much resistance against the imposition of a temporary fee. In 1588 a 45-year-old resident of Vermellar (Salamanca) testified that the council of the place had never charged a fee for its commons except for that year when it levied a fee of 2 *reales* per lot. And he seemed to acquiesce in the necessity of the fee, although the land was of low quality, because the council needed to expend large sums of money on lawsuits and to support men-at-arms.[52] Though the assessment of a fee was usually considered to be extraordinary, in some places the fee had become so entrenched that it had come to be considered the norm. Medina del Campo (Valladolid), for example, had certain common lands called *sernas*, for which the municipal government charged an annual fee of 1 or 2 *fanegas* of wheat per *obrada*, depending upon the location (and presumably the quality) of the lands (Rodríguez y Fernández 1903–4: 565).

Even in places where the fee had become entrenched, the amount might vary depending upon the requirements of the council for that year. The council of Alaejos (Valladolid) made assessments varying from 2 to 6 *reales* per standard lot (the standard lot was 8 *fanegas*) of common arable. In places where there was a long tenure of common lands, the fee might not be assessed every year. In Alaejos, for instance, where tenure was for ten years, the fee was charged only for the first year, and the remaining nine years were free. I have seen one example – there may have existed many others – of a place that assessed a fee not in money nor in grain, but rather in personal service similar to the feudal *corvée*. The place was Montánchez (Cáceres), where this type of unpaid personal labor was called the *dua*, or *las duas*. In 1589 a septuagenarian peasant farmer from the town described the custom in this way:

Those lands are public and common in this manner: the *vecinos* of the town can farm them . . . and in exchange for the right to farm them the said *vecinos* are obliged to give service, and they work without pay in the business of the council, which is to repair bridges, roads, meat markets, granaries, and other public works, and a person who does not wish to perform this free labor will be given no common lands . . .[53]

In those cases where a regular fee was charged for their use, common lands assumed a character much like that of *propios*. In fact, sometimes it is difficult to distinguish the one from the other. True *propios*, however, were never equally divided among the *vecinos* of a place, nor could they be used for the payment of a nominal fee, but rather they were let to the highest bidder or put up for rent at the market price. A municipality that had succeeded in establishing relatively high regular fees for the use of its common lands might succeed in converting the lands into *propios*. Around 1575 the council of Lumbrales (Salamanca) appropriated the local common lands, for which it had assessed a progressively larger annual fee, and used them for several years as *propios*, renting them out to the highest bidder. The lands would almost certainly have remained *propios* permanently if popular indignation had not demanded their return to common status. As one *vecino* explained, 'we liked the lots that we used to receive'.[54]

OTHER COMMONS

The common property of the Castilian municipalities included not only pasture and arable lands, but other resources as well. Many of these other commons were supplied by the *monte*, which in the sixteenth century was still very prominent in the landscape of many parts of Castile. In fact, the economy of some areas, such as the Montes de Toledo, was based upon the utilization of the *monte*, which supplied not only land for pasture and cultivation, but also lumber (for tools and for building), firewood and charcoal (for domestic and industrial purposes), hunting and fishing, medicinal herbs, cork, fruits and nuts, bees (and the flowers to sustain them), ashes (for making soap and cupels), spring water, esparto grass (for making cordage, mats, and paper), and a host of other things. The use of these *monte* resources was usually common, and free. But the municipal governments typically adopted ordinances governing them in the interest of protecting the *monte* and of ensuring that its benefits would be equitably available for all who wished to use them. For example, most places extended a blanket authorization for the cutting of tree limbs for tool handles, but it was usually forbidden to cut down entire trees or to make *rozas*, which threatened to destroy the *monte*, without special permission. The manifold blessings of the *monte* are extremely interesting, and were highly important in many areas, especially to the poor, who could dabble in this and that activity to eke out an existence which, if not comfortable, was at least honorable. The subject would merit a detailed study, and the documentation is amply available in the archives of Castile, both local and central. But here, where I am interested primarily in the world of the agro-pastoralist, I must move on to other topics, returning occasionally to the benefits of the *monte* as it becomes necessary in other contexts.[55]

Water, whether for drinking (by humans or animals) or for irrigation, was considered to be public property for the benefit of the entire community, and as such was controlled by public officials. This view of water rights, which was tempered by the right of individual appropriation through *presura*, was a legacy from the Romans and from the Moslems, who themselves were the heirs of the Roman system. The principle of public water ownership facilitated the development of sizable irrigation works, such as those of Murcia and Valencia. By contrast, in medieval France and Italy, and along the rivers of Old Castile and León, the tendency toward the privatization of water ownership through *presura* resulted in the limitation of the scale of irrigation to small projects, the work of individuals or monasteries (Glick 1979: 73, 97, 101, 330 n. 111; Delano 1979: 181). The subject of irrigation and water rights in Spain would itself justify a weighty tome, and has been the subject of several fine local studies. But in this work I can dedicate no more space to it, because I am concentrating on dryland farming, which was (and still is) the overwhelmingly predominant type of agriculture in Castile. It is significant that water was considered to be common property, whether it came from spring, river, or even from a man-made well. However, certain compromises could be made regarding this principle. For example, the city of Jerez de la Frontera (province of Cádiz, in an area where water was scarce) had the practice of issuing licenses to individuals to dig wells (*pozos*) in the local *tierras baldías*. In theory, the water would be public property, but to compensate the well-digger for his pains, the city allowed him the exclusive use of the well for ten years. After the ten-year period, the water became common, but the digger was given the right of a first turn at the well, in cases of disputes over priority. The cupidity of the crown could also abridge the principle of free water use: in 1586 a royal agent sold to an individual a public well in Medina Sidonia (also in the province of Cádiz).[56]

Another common practice was the right of public gleaning (*el rebusco* and *el espigueo*), which demonstrated a special tolerance and protection for the rural poor. *El rebusco* was the right to gather fallen or forgotten apples, olives, grapes, or other fruits and vegetables after harvest. It enabled the destitute to get some food without begging. The custom of *el espigueo*, which permitted the gleaning of grain after the regular harvest, was general throughout Spain, and seems to have been a prehistoric custom designed to aid the hungry. There must have been some abuses, however, because the law specified that only the old and infirm, women and minors, and others who could not draw regular wages had the right to gather grain in that fashion (Hoyos 1947: 129–30; Guerra 1952: 524; Costa 1898: 277–80). I have earlier dealt with the importance of the acorn harvest in areas with oak forests. Not as widespread, but equally important in some areas, were chestnuts, which were also considered to be a common resource. Chestnuts were used as food for both man and livestock, and the harvest was supervised by municipal governments in much the same way that they supervised acorn gathering. Wild fruits and vegetables were also considered to be common property, wherever they grew. Wild asparagus, artichokes, mushrooms, figs and similar things could be harvested as a common resource even when they grew on 'enclosed' lands that were private property. The criterion was whether or not they were the spontaneous products of Nature.

55

If they were, then they were common, even though they might be located on private land. It should be remembered that, conversely, an individual could own private crops, vines, or even trees that he had planted – on public land. The intermeshing of private and public ownership was highly complex![57]

Nearly all common property was of the sort that was provided spontaneously by Nature. But because of special circumstances, some municipalities came to own other properties which were also treated as commons although they did not meet that qualification. In 1575, for instance, Valle de Sotoscueva (Burgos) owned a water-driven flour mill on the Engaña River. All the *vecinos* of the place could bring their gain to be ground, each being allowed a specified length of time to operate the mill. There was no milling fee, and when the mill needed repairs, the costs were borne by the local government.[58] The town of Salduero, in neighboring Soria province, had not only a common flour mill, but also a common forge and a common water-driven sawmill (García Terrel 1958: 23–5, 109–12). Municipally owned property of that sort, however, was usually treated as a *propio*, rather than as commons.

The ownership of animal dung, which was highly valued as a fertilizer, was ambivalent. When it fell in fields and pastures, it was left to enrich the soil there, whether public or private. The manure that accumulated in animal pens or corrals became the private property of the owner of the pens, if they were private, but became community property if the pens were public. In an era when animals of various species regularly walked the streets, the towns were able to amass large quantities of manure through street-cleaning. The municipal dunghills (*muladares, montones de estiércol*, or *monturios*) were considered to be the common property of all the *vecinos* of the place, who took advantage of them primarily to manure their orchards and gardens (Guerra 1952: 519, 531–2).

3

Other aspects of the communitarian system

In addition to its own common property, the Castilian town often shared common rights on certain lands, or other property, in a form of intercommunal use. It is a bit surprising to see the widespread existence of intermunicipal communalism in Castile, where there has long been a notorious emphasis on the *patria chica* – local rather than national loyalty. Many towns adamantly refused to allow outsiders to use their common lands or even the *baldíos* under their jurisdiction. For example, in 1543 the town of Villaconejos (Madrid) confiscated some land occupied by a priest who was a *vecino* of Ciempozuelos, a village some eight miles down the road. The priest had purchased the land in good faith from a *vecino* of Villaconejos. Actually, how-ever, he had only bought occupancy rights to the property, because it was described as being *baldío y concegil* (common, in other words). In any case, the clergyman lodged a suit to recover his property. The suit was eventually resolved in 1550 by the Chancillería (Supreme Tribunal) of Valladolid, which ruled against the priest. In its successful arguments, the town claimed that it had never at any time permitted outsiders to occupy its common lands, even though they had purchased them from a *vecino* of the place who did have occu-pancy rights.[1]

Such prejudice, and even hostility against outsiders, was wide-spread in Castile, but it coexisted with a remarkable intercom-munalism and intermunicipal cooperation. Intercommunalism had its origin during the Reconquest, when lands were used in common by several settlements in the jurisdiction of a powerful city, or in the zone given to a military commander, bishop, or lord. The settle-ments, later growing into towns, had some commons that were reserved exclusively for the inhabitants of that particular place, but there were other commons that were shared by the inhabitants of two or more places. Throughout Castile in the sixteenth century there existed intermunicipal commons that extended to veritable federations of towns. The lands that were common to inhabitants of one town were clearly distinguished from those common to the intermunicipal union (typically called a *comunidad* or a *comunidad de villa* [or *ciudad*] *y Tierra* by sixteenth-century Castilians, but usually referred to as a *mancomunidad* by modern historians) (Salomon 1964: 143). Belonging to a large intercommunal union could be an important advantage, and the inhabitants of member towns were fully conscious of the fact. When asked where he was from, a person would routinely include not only the name of his village, but also would add that he was a *vecino* of a certain Tierra where he had intercommunal rights, particularly if it had to do with a prestigious city. For instance, in 1542 a resident of the village of Villaureña (Zamora) identified himself as 'a native of the nearby town of La Bóveda, and a *vecino* of Villaureña and of the Tierra of the city of Toro'.[2]

Some places followed the custom of holding a yearly ceremony to reaffirm their membership in the intermunicipal union to which they belonged. For example, the councilmen of the city of Osma and of the towns of Gormaz and Santisteban (all in Soria province) met on 1 May of each year in the village of Olmeda, on the outskirts of Osma. There they attended mass together, and before leaving the church they solemnly reconfirmed and swore to uphold their intermunicipal common rights.[3]

Amando Represa, the director of the Archive of Simancas, has calculated (1979) that in the part of Old Castile comprising the present provinces of Soria, Burgos, Valladolid, Segovia, and Avila, there were as many as 48 *comunidades de villa y Tierra* embracing 1,648 villages in the late thirteenth century. Some were small associations of only five or six villages, there were medium-sized ones such as Medina del Campo, with 50 villages, and some were truly enormous. The largest were headed by the cities of Soria (with 238 villages), Segovia (204), and Avila (305). The intermunicipal community of Soria occupied 2,666 square kilometers – an area larger than the present province of Vizcaya. Although by the late sixteenth century seventy of the Sorian villages had become depopulated, the others had absorbed their inhabitants, and the union as a whole had grown enormously in population and in strength. And in the mountains of Asturias and León there existed numerous large intermunicipal unions, many of which survived well into the twentieth century. For some villages, the intercommunal lands were of paramount importance, for they had no commons for their own exclusive use.

It should not be thought that intermunicipal communal unions were peculiar to Old Castile: they were also important in the present provinces of Madrid, Guadalajara, Toledo, and Cuenca (Salomon 1964: 143–4). And in Badajoz province there was a huge intercommunal area measuring 9 by $7\frac{1}{2}$ leagues. The soil of the region was ill-suited for cultivation, but it was excellent pastureland. This area, which was included in the territory of the Order of Alcántara, had nineteen towns in it who shared pasture rights in various *dehesas* (Casco 1961: 245–7). The other military orders also sponsored the creation of intermunicipal communities, many of them quite extensive. There were many instances of such groupings in the Campo de Calatrava district of the province of Ciudad Real, and in the lands of the Order of Santiago (Quirós 1965: 207–8; Merino 1915: 294–5).

The largest of the intermunicipal unions were formidable indeed, and needed to be organized in a way that would protect the interests of their members. The administrative center was a city or a town, which served as the nucleus of a group of free villages. These were typically organized into districts called *cuartos*, *sexmos*, or *ochavos* (suggesting a division into four, six, or eight), depending upon the size of the community (Valdeavellano 1968: 542–4). For example, the city of Soria and its Tierra formed an intercommunal association comprising over 150 towns and villages in the sixteenth century. The territory was divided into five *sexmos* (notwithstanding the fact that the name literally means 'six'), or rural districts, which roughly corresponded to geographical factors. The pine forest zone, for instance, comprised one *sexmo*. The intermunicipal community was governed by a *junta comunera* (intercommunal council) made up of an elected president called the *procurador síndico general*, five elected representatives (*procuradores* or *sexmeros*) from the five *sexmos*, and an appointed inspector (*fiel*), consulting attorney (*abogado asesor*), and scrivener (*escribano*). For the election of the intercommunal council representatives, each *sexmo* was divided into subdistricts called *cuadrillas*. On a rotating basis, the various *cuadrillas* elected the representative for their particular *sexmo*. The representative, who had to be a *vecino* of one of the villages of the *cuadrilla* whose turn it was to hold the election, was chosen by general vote for a two-year term. The five *sexmo* representatives thus chosen, in turn elected the president (*procurador síndico general*) of the union, who served a two-year term and was chosen by alternation between the five *sexmos*, so that each *sexmo* would have the presidency for two years during every ten-year period. The inspector, attorney, and scrivener of the council were appointed by the elected officials. The council thus constituted would oversee the administration of the intercommunal property of the association, and would place guards to enforce its ordinances regarding the property's use. It is significant that the president and the inspector had the right to attend the council meetings of the city of Soria, where they had a voice and vote. But the intercommunal council should not be confused with the urban council – they were distinct institutions (Represa 1979).

Intermunicipal commons were of several types. Some were limited to the use of the *baldíos* and to reciprocal *derrota de mieses* rights on each other's stubble fields. Others included (or were restricted to) pasture rights in the fellow member town's *dehesas*. For instance, the villages of Cardenete and Yemeda (Cuenca) shared the use of certain pastures for their work animals. And the towns of Cazorla and La Iruela (Jaén) shared about 2,000 *fanegas* of pasturelands. Map 2 shows the arrangement of the commons and intermunicipal commons of the villages of Gerena and El Garrobo (Sevilla). Gerena had the exclusive use of three *dehesas* (1); El Garrobo enjoyed the sole rights to one *dehesa* and an *ejido* (5 and 6); and the two villages shared a large *dehesa* (4) astride the boundary between the two.[4]

The most widespread intercommunal rights were pasture rights, but there existed also many arable commons of an intercommunal nature. For example, in the *encomienda* of Mohernando (Guadalajara) there were over 13,000 *fanegas* of intercommunal arable lands for the use of the *vecinos* of the town of Mohernando and the villages of Humanes, Robledillo de Mohernando, Razbona, and Cerezo de Mohernando (Vassberg 1974: 394). And all the villages of the region called the Tierra del Vino (province of Zamora) shared their arable *tierras entradizas*. The phrase *rejas vueltas* was frequently used to describe reciprocal tillage rights. As a matter of fact, this phrase, which literally means 'turnabout plowing', came to be so closely identified with the idea of intercommunalism that it was even used – quite illogically – to describe reciprocal pasture privileges, even though *pacer a rejas vueltas* referred exclusively to livestock grazing rights, and had nothing whatever to do with plows. Many intercommunal arable lands were exploited through *rozas* in the *monte*.

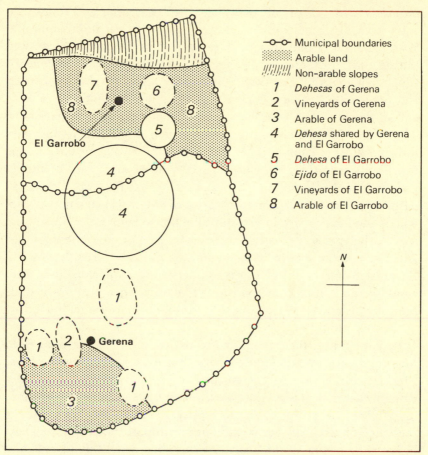

Key:
- —o—o— Municipal boundaries
- Arable land
- Non-arable slopes
- 1 *Dehesas* of Gerena
- 2 Vineyards of Gerena
- 3 Arable of Gerena
- 4 *Dehesa* shared by Gerena and El Garrobo
- 5 *Dehesa* of El Garrobo
- 6 *Ejido* of El Garrobo
- 7 Vineyards of El Garrobo
- 8 Arable of El Garrobo

2. Municipal and intermunicipal lands of Gerena and El Garrobo (Seville province). From an undated map (apparently from the late 1500s) in AGS, CJH, 24 ant. (14 mod.)

And arable rights were frequently included along with pasture and other rights. A much-used formula to describe the broader inter-communal rights was repeated in 1534 by the town of Campo de Criptana (of the Order of Santiago, province of Ciudad Real) with regard to the common lands it shared with nearby Alcázar de San Juan. It spoke of 'el derecho de romper e labrar y quemar y roçar y pastar y abrevar' (the right to plow and farm and burn and clear and pasture and water).[5]

Intercommunal privileges often were broadened also to include the right to use the common *montes*. Such *montes* that could be used both for firewood and for pasture were in some places described by the phrase *de corte y diente*, literally meaning 'of cutting and tooth'. In 1569 a royal agent wrote to the crown about an intercommunal *monte* system in Talamanca de Jarama and its Tierra (an area lying astride the border of the provinces of Madrid and Guadalajara), which included El Casar, Valdepiélagos, Valdetorres, Fuente El Saz, and other villages. He reported that the common lands there were called *comuniegas* 'because the town of Talamanca and villages of its Tierra all comprise one community, and a single entity, and they have no distinct boundaries between them, for what belongs to one town belongs to them all, with regard to *montes* and pastures and all benefits'. It should be said parenthetically that the term *comuniegas*, despite the implication of the words of this royal agent, was not widely used to describe intercommunal lands. Sometimes the mutual *monte* privileges were restricted to certain types of common rights. After a squabble over reciprocal common rights between the town of Zarahizejo and the city of Trujillo (Cáceres) it was decided that there would be no mutual common rights to cut firewood or lumber, or to hunt and fish in the *montes*, but that mutual pasture rights (including for acorns) would be respected.[6]

In some places the season for the use of an intercommunal *monte* took on a carnivalesque atmosphere. For example, the town of Las Mesas, a place with 230 *vecinos* in the province of Cuenca, had a valuable acorn-rich *monte* that was common to a number of surrounding villages. According to the *Relaciones*, in some years the people of these neighboring villages would gather around the *monte* two weeks before the opening of the acorn season. They would build huts and set up camp there as if they were at home, with their women working at their spinning wheels, or sewing, and it was reported that one woman even gave birth to a child during one of these waiting periods (Salomon 1964: 142–3; Hoyos 1947: 26–7).

Amando Represa (1979: 15–16) has written about a highly interesting intercommunal association of foresters called the Hermandad de los Pinares, or the Concejos del Pinar. It comprised two villages in the Tierra of Soria and five from the Merindad de Santo Domingo de Silos (Burgos province). The meetings of the association were held in Canicosa (one of the villages in Burgos) and were attended by elected representatives (*procuradores*) from each village in the association, who were often the *alcaldes* of the villages. By the late fifteenth century the Hermandad was already a venerable institution. The organization directly exploited and marketed timber, using its own carts (*carretería*), which reached the cities of Burgos, Valladolid, Palencia, León, and Zamora, among others. The villagers of the Hermandad did well: a document from the 1480s characterized them as 'abundantly wealthy men'. And the *vecinos* of those same villages were still quite prosperous in the mid-twentieth century, by virtue of continuing the communal system of the local pine forests, although in a modified form.

Consider how complicated the communitarian system could be: a village in the Hermandad de los Pinares, a lumbering intermunicipal union, could also belong to the intermunicipal Tierra of Soria, which conferred intercommunal pasture and other rights. The same village probably also had community lands exclusively of its own, and it is likely that there were some *tierras baldías* within its access as well. Private property coexisted with all these various and sometimes over-lapping forms of community property, but was itself subject to communal exploitation through the *derrota de mieses* and other practices.

And it should be emphasized that the communitarian system existed in seigneurial towns as well as in royal towns. The lords who had jurisdiction over towns were obliged to respect their communal rights. Not all lords did so with equal enthusiasm, of course. Many places, in fact, had to struggle constantly with their lords to preserve their commons. But in general, the lords must have been constrained by custom to respect the system, for fear of losing their subject population through emigration to other places with more attractive common privileges. Throughout the sixteenth century the revenue-starved Castilian crown raised money for its treasury by selling seigneurial jurisdictional rights to many of its towns. But as the formerly royal municipalities fell under the seigneurial system they did not lose their common privileges. The new lords were obliged to recognize the existing communal practices. Sometimes the contract between crown and lord-to-be specifically called for the continuation of the traditional community rights. For example, the document conveying to Don Antonio de Luna the seigneurial jurisdiction over Huétor-Tájar (Granada) declared that the transfer of jurisdiction would in no way affect the town's communal rights, and it mentioned specifically the intermunicipal rights between Huétor-Tájar and the city of Loja (Guarnido 1969: 76). And an intermunicipal communal union could be made up of towns under the jurisdiction of several different lords. The intercommunal system of the city of Guadalajara, for instance, included towns belonging to the count of Coruña, to Juan Hurtado de Mendoza, and to the princess of Eboli.[7]

Intercommunalism even existed on an international scale. In 1559 the Castilian Cortes indicated that there had in the past been reciprocal pasture rights between Castile and Portugal. But the Cortes expressed dissatisfaction over the fact that Portugal had curtailed pasture rights for Castilian animals, whereas Castile continued to grant pasture rights to Portuguese animals, as before (*Cortes*: v, 818). It would be interesting to know more about this type of intercommunalism, and to know to what extent it also existed with France.

PROTECTING THE SYSTEM

The flexible character of community property undoubtedly made it more valuable to the municipalities and to their citizens. But because much of this property could not be clearly defined as to type, and because the history of its acquisition was so often vague or clouded with illegitimacy, it was highly vulnerable to attack from sources seeking to erode the institutions of public ownership, or to exploit them for their own benefit. The problem was aggravated by the fact that there were conflicting laws regarding the use of community property in Castile. These conflicting laws – local and national – account for much of the trouble between individuals, town governments, the crown, and the Mesta. The communitarian tradition was able to maintain its vitality throughout the sixteenth century. But the tradition survived only because it had been staunchly defended, because for centuries it had been under attack from the nobility, the crown, the municipalities, and even from the very peasants who most benefitted from the system.

The most frequent and persistent attacks on community property came from the peasants who were using it. It is not difficult to understand how an individual who cultivated a plot year after year (remember the examples of long tenure) could ultimately come to think that his right to the plot should extend beyond a mere temporary occupancy. Each piece of land has a unique personality, depending on its soil type, surface irregularities, subsurface drainage, and other characteristics. And it often takes years of experimentation before a cultivator can understand its peculiarities sufficiently to derive the maximum benefit from it. Thus, there was a rational justification for a permanent occupation of the soil. In addition, there must have been a certain emotional attachment of the cultivator for a field he had worked and coaxed to produce season after season. Because of these practical and psychological factors, the functioning of the institutions permitting individuals to use public lands produced a strong tendency to infringe upon the principle of public ownership, thus transforming the right of limited and precarious use into the right of extended use, and temporary possession into permanent possession.

Accordingly, in all parts of the two Castiles the *tierras baldías* used by peasants tended gradually to become treated as private property. A frequently used technique to encroach on public lands was for individuals owning adjacent lands to enlarge their own property by gradually moving the landmarkers (*mojones*) into the commons, or by gradually expanding into the commons by plowing an additional furrow or two every year. By the same token, the Castilian peasants made unauthorized use of the common *montes*, especially in the extraction of firewood, charcoal, and lumber. Each individual tried to take as much as he wanted, whenever he wished. And there was a similar tendency for the peasants to misuse the various types of communal pastures available to them (Vassberg 1980).

Members of the nobility also often encroached upon public property to try to enlarge their estates. The success of a municipality in resisting usurpations by such powerful persons varied greatly, depending upon the resources and the determination of the parties involved. A drawn-out litigation to attempt to recover usurped municipal lands might prove so costly that it would be considered better to forfeit the property. Some municipalities simply acquiesced in the usurpation of their lands by a powerful noble, apparently because they despaired of any positive results, or could not bear the costs, or from fear of retaliation, or simply out of respect. A law of 1435 (*Novísima recopilación*, libro VII, título XXI, ley III) tried to remedy this situation by making it obligatory for local councils to seek justice when their property was illegally taken, even if the usurpers were 'caballeros y personas poderosas'. But the conditions that had inspired the law were strong enough to cause it to be broken. Nevertheless, there are numerous examples of municipalities that were successful in using the courts to resist the nobility's attacks on their property. A suit brought by Morón de la Frontera (Seville) against the count of Viana was resolved in the city's favor by the Chancillería of Granada in 1552. But the legal battle took no fewer than eighteen years, and the townspeople were so discouraged at one point that they nearly gave up the fight.[8]

Another way the nobility contributed to the usurpation of public lands was to grant permission for *vecinos* to plow and even to hold as private property a part of the *tierras baldías* that had previously been available for public use. For example, in the mid-1500s the marquis of Villanueva gave the *vecinos* of the town of La Campana (Seville) his permission to clear parts of the local *monte baldío* to plant vines, olive trees, and grain. As a consequence, by the early 1570s there were, dispersed in the *montes* of La Campana, over fifty patches that had been cleared and planted with the license of this noble. Sometimes a town council would join the lord in legitimizing the taking of parts of the *tierras baldías*. One such was the council of Espera (Cádiz), which joined with the duke of Alcalá to make grants of *tierras baldías* to local residents around the year 1530.[9]

The municipalities and municipal officials were also often guilty of usurping public lands. It has already been noted that town councils would sometimes grant their *vecinos* parts of the *tierras baldías*. This can be viewed as complicity by the towns in the usurpation of public lands. On the other hand, it should be noted that under many circumstances, the granting of *tierras baldías* by a municipality was to the distinct advantage of the local community. The councils making such grants might have acted out of a desire to insure that the possession of those lands would remain with their own *vecinos*, because there often existed a lively competition between neighboring towns over the use of *tierras baldías* available for their mutual benefit. The Castilian municipalities saw the *tierras baldías* as lands to be used largely as they pleased. Although they normally reserved them for the common use, there were many municipalities that usurped lands from the *tierras baldías* to add to their *propios*. For example, the city of Ubeda (Jaén) was found in the mid-1500s to have usurped four or five thousand *fanegas* of *baldíos* for its *propios*, renting the lands out as arable.[10]

It was not only the *tierras baldías* that the municipal governments granted to their *vecinos*. A few places (they were rare) granted their common lands in property to the *vecinos* using them, abandoning the communitarian system entirely, at least as far as cultivation was concerned. Such was the case of the town of Cabeza Arados (Ciudad Real), which adopted the system of private ownership in the mid-1550s. The documentary evidence provides no explanation for the change. It might have been to avoid the complications of having to supervise the lottery system, or it could have been to satisfy the demands of the local citizenry. In any case, the town council continued to exercise control over the rotation schedule of those lands.[11] The series of national laws dealing with the subject indicate that it was not an uncommon occurrence for municipalities to alienate their own lands. In 1329 and 1351 the monarchs Alfonso XI and Pedro I forbade local councils to sell or alienate their property. A law of 1515 reiterated the same principle. And the emperor Charles V repeatedly found it necessary to issue new versions of the law, showing that the abuse continued (*Novísima recopilación*, libro VII, título XXI, leyes II, VIII, IX).

Much more prevalent than the loss of community property through its sale by the council was its temporary loss to the community as a whole because of the high-handed and unfair actions of officials of the council. A royal ordinance of 1492 by Ferdinand and Isabella ordered officials of all municipal councils in the realm to return to the municipalities whatever *propios*, lands, pastures, *montes*, *dehesas*, and whatever other things from the common lands or *baldíos* that they had unlawfully taken. And it ordered them not to take the said property any more, under penalty of loss of office and permanent ineligibility for another office in the council (*Novísima recopilación*, libro VII, título XXI, ley IV). Earlier laws, of 1433 and 1436, show that council officials had been taking advantage of their position to rent for themselves the towns' *propios* at cheap rates (*Novísima recopilación*, libro VII, título XVI, ley IV). But the evil persisted in spite of the laws designed to eliminate it. And the situation was made worse by the crown's sale of municipal offices in the last half of the sixteenth century.

The Cortes of 1576 complained to the monarch that sales of the office of *regidor* (administrative official) were causing a hardship on the poor. The offices were bought by wealthy individuals, and whereas the town councils had previously acted to protect community property from despoliation by powerful private interests, when those private interests had bought their way into the local government, they could effectively manipulate it. Control of the town council enabled them to gain for themselves the use of community property. And the poor people were left with no remedy for this oppression, because the rich controlled the election of *alcaldes* (chief municipal officials), to whom they ordinarily would have turned for help, and they had no money to employ the existing alternative remedies for the situation. Despite the importunities of the Cortes, the crown took no action at the time (*Actas*: v, 23–4), and the abuse continued and worsened. The Cortes of 1586–8 again complained to the monarch that the sale of offices had allowed the buyers to become lords of the towns, and that they were able to take for themselves the *propios*, firewood and common lands, and even to usurp the crops of individuals, leaving the poor with no recourse. At the request of this Cortes, Philip II promised not to sell any more offices 'except in cases of necessity', and to allow the local councils to repurchase for themselves the offices that the crown had sold (*Actas*: IX, 402–3). Unfortunately, the 'necessity' of Philip II was chronic; and the sales and the abuses continued.

Yet, despite abuses by unscrupulous municipal officials and despite usurpations by peasants and nobles, the communitarian system in sixteenth-century Castile generally was able to maintain its viability. The abuses were numerous and glaring, and they took their toll over the century. Moreover, during the reign of Philip II the crown developed a new fund-raising program (described in chapter 6) which was highly prejudicial to communitarianism. Nevertheless, on the whole, the system continued to function more or less well, thanks to the weight of tradition and thanks to the force of local and national laws protecting it.

The municipalities adopted ordinances, submitted to the crown for its approval, regulating the use of their various commons and *propios*. The local rules for community property comprised a part of the general municipal ordinances. However, places with especially valuable property of a special nature would usually gather into one collection all the regulations governing that particular thing. For example, Trujillo (Cáceres) had its *monte* ordinances, as did Andújar (Jaén). La Puebla de Montalbán (Toiedo) had its *monte* cutting ordinances, and the city of Soria adopted a special set of ordinances for its new (following fires or massive cuttings) *montes*. The various municipal ordinances specified the exact fine to be levied for each infraction of the rules. For instance, the new *monte* ordinances of Soria included a complicated schedule of fines for various types of animals, in various sized herds, who entered the *monte* during its vulnerable early growing period: for bovines, horses, mares, or mules – 20 mrs per head by day and 30 by night; for asses – 5 mrs per head by day and 10 by night; for sheep – 1 mrs for up to 100 head, and for over 150 head it was 150 mrs by day and 300 mrs by night; and so on. From time to time the municipalities would modify their fine schedules, usually to increase them as they were made obsolete by inflation or by other changing conditions. Some penalties were extremely harsh – the reader might remember from earlier in this book that Cáceres had an ordinance specifying a hundred lashes and six years in the galleys, in addition to damages, for cutting down or burning trees in its *montes*.[12]

Not only did the municipalities punish those who harmed the *monte*, some places even took steps to promote the reforestation of denudated areas. The city of Trujillo had laws giving it the authority to compel the *vecinos* of its Tierra to plant and maintain new *montes*.[13] Beginning in 1539 the city of Zamora sponsored the planting of thousands of trees (mostly poplars and pines) to restore its common woodlands – a program which was continued into the seventeenth century. And the council of the small village of Alvala (in Toledo province near the confluence of the Tajo and the Guadarrama) organized the planting of acorns in the mid-1560s to restore an oak *monte* in its territory. The extensive pine groves (*pinares*) between the Duero and the Sierra de Guadarrama were begun in the late fifteenth and in the sixteenth centuries. Pine was preferred over broadleaf trees because it was fast growing and because its resinous branches made it less susceptible to damage by livestock (García Sanz 1977: 32; Domínguez 1973b: 160–1; Hopfner 1954: 415).

Many examples can be found of municipalities who were quite heroic in the defense of their community property, even in the face of unfavorable odds. In 1584 the governor of the powerful duchy of Feria ordered the town council of Salvaleón (Badajoz) to give a license to the warden (*alcaide*) of the local fortress to permit him to build pig pens and to cut firewood and lumber in one of the town's common *dehesas*. The council balked at the order on several grounds: first, the *alcaide* had not been granted *vecino* status (although he had lived there for two years); furthermore, the *alcaide* owned so many livestock that their presence in the *dehesa* would be prejudicial to the interests of the other *vecinos*; and finally, it was against the town's ordinances for anyone to build pig pens in that *dehesa*. When the council refused the license, the governor threw all the councilmen in jail. But they continued to withhold their assent, and appealed to the Audiencia (Supreme Tribunal) of Granada, which ordered them released. A suit resulted, and in 1586 the Audiencia ruled in favor of the town, despite a protest and an appeal from the duke. The settling of grievances through the courts was so lengthy, expensive, and uncertain that some councils resorted to violence to achieve quick justice. In 1563, for instance, the council of the village of Puebla de Azaba (Salamanca) rang the bell for a town meeting. And when the *vecinos* had assembled in front of the church, the council organized a party of some thirty men to tear down a wall of a certain building on municipal property, and to remodel the structure for use as the village corral. The owner of the demolished building protested vigorously, and brought suit against the village, but in the meanwhile the village had its corral.[14]

The municipalities appointed guards to protect their community property and to denounce violators of ordinances governing its use. There were many local variations in the names for these guards. In most places they were called *guardas del campo* (guards of the countryside), a title general enough to cover a broad jurisdiction. Some places called them simply *guardas*, or *alcaides del campo* (wardens of the countryside), or if they were mounted they might be called *caballeros del campo*. For more specialized duties there were *guardas del monte*, also called *guardas montaneras*, *montaneros* (foresters), or *caballeros de sierra* (mounted foresters). In parts of Extremadura, the foresters were called *montarazes* or *guardas de la montarazia*. Another specialized title was *meseguero* or *mesequero*, also called *mesequero del pan* or *guarda de la meseguería*, named after the *mies* (ripe grain) which these guards were to protect. And there were *guardas del verde* (of the green), whose task was to protect pasture.

The municipal guards watched over not only community property, but also private property, to keep animals from damaging crops, and to ensure that *derrota* rights were being observed. The guards, who were normally selected annually by the municipal council, had to swear by the cross and by the saints to uphold the local ordinances, and to discharge their duties honorably. In some cases the positions were auctioned, or rented each year to the highest bidder, who would then have a right to a specified percentage of the fines collected that term. This was true of the city of Trujillo, where the task of policing the *montes* was assigned to two *mayordomos*: one *de cortos y quemas*, in charge of cutting and burning violations; the other *de la montarazia*, charged with supervising the acorn harvest. Each *mayordomo* had a number of city-paid guards and constables (usually called *guardas* and *alguaciles*, but sometimes *fieles* and *corredores*) to do the actual patrolling, both on foot and on horseback. During the acorn season, the city would also send out its councilmen and other officials to help the regular guards (Vassberg 1978: 52–3). When the guards discovered a violation, they would report it to their *mayordomo*, who would denounce the violator to the city government. Unless the accused contested the charge, the city would levy a fine with no further hearing, according to the rates specified in the municipal ordinances. Occasionally the guards would arrest the guilty party and bring him to the town jail. Far more common, however, was for the guards to confiscate some or all of the animals involved in the violation, and to herd them back to the town corral, where they would be held in lieu of fines, pending the resolution of the case. Such seized animals were called *prendas* (security to guarantee payment of the fine). The security could also be inanimate objects (called *prendas muertas*) such as tools (used, for example, in illegal cuttings), blankets, weapons, and articles of clothing or other personal effects. If animals were seized as security, the town's justice officials might agree to exchange them for some inanimate object valuable enough to cover the amount of the fine. Impounded animals would not be released, however, until a fee was paid for their keep, because it could be quite expensive to supply them with feed and water.[15]

The smaller municipalities would not need a special *mayordomo* to supervise their guards. In Arjona (Jaén), for example, the guards were required to report violations in person to the scrivener (*escribano*) of the town council, who would inscribe the information into the municipal records. It was the practice in Arjona for the guards to collect a fine on the spot, and for the town council additionally to assess a like amount against the violator. If the violator failed to pay this amount, the town officials would confiscate some of his property to sell in public auction to raise the necessary amount. The ordinances of Arjona stipulated that the town's guards were to make the rounds of all the properties of the territory at least once a week. And to make sure that they were diligent in policing the private property of the area, the ordinances required the guards to report any damage to the owner within three days, under pain of paying the damages themselves, plus a fine of 100 mrs. Being a guard was a difficult business, since it involved both diurnal and nocturnal vigilance. And in some cases it involved spending several days and nights in the field. For instance, the city of Soria had six guards to police its new *montes*. These were supposed to provide a continuous surveillance over the area. Every Friday three of the guards would go into the city to make a report of damages and fines while the other three remained in the field guarding the *montes*. The following week it would be their turn to report. Thus, each trio of guards would report to the city government every two weeks; the rest of the time, presumably, they were on duty out in the *montes*.[16]

Not all fines were monetary. A widely used fine was the *quinto*, literally a fifth of the intruding herd or flock, but often moderated to only a tenth, or even less. There were many variations to the *quinto*. In Soria, the full *quinto* was enforced against hogs or goats who damaged the new *monte*, but it was not applied at all to horses, cows, or other larger animals, who paid a monetary fine instead. And even in the case of hogs and goats, if less than five animals were involved in the violation, the *quinto* could hardly be assessed, so a monetary fine was levied in its place. In some places, the idea of a proportionate fine was dropped in favor of a stipulated number of animals for each flock involved in a violation. The ordinances of Trujillo, for instance, set a fine of two head from each flock of sheep illegally entering the city's *caballerías* by day, and four head if by night. And there were places where the *quinto* was no longer collected in kind, but was computed in money instead, although the old term *quinto* was retained for the fine.[17]

As an incentive to the diligent reporting of violations, the guards were normally given a proportion of the fines they brought in, in addition to a salary. Each municipality had its own formula for this. In Soria, two-thirds of the fines went to the city treasury, and one-third to the guard who reported the infraction. The one-third share for the guard was a widely followed practice. In Trujillo, however, in certain cases the guard received only one-fifth of the fifth (*quinto*, of animals) brought in by him. And in Arjona, the guard's share was one-half of each fine up to 400 mrs, with everything in excess of that amount going to the town. If the guards were not prompt in making arrests or in reporting violations, they might lose their share of the fines, because most municipalities' ordinances allowed ordinary private citizens to report infractions of the law and to receive a percentage of the fines, if the guards failed to do so within a reasonable length of time. The ordinances of Andújar (Jaén), for example, gave the person who denounced unreported violations a quarter of the fine; and in Trujillo, the denouncer received a one-third share. What was the income of a municipal guard? I have seen only one reference to a salary: that one was for one of Trujillo's guards, who was paid 3,740 mrs for five months' salary in 1594, which amounts to 25 mrs per day.[18] If that guard received a substantial additional amount as a share of fines (which was not made clear in the document I used), his income would probably have been considerably above that of the average rural inhabitants with whom he came into contact; because, according to the *Relaciones*, the average daily income of *vecinos* in the neighboring province of Toledo was less than 38 mrs, and in certain poor regions it was below 12 mrs (Silva 1967: 28–42).

The municipal guards had a difficult task. The town councils realized this, and employed many devices to try to ease their burden. One widely used scheme was the organization of the fields of the locality into compulsory blocks or districts (*hojas* or *pagos*) where everyone would plant, or fallow, according to the same rhythm. This system had important advantages over the alternative subdivision of the territory into tiny parcels of mixed planting and fallow: since all the planted fields were together, it was easier to protect the crops from grazing animals; and since all the fallowed fields were together it made herding and pasturing animals more efficient. Hence, in many places it was forbidden to plant outside the designated block for that year. Many towns also established planting zones for vines and orchards. Some municipalities made planting in these *pagos* obligatory; others provided protection (by local ordinances, and the guards to uphold them) only for those crops planted within the special areas, and disclaimed responsibility for any damage done to fields on the outside (García Fernández 1964: 142–3; García Sanz 1977: 30–4). Another aid to maintaining the integrity of crops was the widely followed practice of organizing all the animals of a place into a single herd, which could be more easily watched than many tiny groups of wandering animals. Still another expedient was to require the animals of a place to wear bells. I do not know how widespread the requirement was, but the ordinances of Arjona (Jaén) of 1537 stipulated that each yoke of oxen or cows taken to places where they might cause damage had to wear a bell (*cincirro* – the modern spelling is *cencerro*) 'with its clapper not stopped up', and likewise each flock of sheep or goats had to have audible bells (*esquilas y cincirros*) that would ring to indicate where the animals were going, to make it easier to avoid damage to crops and other things. The animals of El Burgo (León) also wore bells.[19]

73

The guards experienced all sorts of difficulties in dealing with malfeasants. In 1589 a guard of Molina de Aragón (Guadalajara) testified that he was having considerable trouble apprehending violators of the law along the border of the neighboring kingdom of Aragón, because the local people conspired with their friends and relatives across the border so the latter could avoid capture and fines. The guard told of one such incident: he was about to seize a certain flock of Aragonese sheep illegally pasturing in his territory, but before he reached the herd he heard the voices of Castilian shepherds calling out to warn their Aragonese friends that the guards were coming, upon which the violators fled with their animals across the border, where they were safe from capture, being out of his jurisdiction. Sometimes the guards (like law enforcement officers throughout history) were physically attacked. In 1549, for example, the guard of the little village of La Revilla (Burgos) found a flock of several hundred sheep illegally grazing in the local *dehesa boyal*. He immediately went to assess a fine or to take some animals as security. But the sheep, which were from a neighboring village, were being watched by a couple of brothers who had a huge mastiff which they set on the hapless guard. The dog kept the guard at bay long enough for the brothers to escape with all their sheep. After that, to the mortification of the guard, the brothers went around bragging that they could graze their sheep anywhere they wished with impunity, because their vicious dog would take care of the guard.[20]

The danger of physical attack could also come from humans, of course. A forester of the city of Soria discovered this in 1528. In the early morning one day in March the forester and a helper apprehended a herd of over thirty cattle illegally pasturing in the *monte*. The cattle were being watched by a boy, but he fled when the guards appeared, so they began herding the animals to the city's corral, as security for a fine. But they did not get far, because the boy had run to fetch the animals' owner, a violent type who galloped up on horseback fulminating curses and insults, and threatening the guards with a lance and a sword so that they finally had to abandon the cattle and flee themselves. And in Arjona (Jaén) armed lawbreakers caused so much trouble for the guards that an ordinance was adopted in 1537 making it illegal for anyone herding animals to carry 'a lance, spear, goad, dagger, crossbow, cutlass, or any other arm except a knife (*cuchillo corvo*), on pain of the loss of the weapon and a fine of

200 mrs'. But one questions whether the ordinance actually deterred malfeasants from bearing arms.[21]

Most municipal guards seem to have performed their duties conscientiously. But guards were not saints, and some fell into the temptation of taking advantage of their position of power. Some abuses of authority were merely the result of excessive zeal, or punctiliousness. Another understandably widespread abuse was for the guards to show favoritism, particularly to municipal councilmen (who appointed them and paid their salaries). Inevitably, there were also charges of brutality, both in the handling of human prisoners and in the treatment of animals. The guards of the city of Toro, for example, were accused of the unnecessary use of manacles to bring in prisoners. And on one occasion the guards of Serradilla (Cáceres) seized about a dozen cattle and put them in the town corral, where they were reportedly kept without food or water for three or four days. Many allegations of brutality were undoubtedly exaggerated, but the charge in the case of Serradilla has the ring of truth, because one cow died. Another common abuse was bribery. A guard who apprehended a violator might insinuate that it would be cheaper to pay a small bribe than to pay the fine. If the suggestion for a bribe was initiated by the violator rather than by the guard, the effect would be the same: the guard would be richer, the municipal treasury would be poorer, the depredation of property would go unpunished, and respect for the law and its enforcers would be undermined.[22]

The temptation for the guards to accept, or even to demand bribes was much greater in those places where the guards got their offices through competitive bidding. In 1566 it was reported that the guards of Chinchilla de Monte Aragón (Albacete) publicly acknowledged that they paid as much as they did for their position only because they knew that they could recoup their investment by accepting bribes. Unfortunately, it was not only the guilty who made illegal payments to guards. There is considerable evidence of extortion: unscrupulous guards would intimidate the innocent into paying bribes (or protection money) to avoid the nuisance and expense of having to defend themselves against trumped-up charges. This sort of abuse led an indignant *vecino* of the village of Adobe (Guadalajara) to say of the guards of nearby Molina, 'They are not guards, but thieves . . . who come not to guard . . . but to see what fines can be levied; and not only do they exact fines, they also make the peasants give them grain, and salt pork (*tocino*), and cheeses, and other things.'[23] Such flagrant misconduct, however, must surely have been extraordinary. Most guards lived, with their families, in small towns and villages. In that setting, they would have been under constant scrutiny by the local community, and there would have been powerful social pressures for them to conduct themselves honorably, even in the absence of official restraints.

BOUNDARY INSPECTIONS

Periodically, the municipal governments would order an inspection tour (*visita de términos* or *visita de inspección y amojonamiento*) of the boundaries of the locality's territory. There were two major concerns in these inspections: first, that the integrity of the various municipal properties was being maintained; and second, that the dividing line separating the territories of different municipalities had not been altered. Territorial and property boundaries were marked in various ways. The boundaries often followed easily identifiable natural features such as rivers, unusual rock formations, or large trees. But these were not always available, so man-made boundary markers were also used. Buildings, walls, or corrals could serve the purpose, but the most widely used artificial landmark was the stone *mojón* (marker). At regular intervals the council of a municipality would appoint a boundary committee, who would make the rounds checking the landmarks, straightening them if necessary, and replacing them if they were missing. When inspecting the boundary between one town and another, it was customary for the boundary committees from the two municipalities to meet, and to check jointly the landmarks of their common boundaries, and of the intermunicipal commons shared by them. The composition of these municipal inspection committees normally included two councilmen (*regidores*) and the local *corregidor* or his lieutenant. Castillo de Bobadilla (1608: II, 946–8) recommended that the *corregidor* should make the inspection tour in person when the boundaries of commons and *propios* were to be rectified, because the full weight of his authority would be needed against those powerful interests who so often were guilty of usurping municipal property. Neither the *corregidor*, nor his lieutenant, nor the councilmen who made these inspection visits were paid a special salary, nor did they get their meals paid while performing this service, because it was considered to be a regular part of their duties. The inspection tours were normally made during seasons when there was no urgent work to be done in the fields. In fact, it was illegal to make them during the harvest months of June, July, and August, so as not to disturb the peasants during this crucial period. The spacing of inspection tours varied from place to place. The Cortes (*Actas*: v, 123–4) recommended annual inspections, and even called for holding back part of the salary of *corregidores* and municipal officials who failed to make yearly tours. Nevertheless, many places did not think it necessary to perform the task so frequently.[24] Trujillo, for example, had its inspections only once every six years (Naranjo 1922–3: 1, 355–6).

THE LAW OF TOLEDO

Despite ordinances and guards to enforce them, despite periodic inspection tours, and despite fines and other penalties, many municipalities discovered that they were unable to deal successfully with usurpations of their commons and *propios*. Even when a town took vigorous action against malfeasants, the effort was frequently wasted, because the usurper would simply reoccupy the same lands at the earliest opportunity, leaving the town still despoiled of its lands, and the poorer for its fruitless investment of time and money. In the Cortes of Toledo of 1480 the municipalities requested the crown's assistance in dealing with such usurpations. The result was the Law of Toledo (1480), which remained the basic instrument of royal protection of community holdings throughout the next century. This law was designed to make it possible for municipalities to recover their lost property despite the resistance of powerful local interests, who themselves were often guilty of the usurpations. The Law of Toledo ordered *corregidores* and other royal justice and investigative officials to receive complaints from the municipalities about usurped property. The official was to act as an extraordinary judge, summoning the accused parties to prove within thirty days the legality of their possession. In the meanwhile, the judge would undertake an investigation using witnesses and written evidence. At the end of the thirty days, he was to pronounce his verdict, and if he found that the municipality had indeed been despoiled of its property, he was to make immediate restitution. The law stipulated that if the convicted usurper resisted the order of restitution on the basis of spurious legal claims, he was to forfeit not only his claim to the property, but was also to be divested of any royal or local governmental post. And if he had no such office, he was to have one-third of his property confiscated for the crown. If the investigation proved that the usurper had possessed no legal claim whatever to the property in question, he was to be fined twice its market value. The law further contained safeguards designed to keep usurping parties from hiding behind extended litigation, and it designated the royal council of finance as the sole court of appeal (*Novísima recopilación*, libro VII, título XXI, leyes II, v).

The practical application of the Law of Toledo proved that more time was needed for investigation, and that pending litigation could be a problem. Consequently, the law was amended to allow seventy days for resolving cases, rather than the original thirty. A case was to be suspended if it was discovered that there was previously initiated litigation pending on the property, and was to be turned over to the magistrate before whom it was pending. But the matter of pending litigation proved to be a troublesome loophole through which usurpers of community property could maintain their illegal possession and impede the resolution of charges against them. A new law of 1552 attempted to eliminate this loophole by providing for the restitution of usurped property despite appeals if the legal claim to the land post-dated the year 1542. It further ordered magistrates to personally resolve any pending litigation, unless it was pending before one of the Chancillerías. This sealed one loophole, but opened another. Now the favorite method of resisting the Law of Toledo became to tie up the property in litigation at the Chancillerías, and despite the combination of local and royal efforts, it remained difficult to enforce the Law of Toledo (*Novísima recopilación*, libro VII, título XXI, leyes VI, VII).

Municipalities with especially frustrating land problems could petition the crown to send a special magistrate with legal training and experience (*un juez que fuese de letras y experiencia*) to help them enforce the law. The monarchs of Castile had been providing special agents for boundary cases for over a generation before the passage of the Law of Toledo. But after the passage of that law the commissioning of such magistrates became more and more commonplace. They were called *jueces de términos* (boundary magistrates), and were dispatched at the request of a municipality, with a royal commission specifically to enforce the Law of Toledo. Badajoz received such a magistrate in the 1480s (Rodríguez Amaya 1951: 445–59), Córdoba had one in the 1530s, and so on. The boundary magistrates, who were individuals with the licenciate or the doctorate, were aided by a special scrivener (*escribano*) attached to the commission, and sometimes also by a prosecutor (*fiscal-alguacil*). The salaries of all these boundary commission officials were paid out of the fines levied by the commissioner against violators of the Law of Toledo. In places where there were many cases to hear, the royal boundary commission might have to sit for many months. For instance, the commission for Jerez de la Frontera began operating in late 1551, and did not conclude until March of 1553. But even the best efforts of the royal boundary magistrates could not permanently halt the usurpation of municipal property.[25] Castillo de Bobadilla (1608: II, 947) wrote 'I never saw the place where most of the rich had not violated [the Law of Toledo] many times, nor did I ever see anything more commonplace than for each of them to take community property for himself, nor did I ever see such a lack of enforcement of the infinite number of remedies that are provided to correct the situation.'

THE MESTA

No discussion of the communitarian system of Castile would be complete without a section devoted to the role of the royal Mesta (association of livestock owners). The privileges of the Mesta are well known, thanks to Julius Klein's classic study (1920) of the organization. Hence it is not necessary to spend much time repeating them here. The Mesta's *cañadas* (especially designated trails for transhumant flocks and herds) could be used by local as well as by migratory animals. They were regarded as common lands, but they were exclusively for pastoral purposes, and could never be plowed. There were many conflicting laws about the Mesta, and the attitude of the municipalities toward its seasonally moving flocks varied, depending upon local pasture resources, the size of local herds, and the strength of the local government. The *montes* and *baldíos* were opened to the Mesta flocks by the earlier royal charters of the organization. However, the term *baldío* was ambiguous, and some towns were able to assert their authority over the local *baldíos*, insofar as they used them as local commons. During the Middle Ages the local commons – as distinguished from the *tierras baldías* and *realengas* – were usually recognized as being reserved for the use of local cattle. As long as the pressure on local pasture resources was slight, there were no grave problems over grazing rights. There was litigation over the question of Mesta access, but the towns generally were successful in establishing their rights. But as the size of herds increased, and as the Mesta grew in power, its itinerant judges (*alcaldes entregadores*) became ever more bold and arrogant in their treatment of local inhabitants and local governments. And by the beginning of the 1500s the Mesta flocks were regularly invading town commons, even such special pastures as the *dehesas boyales* and *carniceras* (Klein 1920: 92–3).

The monarchs of Castile, particularly Ferdinand and Isabella, increased the privileges of the Mesta because of the association's importance to the lucrative external wool trade. An infamous law of 1501 declared that all lands upon which the migrant flocks had ever grazed were to be reserved in perpetuity for pasture, and could never be used for any other purpose – a measure clearly detrimental to arable agriculture. This pro-Mesta policy was continued by the first Habsburg ruler: in 1527 a royal decree stipulated that local governments could not deny their commons to the Mesta flocks, and that if the flocks damaged cultivated fields, the stock owners would be liable only for damages, and not for fines or for other 'vexations'. The Mesta was at the height of its power during the reign of Charles V, its flocks numbering some three and a half million head. These animals and the Mesta judges were undoubtedly the source of much misery for the local people with whom they came into contact. Many a grain field was ravaged, many a peasant was unfairly harassed, and many a local pasture was stripped by the invading flocks (Huetz 1967: 637; Gómez Mendoza 1967: 501–2, 508).

This high-handed treatment spurred an intense anti-Mesta reaction on the part of the towns and the peasants. At the same time, around mid-century, the crown stopped favoring the organization as it had before: the Castilian economy had become more complex after the opening up of the American market, and wool had lost its preeminent position to grain, wine, and olive oil. The Cortes now assumed an increasingly anti-Mesta posture, and the Chancillerías began handing down decisions that tended to favor the extension of agriculture at the expense of the old pastoral prerogatives. And for various reasons, the number of animals in Mesta flocks dropped to around two million head by the end of the sixteenth century. The final step in the reduction of the power of the Mesta came as a result of the conditions placed on the monarch by the Cortes before it agreed to approve the *servicio de millones* (special tax to rebuild the Armada after the debacle of 1588). The Mesta judges lost most of their power, and the importance of the stock owners' association was greatly diminished (*Actas*: v, 246).

Because of the nature of the organization, the Mesta had an adversary relationship with agriculturalists living alongside its routes. The Mesta saw the plow as a threat to its *cañadas* and pastures, and local peasants saw the Mesta flocks as a menace to their fields, vineyards, and orchards. It is tempting to describe the resulting conflicts as being the manifestation of a natural animosity between stockmen and farmers. There was undeniably a sustained antagonism between the owners of migratory flocks and the local agriculturalists of the areas through which they passed. But this was not, strictly speaking, an arable–pastoral conflict, because the typical Castilian peasant had both cultivated fields *and* animals. The grain farmer needed animals for draft power, meat, dairy products, and wool and leather; and the stock raiser needed fields to provide grain for his bread. For the peasant, then, there was a complementary, rather than an antagonistic, relationship between stock raising and arable agriculture. The *derrota de mieses* and the *dehesa boyal* are proof of this complementary relationship. The intruding Mesta flocks, however, disrupted the local equilibrium. They competed with local animals for pasture, and the conflicts which ensued engendered countless legal battles. In fact, much (if not most) of the litigation between the Mesta and local interests reflected not a pastoral–arable conflict, but rather a rivalry between local and transhumant pastoralism.

For example, throughout the late 1400s and the entire 1500s the city of Trujillo maintained a running feud with the Mesta, whose animals wintered in the area. In the year 1500 the Chancillería of Granada resolved in favor of the city a suit over whether or not the migratory herds had the right to pasture gratis in Trujillo's common *dehesas*. In the same year Trujillo agreed to allow the Mesta herds free passage in the Berrocal (a rocky area) adjacent to the city, so long as they entered one day and left the following day. If the animals lingered beyond that, they could be fined by the city for trespassing. The Mesta regularly secured the pasture rights it needed through rental agreements with Trujillo, but there continued to be trouble over conflicting interpretations of local ordinances and Mesta privileges. In repeated confrontations with the Mesta, the city acted arbitrarily, subjecting the shepherds and their flocks to various forms of harassment. The Mesta defended its ancient prerogatives as best it could, but its star was on the wane: the Chancillería often ruled against it. The Mesta frequently complained that sheep and shepherds were being mistreated by officials from Trujillo. There were numerous examples of deliberate plowings of Mesta trails and pastures, and of the usurpation of Mesta pastures. The city and its *vecinos* acted in an arrogant and overbearing manner toward the Mesta, often getting the best of it through deception, through brute force in the field, and through legal maneuvers in the courts.[26]

Trujillo, of course, was an extraordinarily powerful (and litigious) city. Smaller and weaker municipalities were less likely to fare well against the Mesta. In 1586, for instance, the Chancillería of Granada ruled that the town of Monroy (Cáceres) had to allow Mesta animals pasture rights in its *dehesa boyal*. And in 1590 the town of Navacerrada (Madrid) lost a case before the Chancillería of Valladolid, in which it had tried to exclude Mesta animals from an *ejido*. But other small municipalities were victorious against the Mesta, especially in the second half of the century, as in the case of Aliaguilla (Cuenca), which in 1591 won from the Chancillería of Granada recognition of its right to keep Mesta flocks from using its three *dehesas boyales*. And as the century neared its end, some small municipalities felt confident enough to treat the Mesta in a high-handed, arrogant manner. For example, in 1583 the council of Arnedo (Logroño) suddenly voted to increase its fines tenfold, and it ordered the decapitation of animals illegally invading the pastures and fields of its territory.[27]

Some historians, awed by the spectre of Mesta excesses during the zenith of the association's power, have concluded that early modern Spanish agriculture was ruined by depredations of migratory flocks. But that is simply not true. It is likely that only a minority of Castilian peasant farmers ever had their crops damaged by Mesta flocks. Furthermore, the available evidence clearly indicates that arable agriculture was generally victorious over pastoral interests in the sixteenth century – overwhelmingly so during the reign of Philip II. Nearly all of the lawsuits that I have seen between the Mesta and agriculturalists originated because of illegal plowings of *cañadas*, *dehesas boyales*, or other areas that traditionally had been reserved for pasture. The evidence that I have seen, in suits in the two Chancillerías and in the Mesta archive, suggests that the Mesta was tenacious in the defense of its traditional pasture rights, even when the bias of the courts was distinctly in favor of the expansion of cultivation. But members of the Mesta seem to have been normally quite willing to pay damages and fines when their animals strayed into established cultivated fields. The *baldíos* constituted a grey area, claimed as pasture by the Mesta, and claimed as potential arable by land-hungry peasants. And it was the question of new cultivation in the *baldíos* that generated most of the antagonism between the Mesta and agriculturalists, and most of the legal battles between the two.[28]

THE IMPORTANCE OF THE COMMUNITARIAN SYSTEM

By now it should be amply clear to the reader that the communitarian system in sixteenth-century Castile was not merely a decrepit vestige of the medieval past, nor was it a local aberration restricted to a few isolated districts that were out of tune with the rest of the country. Rather, it was a vital part of the fabric of society. But exactly how important was it? Unfortunately, that question is difficult to answer. We know that the towns described in the *Relaciones* rarely lacked community property. The *Relaciones* show that Castilian villagers of the late 1570s found the different forms of public ownership to be highly beneficial, and of great importance to their economic welfare. They never thought that they had too many commons or *propios*, but rather tended to want to increase them in size and number. Many towns bought, or even rented property for this purpose. And the villagers always lamented any loss or contraction of their common privileges. This strong popular attachment for the communitarian system is hardly surprising, for the system sustained both stock raising and cultivation, and constituted a keystone of the social and economic structure of rural life. But the dependence of a Castilian municipality on community-owned property varied greatly from one place to another. It would be splendid to be able to present here a set of accurate statistics breaking down municipal territories of various regions into privately owned and public lands, with subdivisions of the latter into various categories for comparative purposes. But unfortunately, it is not possible to do so: the surviving quantitative information is incomplete, geographically spotty, and of inconsistent quality. It seems that most places had a hybrid property structure in which private property and public property coexisted. The structure could be very complicated: a hypothetical town could have a juxtaposition of seigneurial property, ordinary private property, municipal property of various kinds, and intermunicipal property. The crown lands added an additional complication, and do not forget that even 'private' property was subject to public use through the *derrota de mieses*, and other practices.

One must be cautious in interpreting documentary assessments of the proportion of community-owned lands of a place, because to sixteenth-century Castilians virtually every field in a territory was 'public' and 'common' through the *derrota de mieses*. This can easily lead to misconstruction or exaggeration. For example, a local historian, writing in the mid-twentieth century about the old land-holding system of Badajoz ,concluded that virtually all of the territory of the city consisted of communal lands, because the 'private property' rights in the area were essentially limited to the right to plant and to pasture on the lands, and even these were subject to limiting restrictions (Rodríguez Amaya 1951: 438).

We know that there existed some villages where there was little community property, and where nearly all the land was in private hands (Vassberg 1974: 400–1). But this seems to have been highly unusual. According to the Cortes of Madrid of 1563 (*Actas*: 1, 331) it was 'notorious that the *baldíos* and other public and common lands were the most important thing that the towns had for their sustenance and preservation'. Now, it must be admitted that the Cortes were often guilty of hyperbole. However, it seems quite clear that there were many places where most or even all of the land in the locality was indeed community property of one sort or another. For example, in 1584 a royal magistrate conducted an investigation that showed that in the town of Castrillo (apparently Castrillo la Guareña, in Zamora province) nearly the entire territory was common or *baldío*. During a similar investigation in the village of Brincones (Salamanca) a sexagenarian *vecino* of the place testified that the entire territory was common pasture for local livestock, except for one small plot of about a *fanega* in area. And the *vecinos* of Castroverde de Campos (Zamora) reported in 1584 that they had nothing with which to sustain themselves but their periodically allotted common arable lands. A similar situation existed in the village of Piedras Albas, in the province of Cáceres near the Portuguese border. There the *vecinos* reported that their only livelihood was growing grain, and the only lands they had for this purpose were *tierras baldías*. Even down in Málaga province, the *vecinos* of Teba claimed that all the lands in the territory were 'public and municipal and common and *baldíos*'.[29]

Even if we allow for exaggeration, there can be little doubt concerning the dominant role of the communitarian system in the aforementioned places. But even in other towns, where community property represented only a minority of the total resources, its impact could nevertheless be tremendous. Where there were common arable lands, everyone could attempt to improve his standard of living by farming them. The exploitation of even a small amount of community land could significantly advance the well-being of a peasant with marginal property resources of his own. Consider the example of the town of Quesada (Jaén). The municipal government supervised the use of a large block of arable *baldíos*, which the *vecinos* of the place could freely use in lots of up to 10 *fanegas*. Unfortunately, we do not know what percentage of the town's territory these *baldíos* comprised, but in 1569 the population of Quesada was 1,400 *vecinos*, of whom about 800 were independent peasant farmers (*labradores*). And over 700 of these peasant farmers – practically all of them – had lots in the *baldíos*, thus benefiting from the free use of those lands. In Villarramiel de Campos (Palencia) there existed a similar situation. In 1584 the town boasted some 1,340 *obradas* of common arable lands that were allotted for life to all the resident married *vecinos* of the place. In this instance, we know that these particular commons made up about a quarter of the area of the local territory. And much of the remaining three-quarters must have also been community property, in the form of pastures, *ejidos*, and so forth.[30]

It is commonplace for documents dealing with common lands and *baldíos* to stress the importance of the fact that no rent needed to be paid for their use. Quite clearly, that was one of their most attractive features – they allowed the ordinary peasant, who had meager resources, to utilize lands without having to worry about either rent or the responsibility (and expense) of land ownership. One can find abundant documentary evidence from all parts of Castile indicating that these lands were exploited in preference to privately owned lands, precisely for that reason.

The communitarian system was considered to be an essential part of Hispanic society. Therefore, when the Americas were colonized, it was considered perfectly natural that the various institutions of public ownership, like other institutions of the Castilian motherland, should be transported to the New World (Fabila 1941: 8, 13, 15). It would be fascinating to study the fate of the transplanted *propios*, *ejidos*, *dehesas boyales*, and other types of community property in the

exotic setting of the western hemisphere, particularly as they inter-
acted with pre-existing native institutions. But here we can only
mention the transatlantic voyage of the Castilian institutions as proof
of their vitality and of their importance to the Spanish culture of
the day.

THE SURVIVAL OF THE COMMUNITARIAN SYSTEM IN LATER SPAIN

Although the communitarian system suffered many vicissitudes,
and although it sustained attacks from various sides (about this,
more later), the system was too deeply rooted in the habits and
in the economy of rural Castile to be quickly eradicated. The mid-
eighteenth-century Catastro de Ensenada, which was the first comprehensive statistical survey of the nation's resources, showed that
community property was still very much alive. In the district of
La Armuña (Salamanca) twenty out of thirty-three towns and
villages still had common arable lands (Cabo 1956: 119–23). And
in the Subbético district of the province of Córdoba, every town had
propios and commons, about a quarter of which were in arable, and
the remainder in pasture (including *monte*). In that district, the town
of Priego alone owned 12,730 *fanegas* of community lands scattered
in about twenty different blocks (Ortega Alba 1973: 634–6). And
up-river, in the neighboring province of Jaén, the municipalities had
also retained large amounts of *propios* and commons. Little Baños de
la Encina had 14,000 hectares – an impressive legacy for a village of
only a couple of thousand inhabitants (in 1595 it had 1,336, and was
probably not much larger in the mid-1700s) (Higueras 1961: 121–77).
The Catastro revealed that over half of the land in the territory of
Salduero (Soria) was common (1,451 *yugadas* out of 2,500), but most
of this was *monte* or *dehesa boyal*. Most of Salduero's cultivated land
was privately owned, although the town did own 20 *fanegas* of arable
(García Terrel 1958: 25–5, 109–12). And in the Corregimiento of
Cáceres there were 242,205 *fanegas* of *baldío* commons (in *monte*) out
of a total area of 488,196 *fanegas* (Martín Gil 1938: 36). The proportion of community property in the mid-1700s was undoubtedly
much lower than it had been back in the sixteenth century, because
the general trend, for centuries, had been toward the individualization of land ownership.

The decisive blow in the destruction of Spanish communitarianism

came in the nineteenth century, with the state-directed disamortization of ecclesiastical and municipal lands. The disamortization
process revealed the existence of numerous municipalities where the
totality of the territory was still collectively owned, with no private
property other than houses and adjoining garden plots. Joaquín
Costa (1944: 250–83) cited numerous such villages between the
Duero and Tormes rivers (Zamora) in Old Castile. And in the Sierra
de Urbión (Soria) there were still a number of villages subsisting
almost exclusively on the exploitation of community-owned forests.
Costa even found some villages in southern Spain where the land was
almost 100 percent communal. In Extremadura, as the disamortizations began, the little village of Almaraz (Cáceres) still had about
800 *fanegas* of arable commons which were divided into 80 lots and
periodically apportioned among the *vecinos* of the place (Corchón
1963: 258–9, 311–12). And in the province of Almería, a count
revealed that over 99 percent of the live oak trees of the area were
still common, rather than privately owned (Toro 1849: 257–64). All
this was before the state-directed forced disamortization of commons.
But even after the expropriations there remained some living frag-
ments of the communitarian past, mainly in isolated mountain zones
that had escaped the notice of the government, or that were considered to be too trifling to worry about. Near the end of the nineteenth century Costa found villages that still practiced the periodic
distribution of common arable land in several places in Old Castile.
And he wrote (1944: 250–83) that the custom of the free use of
community lands (*baldíos*) for the plowing was still in use in many
areas, including La Mancha, Andalucía, Asturias, Navarra, and
Cataluña. The poor, isolated villages of the Campo de Aliste (Zamora) had also been able to retain many of their communal customs,
and had retained some of their lands, despite the disamortizations
(Méndez 1900: 35–74).

One would think that by the mid-twentieth century the progressive
evolution of society would have caused the vestiges of the communal
past of a bygone era to have completely disappeared. Not so: a
surprising number of the old customs have survived. The most basic
is the collective right to use forests and pastures, and this custom
persists in many parts of Spain, particularly in the mountains of the
north (Hoyos 1947: 18–23). An outstanding – though certainly not
typical – example of communal survival is the village of La Aldea del
Puente (León). Here community property is not a marginal residue

but still an element of prime importance. In 1970 it occupied 46 percent of the local territory, and included forest, grazing land, and arable. The *derrota* was even still observed there (Ferreras 1971: 713). Elsewhere in the province of León there still exist mountain villages organized into intermunicipal unions with shared pasture rights in certain areas. And the village of Llánaves (León) in the 1950s continued to practice the periodic division of arable lands, following precisely the centuries-old custom (Martín Galindo n.d.: 7–26).

The La Armuña district of Salamanca province also had villages still employing the old periodic allotment of common arable, although the amount of land had dwindled to a fraction of its former size. In La Armuña common rights to acorns and firewood were also still observed in the 1950s (Cabo 1955: 412–13). The geographer Antonio López Gómez (1954: 566) studied the surviving agrarian collectivism of the mountain village of Valdelaguna (Burgos) in the 1950s. He found that the village made allotments of common arable every eight years, of parcels organized into two *pagos* (planting districts) which were sown alternatively in a biennial schedule (the time-honored *año y vez*). The *derrota de mieses* was still followed, not only on the communal fields, but on private plots as well. About 15 percent of Valdelaguna's community lands were arable; about 35 percent was in pine forest; and most of the remainder was pasture. These proportions show that the local economy was highly dependent on the pastoral sector and on the exploitation of the local forests – a situation that probably had not changed appreciably since the Middle Ages. In another area, the Campo de Arañuelo (made up of parts of Cáceres, Toledo, and Avila provinces), the old community ownership seemed to have vanished, but there were reminiscences of the old system in the current separation between cultivation rights and pasture rights to the same plot of land. Frequently, one person farmed the land, but a different person rented pasture rights to it for the period when it lay fallow – purchasing what had once been a common right through the *derrota* (Corchón 1963: 260).

In the mid-twentieth century, even in those areas where communal ownership was still important, it was losing ground to the institution of private ownership. The reason is that private ownership provides a far greater incentive to invest the capital needed for improvements to bring about higher yields. Because of this, in most areas (the Tierra de Sayago district of the province of Zamora is a good example) (Cabo 1956: 637–9) the communal property is now limited to mountainous or forested areas, and the survival of these is sometimes due to the intervention of the national government, which has declared them to be 'of public utility'. It should be mentioned that the state has also encouraged another type of collectivism: by 1969 there were 224 agricultural cooperatives operating in the eight provinces of Old Castile. They had about nine thousand members, and cultivated nearly four million hectares of land. But this represented only 2.65 percent of the total cultivated land of the area. Ironically, the government, having once forcibly disamortized communal lands, now finds itself faced with considerable resistance to the idea of giving up individual land ownership to join a cooperative (García Fernández 1970: 5–9).

THE COMMUNITARIAN TRADITION IN THE REST OF EUROPE

Spaniards, and Hispanists, are fond of proclaiming that Spain is different. It is unique, of course, but community property was by no means peculiar to Castile. Similar practices and institutions existed in most of Europe from medieval times down to the nineteenth century. This is not the place to study the details of the property-holding systems of the rest of Europe. But there, as in Castile, the extent of public ownership and public control varied widely from place to place. As one would expect, Portugal had a communitarian system quite similar to that of its neighbor to the east. And many of the same institutions can also be found in France and Italy. But the communitarian system was not limited to Latin Europe: the Celtic and Germanic areas – Britain, Germany, the Netherlands, and Scandinavia – also had their commons and other customs that in many instances were remarkably like those in Castile. And the collectivist tradition of eastern Europe is well known. In all these areas, communal practices thrived and decayed at different periods, depending on local conditions. Noble and peasant usurpations were everywhere a problem, as was royal covetousness. Nevertheless, the communitarian tradition seems to have remained generally strong until the mid-eighteenth century, after which most governments began encouraging a transition to private ownership, on the grounds that the change would bring about an improvement in agriculture.[31]

4

Private property ownership: the privileged estates

The communitarian system – itself highly complex, as we have seen – was juxtaposed with various types of private property ownership to form a sort of hybrid property structure. The system of sixteenth-century Castile contained many medieval elements alongside modern property holding forms – the seigneurial system superimposed upon relatively free villages, the traditional communitarianism side by side with modern private property ownership, and a vigorous expansionist ethic coexisting with the old subsistence mentality. The overlapping of private and community property ownership formed a complementary, and relatively harmonious relationship in the typical Castilian village, and constituted the economic basis for rural society. Historians have made much of the inequitable distribution of land-ownership between the nobility, the clergy, urban investors, and the peasantry. But as Slicher van Bath has noted (1963: 310), the question of ownership is complex, because several different parties can have rights to the same piece of land. And sometimes the rights of the nominal owner are eclipsed by the rights of tenants or others with claims to the produce from his land. When we begin to study the reality of sixteenth-century Castile, we discover that many of the old generalizations and stereotypes break down. The situation was far more complicated than most historians have thought.

Virtually every writer dealing with the subject has concluded that landownership in early modern Castile was overwhelmingly dominated by the privileged estates: the nobility and the clergy. It is possible that this view corresponds to the reality of the situation. But it should be recognized that it is based on extremely fragmentary evidence. It is supported primarily by extrapolations of data from the mid-eighteenth-century *catastro*, and by polemical contemporary sources that are quite obviously distorted. It is undoubtedly true that the church and the nobility owned a disproportionate amount of land in Golden Age Castile. But they did not own as much of Castile as is commonly believed.

In this chapter, I separate the property of the privileged estates into three categories, pertaining to the nobility, to the church, and to the military orders. The division is not altogether satisfactory, for there is considerable overlapping, and the first two categories are quite heterogeneous. Furthermore, it omits the king, who was the single most important landowner in the land, because I have already dealt with crown lands in chapter 1. And it veils the fact that the crown, since the days of Ferdinand and Isabella, controlled the military orders. Nevertheless, if we keep in mind the limitations of the categories, we can find them useful to help us understand the landholding situation of the day.

THE NOBILITY

The Spanish nobility were supposed to be the descendants of the Visigoths and other Germanic knights who took part in the Reconquest. It was believed that this group possessed certain special qualities which entitled them to be set apart as a privileged caste. Those special qualities might not be visible, so the theory went, but they ran in the blood, and eventually they would emerge, if not in the present generation, then in their descendants. Noble status could also be conferred by the crown, theoretically in recognition of those 'special qualities' in the recipient. However, in practice ennoblement by act of royal power normally followed some sort of service to the crown. And by the reign of Charles V privileges of nobility were openly sold to whoever could pay for them, as a means of increasing royal revenues. *Hidalguía* (noble status) was desirable because it conferred not only social prestige, but also immunity from direct royal taxation, and certain legal privileges as well.

The Castilian nobility of the Golden Age was by no means a homogeneous grouping. Antonio Domínguez Ortiz (1971: 108–19) has divided them into no fewer than five categories, ranking from the powerful grandees and other fabulously wealthy titled aristocrats, down to impoverished *hidalgos* who had to work by the sweat of their brow to keep from starving. This reflected enormous differences in property ownership. Consequently, it is misleading to treat 'noble property ownership' as if the nobility represented a unified group of economic equals. Because the Reconquest started in the north, and only gradually moved south, there was an unequal geographical distribution of the Castilian nobility. In the far north nearly the entire population claimed *hidalgo* status, and was accepted as such. In Asturias, for example, 75.4 percent of the *vecinos* were *hidalgos* in the sixteenth century, and in the Trasmiera district of the old province of Burgos it was 84.8 percent. Few of these were titled nobility, and most of the population – though noble – was made up of ordinary working people. Naturally, these included peasants, most of whom had little or no property. At the other end of Spain, in Andalucía the proportion of nobles was very small. In the province of Córdoba it was barely over 1 percent, but the Andalucían nobles enjoyed outstanding social and economic advantages, often owning large estates. Between these two extremes, in the Castilian heartland, the percentage of *hidalgos* varied from place to place. It was only about 2.5 percent in the city of Ciudad Real and its territory. And in the rural villages of New Castile, it ranged from 0.6 percent in Guadalajara province, and 1.2 percent in the province of Madrid, to 2.2 percent in the province of Toledo (Ruiz Martín 1967: 189–202). Of course, all sections of the country had both rich and poor *hidalgos*, and the rich ones tended to reside in cities, rather than in rural villages (Phillips 1979: 100–8; Gerbet 1972: 301–3).

The nobility is always linked with the seigneurial system, although only a tiny minority of nobles were actually seigneurs. It is well known that feudalism did not take deep root in Castile, because the crown never surrendered its control of the national territory as had happened in France and in other European countries. The political and legal power of the Castilian nobility was considerably reduced by Ferdinand and Isabella, but these monarchs left intact the nobles' great socioeconomic power. When the Habsburg period began, about half of all towns in Castile were under the seigneurial jurisdiction of some lord. The proportion of total population under seigneurial jurisdiction, however, was considerably less, because most of the larger towns were *realengo* (under the direct authority of the crown) or were under the royally-controlled military orders. The most powerful type of noble control was *solariego*, a medieval system where both the land and the seigneurial jurisdiction were owned by the lord. But by the sixteenth century, there remained few places in Castile that were *solariegos*. Most were merely under the jurisdiction of the seigneur. And in the typical seigneurial village, the lord owned only a part of the land – sometimes only a fraction of the area under his jurisdiction. That does not mean that the lords were weak, however, for they tended to be large property owners. And although it was not necessarily financially profitable to have seigneurial jurisdiction *per se*, the crown had no trouble finding buyers of jurisdictional rights, because lordship conferred considerable social prestige. The perennially bankrupt Charles V and Philip II raised money for the royal treasury by selling towns to prestige-hungry nobles, and even to non-noble social climbers. Seigneurial jurisdiction conferred upon them the right to appoint or confirm the officials of the town council, to issue decrees and ordinances, and to hold a court of first instance. But the sale of jurisdictions did not in itself affect the landholding system (Domínguez 1971: 155–6; Salomon 1964: 160–5, 189–212; *Actas*: v, 19–20; Guarnido 1969: 63–5).

SEIGNEURIALLY SPONSORED SETTLEMENT

There is evidence that in some places the existence of large blocks of land in the hands of the nobility retarded the post-Reconquest resettlement of the country. The seigneurs sometimes placed restrictions on hunting, woodcutting, pasturing, cultivation, and other activities. Furthermore, they exacted tribute from colonists moving into their domain, which tended to make seigneurial lands less attractive than lands directly under the jurisdiction of the crown. But many lords realized that they needed settlers to develop their lands, and to pay them tribute. Consequently, they extended liberal benefits as an inducement to colonization. In the fifteenth and sixteenth centuries, for example, the Valley of the Pusa (a tributary of the Tajo, in Toledo province) was in the domain of lords who allowed settlers full ownership of the lands they cleared and plowed (*rozas* from the *monte*). In exchange, they had to pay the lord a tribute, called the *terrazgo del pan*, of one-twelfth of the grain harvest, in recognition of his authority. Colonists were also given ownership of lots for houses, and of land for orchards, vineyards, and gardens, with no *terrazgo*. The result of this liberality was a population explosion, and the seigneurs granted more and more lands to the increasing numbers of peasants who cleared and cultivated them. Thus the settlement of lands under seigneurial jurisdiction involved the alteration of the landowning structure, to the benefit of the peasants. There was a restriction to their rights of ownership, however: they were not to sell their property to outsiders, *hidalgos*, clergy, or anyone else who might claim exemption from the *terrazgo* (Jiménez 1951: 568–9, 1971: 86–98; Palomeque 1947). A similar process developed in the village of Benamejí (Córdoba) in the first half of the sixteenth century. The settlement did not prosper so long as the inhabitants were obliged to rent lands from the lord of the place. But it grew nicely after the seigneur granted each *vecino* 60 *fanegas* of land. This amount had to be cleared from the *monte*, and had to be plowed within two years. And thereafter, each landholder was required to plant at least half of his property each year, otherwise it would revert back to the lord. Each *vecino* was also allowed land for vines and olives. Many new settlers came to Benamejí from Burgos to take advantage of this 'homesteading' opportunity. Again, the landholdings of the noble seigneur were reduced, but that turned out to his ultimate advantage because of the increased tribute (Ortega Alba 1973: 608–9).

Noble lords with unpopulated lands also attracted settlers by offering them lands through the *censo enfitéutico*. This was a contract derived from the ancient Roman emphyteusis, now modified to serve new historical conditions. In this system, families of tenants were given a certain area of land and were encharged with clearing and cultivating it. All they had to pay the lord and landowners was an annual rent (*censo*), which was originally payable in produce, but by the early modern period had usually been commuted partly or wholly to coin. The amount of the yearly payment was specified in the contract, and was originally considered to be a substitute for the medieval work-rent (*corvée*) due to the seigneur. It was not at all related to the possible profits resulting from the exploitation of the land. Its significance was that it marked the peasants' recognition of the lord's ownership of the land. Lands held through the *censo enfitéutico* could be passed from father to son. They tended to remain in the family, because rates had been low to begin with, and shrank dramatically in real terms with the price inflation of the sixteenth century (Salomon 1964: 159).

The *censo* leaseholders who most gained from this were those whose contracts had been drawn up in the fifteenth century or earlier. The landowner could not adjust the annual payments to compensate for the price rise; he was bound by the archaic rate specified in the contract. This type of contract was also called the *censo enfitéutico perpetuo* or the *pensión perpetuo*, because of the perpetual rights it conferred. Lands held by peasants through these contracts could not only be willed to their descendants, but could even be sold, traded, or mortgaged. The landowner, however, might reserve the right to collect a tax each time the property was sold. This tax, the *laudemio*, could be as much as one-third of the purchase price, or as little as one-tenth. And, of course, the owner had the right to repossess the land if the annual payments were not made. But the terms of the contract normally did not permit repossession until after several years of non-payment. A grace period of from two to four years seems to have been common. Peasants who held lands under *censo enfitéutico* contracts were fortunate indeed. They had secure tenure and low payments, placing them in a relatively much better position than ordinary tenants with short-term rental agreements. The *censo enfitéutico* leaseholder was, in fact, the *owner* of the right to *use* the land – a right which he and his successors could enjoy in perpetuity so long as they continued to make the annual payments. The person who received the payments was the theoretical, and ultimate, owner of the land, but he had relinquished his right to use the property in exchange for the annual fee. Through the *censos perpetuos*, the noble landowners had given up part of their property rights, in effect creating a class of quasi-proprietor peasant leaseholders. In the fifteenth and early sixteenth centuries, landowners had liked the *censo enfitéutico*, because they found it more convenient and reliable as a source of income than working the land themselves (Guarnido 1969: 87; Nader 1977). After the mid-1500s, however, it lost favor, and more agile contracts such as medium-term leases took its place. García Sanz (1977: 286–96) found that most *censos enfitéuticos* in the Tierra of Segovia were finalized in the fifteenth and early sixteenth centuries. In fact, he did not find a single one dated after 1550. But although no new *censos* of this type were drawn up, those already established endured – with few exceptions – far beyond the Habsburg period. Many survived down to the twentieth century, long after the abolition of the seigneurial system.

It would be splendid to be able to establish a statistical inventory of noble property, giving the percentage that was alienated through the *censo enfitéutico*. But alas, we do not have the data to do so, nor could the data ever be collected for the whole of Castile, because of gaps in archival materials. Some local statistics have been gathered, but there is no way to know how representative they are. Victoriano Guarnido Olmedo (1969: 87) has made a detailed study of the town of Huétor-Tájar (Granada), which was under the seigneurial jurisdiction of the Luna family. The Lunas eventually alienated *all* of their property in the area – both urban and rural – through *censos enfitéuticos*. They did not contract them all at once, but rather in a piecemeal fashion, according to their economic needs. Like most Castilian nobles, they were deeply in debt, and constantly were looking for new sources of income. Helen Nader (1977) found a similar situation on the Mondéjar estates in the provinces of Granada and Guadalajara, as did Abelardo Merino Alvarez (1915: 249–51) in the kingdom of Murcia, where the old *solariego* estates were gradually converted into farms let out through *censos enfitéuticos*, thus reducing the lords to mere *rentiers*.

SEIGNEURIAL DUES

There was often no clearcut differentiation between feudal dues and land rents, because the landlord was often also the seigneur. This ambivalence caused interminable litigation, particularly after the nineteenth-century abolition of seigneurial jurisdiction. There were certain dues that were unquestionably feudal in nature: tolls on passage by boat, road, or bridge; and monopoly rights on ovens, mills, and wine or olive presses. In some parts of Andalucía, for example, the lord required that all olives be brought to his mill for pressing. This led to frequent protests and lawsuits (Domínguez 1971: 157–61). But the various tolls on commerce were more annoying to merchants than they were to peasants, because most peasants lived out their lives in a semi-closed economy. One of the most irritating obligations of the feudal era was personal service. But this had never been onerous in Castile, and was practically extinct by the mid-sixteenth century. In most places the peasants had been able to arrange with their lord to substitute cash or grain payments in place of personal service. The villagers of Torremormojón (Palencia), for example, had contracted in 1374 to pay their lord 200 *cargas* of grain every year instead of working without pay with their animals in his fields. Noël Salomon (1964: 193–8) found no proof in the *Relaciones* of the continued existence of personal service in New Castile. But it certainly had existed there earlier, for in the second quarter of the sixteenth century the peasants of the *señorío* of Valdepusa (Toledo) were still obliged to transport grain for their lord (Jiménez 1971: 100–1). And personal service of various kinds was still being demanded by lords in the province of Valladolid in 1537 and in Burgos in 1551, but their vassals had taken them to court to demand their freedom from such archaic requirements, and it is clear that they were on their way out.[1]

The Castilian vassal was theoretically obligated to find lodgings for his lord and the lord's retinue. But that feudal requirement, like the one of personal service, had practically disappeared by the late 1500s. And where the obligation still existed, it was normally commuted for a small cash payment. Nor were Castilian peasants burdened by seigneurial hunting preserves, or by the excesses of aristocratic hunters. There were few hunting preserves: the hunt was normally free and open to all, and was frequently under the control of the local councils. The Castilian peasant under seigneurial jurisdiction did have certain feudal dues to pay, to underscore the traditional loyalty owed by the vassal to his lord. There was the *humaje* (or *fumadga*, or *fogaje*) – a tax on every family head (literally, on every hearth); and there was the *martiniega* – a tax due to the lord on St Martin's Day (Weisser 1976: 25, 131 n. 13; Jiménez 1971: 100–1). But these amounted to only a few *maravedís* per *vecino* per year. The *fuero*, or *pecho forero*, an annual tax which every *vecino* in a *solariego* village had to pay to his lord, was also nominal. Salomon calculated (1964: 190–4, 214–16) that it amounted to between 14 and 33 mrs per family in the provinces of Madrid and Toledo. There was sometimes also the *infurción* – an annual tax in some places limited to one chicken for the lot where a *vecino* had built his house. And the peasants of La Puebla de Montalbán and Menasalbas (Toledo) were required to pay their lord, the count of Montalbán, a *treintena* (one-thirtieth) of their harvest. All of these duties were linked to the occupation by the peasant of lands over which the lord had jurisdiction. There were exceptions, of course, but for the average Castilian peasant living under seigneurial jurisdiction (in both Old and New Castile), the sum of feudal dues that he had to pay to his lord was rather trifling.[2]

THE CHOICE BETWEEN *SEÑORÍO* AND *REALENGO*

The feudal system certainly contained abuses and injustices, but in all fairness, we must admit that it also could provide a safeguard for the community, especially if the lord was powerful and influential. Many lords established fairs and freemarkets to invigorate the economy of their towns. Others founded churches or universities.

97

More importantly, the lords, in their own interest, tried to preserve their vassals from the worst effects of billeting or tax collecting. Nevertheless, there was perpetual strife between some towns and their lords, which often led to lengthy lawsuits. The lords usually blamed these suits on certain 'troublesome' citizens who had their own interests in mind, rather than those of the community. And it is true that the 'trouble makers' were often *hidalgos* and prosperous townspeople who disliked being vassals of a lord. But as Antonio Domínguez Ortiz has observed (1971: 158–61) the common people do not seem to have been much bothered by their seigneurial status. The ordinary working man usually seems to have preferred a powerful lord to one of lesser stature, and a resident lord to one who governed through a *mayordomo*. *Señorío* status could confer other advantages: regardless of whether the lord was the owner of the land (*solariego*) or merely had jurisdiction over it, the weight of custom prevented him from evicting the peasant from the land he worked. This security – the right to remain on his land – was of the greatest benefit to the peasant; but the other side of the coin was that it acted as a restraint upon the lord, limiting his options.

Nevertheless, the great majority of towns seem to have preferred to be *realengos* – directly under the authority of the crown. Thus, there were tens of thousands of discontented Castilians when Charles V and Philip II sold seigneurial jurisdictions to raise money. Even though they were certainly not 'always reduced to economic slavery by the domanial and manorial system', as Defourneaux would have it (1970: 98), the peasants usually seem to have favored *realengo* status. This preference is reflected in several Castilian proverbs. Hernán Núñez, in his *Refranes o proverbios* (1555), cited: *En lugar de señorío no hagas tu nido* (Don't build your nest in a seigneurial town); and *En la tierra del rey, la vaca corre al buey* (In the king's territory, the cow chases the ox), meaning that in royal towns justice was meted out equally to both rich and poor (cited in Salomon 1964: 205, n. 2). There exists also an old proverb (of unknown vintage): *En tierra de señorío, almendro o guindo; en tierra real, noguera o moral* (In seigneurial lands, almond or cherry; in royal lands, walnut or mulberry), which the editor of the collection of proverbs (Bergua 1968: 202) takes to mean that it was better to settle in royal, rather than seigneurial lands. However, it could also be interpreted to mean that there was little real difference between the two. Some towns, however, were so distressed at being sold into *señorío* status that they went into debt to purchase their return to royal jurisdiction (a good business for the crown, since it could get money not only from the sale of *señoríos*, but also from allowing towns to return to *realengo* status). Other towns that were sold into seigneurial jurisdiction acquiesced in their new status, but lost much of their population through emigration to freer areas. This was true of El Acebrón (Cuenca), which the crown sold into the seigneurial system in 1575. By 1597 it had lost over half of its population to nearby *realengo* and military order towns. But we should not conclude that *realengo* status was always preferable to *señorío*, because there are also examples of the opposite tendency. Late in the reign of Philip II the *corregidor* of Carmona (Seville) reported that many peasants had left the crown towns of the area to go live in seigneurial villages, because of the oppressiveness of royal judges and high taxes in the former. Thus, in the final analysis, it seems that the quality of life under the seigneurial system depended upon the character of the lord: if he was benevolent, *señorío* status might actually be an improvement over *realengo*; but if he was oppressive, it was unquestionably worse.[3]

THE ORIGINS OF NOBLE PROPERTY OWNERSHIP

We have already seen that it is often difficult to separate seigneurial jurisdiction from mere landownership. The reason is that the monarchs of the Reconquest often granted the two simultaneously, and even when they did not, in many cases the language in the grants of jurisdiction was vague enough to be construed to include land-ownership as well (Valdeavellano 1968: 518–22). The royal grants of land recognized the hierarchical nature of Castilian society: not only the division between nobles and non-nobles, but also the differentiation between the upper and the lesser nobility. When Almería was reconquered, for example, in 1489, the *comendador* of León, Don Gutiérrez de Cárdenas, received 109.5 *tahullas* of land in addition to 1,163 fruit trees and 3,058 olive trees. By contrast, the 140 knights of the lesser nobility (*escuderos hijosdalgo*) who also participated in the Reconquest of the area received an average of only 14.7 *tahullas* of land, an unspecified number of fruit trees, and only 45 olive trees. Non-nobles received even smaller allotments, of course. The same thing was true in the post-Reconquest division of lands in the present provinces of Málaga and Granada. The higher nobles received large estates, the ordinary *hidalgos* got medium-sized to small farms, and the commoners were given small plots. In Baza (Granada), for instance, 77 percent of the *vecinos* of the post-Reconquest resettlement were allotted only one-third of the cultivated area, whereas a single individual (from one of the great Castilian noble families) got nearly 10 percent of the total. Thus, from the outset of Castilian rule, these areas were characterized by latifundios owned by the nobility and by minifundios owned by commoners. And it had been so since the early days of the Reconquest (Bosque 1973: 489–90).

After the grants of the Reconquest, from time to time the crown made additional grants of lands to the nobility, and to other parties, in recognition of services rendered. Almost inevitably, these lands were granted from the *tierras baldías*. In 1530, for example, the crown ordered the *corregidor* of Guadix (Granada) to give Alonso de Mérida, the warden of the fortress at nearby Lapesa, title to 400 *fanegas* of land taken from the local *baldíos*. And in early 1531, Mérida, who had solicited the grant, selected the land in six different blocks in the environs.[4] According to Joaquín Rodríguez Arzua (1963: 391–2) the crown made so many such grants in the sixteenth century around Ciudad Rodrigo (Salamanca) that noble-owned latifundios came to dominate the local landowning picture. Now, noble-owned estates must certainly have been prominent in Ciudad Rodrigo long before the 1500s, but it is possible that new royal grants in that century made their share of the local landownership flagrantly disproportionate for the first time.

OTHER FACTORS IN THE GROWTH OF LATIFUNDIOS

It should be remembered that there had been latifundios in Spain long before the Reconquest. Some had existed since Roman times, and others were formed during the Visigothic and Moslem periods. Many were created in a piecemeal fashion, through the gradual amalgamation of smaller holdings. Since Roman times the question of latifundios has aroused strong emotions (Delano 1979: 96, 98, 104). Many observers have accepted as an article of faith the postulate that the latifundio is a malignant institution. Individuals with this anti-latifundio bias have tended to ignore the fact that many estates have been painstakingly built up over several generations. In fact, in any relatively free economic system, there is a tendency for the individual to try to increase the size of his estate. That is surely a healthy goal. Of course, there are also large estates that come into existence suddenly, as the result of political favors, and it is these that really deserve the opprobrium of critics. One should also bear in mind that the size of what could be called a latifundio varied depending on land use. Ranching, for example, requires far more space than viticulture. And it should be noted that a large estate was not necessarily held as a single bloc of land. In fact, it was more common to find it made up of a number of parcels of land, some quite widely spaced.

Recent research (Yun 1980: 34–5, 298–304) has demonstrated that in the province of Córdoba, there was a continuous growth of latifundios during the fifteenth and sixteenth centuries. Alongside the large estates formed as a result of the Reconquest grants, new ones were created, through purchase, through additional royal grants, and through the usurpation of *tierras baldías* and other public lands. There were good economic reasons to explain the expansion of large estates at the expense of small productive units. Some Cordovan soils required deep plowing of the sort best performed by large teams of oxen or mules that could only be financed by large operators. More importantly, only the large producers with substantial resources could afford to store their grain in silos to wait for prices to rise above the inevitably low harvest-time levels. And the owners of large estates were often also the owners of mills, which gave them another competitive advantage over their smaller neighbors. When the smaller peasant operators were forced to flee the area because of famine or indebtedness, their property was left to the mercy of the owners of the large estates, who had been better able to weather cyclical difficulties in agriculture. If the indebted smaller operators did not sell their property to their more prosperous neighbors, which they often did, their lands were nevertheless absorbed into the adjacent latifundios.

We find a similar story of the gradual growth of latifundios wherever we turn. For instance, in Guadalajara the Mendoza family bought up nearby farms, pasturelands, olive presses, and fulling mills to add to their estate (Nader 1979: 115). In Ciudad Real, the nobility were active purchasers of grainland and olive trees (Phillips 1979: 43, 65–7). And in Badajoz, many large estates were formed, or expanded, when the largest property owners of an area would take advantage of some calamity, such as war or plague, to encroach on the common lands of the local village. If the village became depopulated, which sometimes happened, its entire *término* would be swallowed up into the latifundio (Rodríguez Amaya 1951: 433–7). We also find a progressive accentuation of the concentration of landownership in the province of Segovia, largely because of purchases and of foreclosures on mortgaged peasant property (García Sanz 1977: 269). And in Huétor-Tájar (Granada) the holdings of the Luna family, which were already large as a result of Reconquest grants, were broadened through a series of purchases in the period 1490–1580. Furthermore, in 1586 the crown gave Don Antonio de Luna the right to appropriate for himself the property of the Moriscos, who had rebelled in 1568–70. In some parts of the kingdom of Granada the absorption by the nobility of Morisco property had occurred much earlier. In Darro (Granada), for instance, whereas the landholding system had originally been dominated by the traditional Morisco minifundia, already by 1570 the entire area was the property of Doña Elvira Carrillo. One should remember (chapter 3 above) that unscrupulous nobles were often able to add to their estates through the usurpation of municipal lands and *tierras baldías*. And in some cases, they were even able to seize with impunity the property of individuals. Don Alvaro de Luna is a good example: around 1490 he brazenly despoiled the property of an *hidalgo* who had participated in the Reconquest in Huétor-Tájar. The authorities of the area were cowed, and acquiesced in the usurpation. Don Alvaro then managed to get *cédulas* from Ferdinand and Isabella empowering him to take possession of the lands that had been allotted to three other Reconquest warriors (Guarnido 1969: 30–9, 51–4).

The Castilian nobility invested in land, even without seigneurial jurisdiction, for the prestige that accrued to landownership, and also because land was a secure investment. It was not always a profitable investment in all parts of Castile, however. For example, after the Reconquest of the kingdom of Granada (1492), there was general optimism about the area's potential as an agricultural producer. The marquis of Mondéjar, accordingly, bought several estates there, but was soon disillusioned, because during the first decade of the 1500s Andalucía suffered the worst agricultural crisis in its recorded history. The crisis, which began because of unfavorable weather conditions, was aggravated by Moorish attacks on the coast and by a steady flight of the Andalucían Moriscos to Africa. Consequently, the marquis sold or traded off his Granadan estates. But the marquises of Mondéjar continued to be interested in agricultural investments,

and purchased a number of estates, both with and without seigneurial jurisdiction, in the Tajo River area (Nader 1977). The social
and investment value of landownership caused the *conquistadores*
returning from America, and their descendants, to invest heavily in
agricultural estates. The Pizarros, for example, were from a rather
modest *hidalgo* family of Trujillo (Cáceres). But with their loot from
Peru they were able to vastly enhance their socioeconomic position
by purchasing both jurisdictions and estates around their home town
and elsewhere in Extremadura (Vassberg 1978: 51, 56).

GEOGRAPHICAL DISTRIBUTION OF NOBLE LANDOWNERSHIP

From his study of the *Relaciones*, Salomon (1964: 182) concluded that
in New Castile the concentration of noble landownership was most
pronounced around large cities such as Madrid and Toledo, and that
it was beyond the 'urban tentacles' that peasant landownership was
most likely to flourish. The same thing was probably also true of the
rest of the Castilian territory, because the noble elite would have
preferred to have their estates as near as possible to their urban
mansions, to gain the maximum advantage from them. The aristocratic families of Trujillo, for example, liked to spend a good part of
the year in the rustic atmosphere of their estates, where they hunted,
enjoyed the open air, and even ate out of doors when the weather
was good (Vassberg 1978: 50). The cliché that Andalucía was
dominated by the large estates of the nobility is undoubtedly true.
In 1566, for instance, the town of Castro del Río (Córdoba), a place
with 1,350 hearths, reported that all the *cortijos* (estate farmsteads)
of the area were owned by nobles from the city of Córdoba, or by
other absentee proprietors.[5]

There is reason to believe that noble landownership may have been
less important in northern Castile, despite the fact that the proportion of *hidalgos* was higher there. In the La Bureba region of Burgos,
for example, noble-owned property was not predominant. There
were a few important nobles with property in dozens of local villages,
but there was no single great noble estate. Noble-owned property in
the area was fragmented into small parcels, because it coexisted with
the predominant peasant minifundios (Brumont 1977: 36–7). The
La Bureba region, however, may not have been very attractive as a
focus of noble investment, because it was relatively isolated. In a
more accessible location, the village of Casasola (Zamora), which

had 165 *vecinos* in 1569, reported that virtually all of the local arable and pasture lands were owned by nobles and other wealthy people from the nearby city of Toro – the same condition reported in Castro del Río, and for the same reason: proximity to an important city.[6] But we can find no hard and fast rule for this, for there was wide variation within regions. The La Sagra district, which lies a short distance to the northeast of the city of Toledo, is a good example. Our statistics come from the mid-eighteenth-century *catastro* survey, but there is good reason to believe that the situation was quite similar in the late 1500s. The *catastro* indicated that the nobility owned no land whatever in Azaña; 18 percent of the total land area in Bargas; and 37.9 percent in Villaseca (Carrillo 1970: 442–59).

CHARACTERISTICS OF THE LATIFUNDIO

Landownership was of paramount importance to the Castilian nobility. Their land furnished them with the products necessary for subsistence, and ideally it also yielded a surplus that could be used as a means to the acquisition of additional wealth. This additional wealth could be converted into more land or animals, or it might be used for non-agricultural purposes. Members of the upper nobility who owned large estates only rarely engaged personally in farm work. They were a class of consumers, rather than producers; consequently, the class could survive only so long as it remained a small minority. The landowning elite had to struggle continuously to maintain a minimum size of estate. This was not easy, because in the normal order of things their holdings tended to become fragmented through inheritance and by sales to raise cash during economic emergencies. To guard against this fragmentation, the nobility attempted to safeguard the integrity of their property by establishing *mayorazgos* – entailed estates, or perpetual trusts, that were legally inalienable, and had to be passed intact to succeeding generations of heirs (Clavero 1974: 211–39). In practice, however, the holder of a *mayorazgo* could find various ways to sell or transfer this supposedly inalienable property, when it suited his purposes. For instance, Helen Nader has demonstrated (1979: 20, 113) that the Mendoza family was able to move property in and out of its *mayorazgos* to raise the capital necessary for adding new sections to them, and to provide various sons with an equitable inheritance.

The large landowners of Castile did not normally play a personal role in the operation of their estates. Even those who treated their land primarily as an investment rather than a social asset, usually preferred not to directly manage the agricultural production on their lands. They let their grain lands to tenants, often on a permanent basis through *censos enfitéuticos*, to provide them with a dependable income, and to free them from the day-to-day responsibilities of running a farm. The tenants often paid grain as a portion of their lease rents, and the landowners were able to sell this grain, just as if they had actually grown it. But the landowners typically encharged a steward (*mayordomo*) with the task of collecting the grain rent, and of selling it in a nearby market, if it was to be converted into cash. In the system just described, the proprietor of an estate was an absentee landowner – even in the unlikely event that he lived on his estate – because he left the managerial decisions affecting the production of crops up to the peasant who actually worked the land (Nader 1979: 113–15). Noble landowners seem to have paid more attention to the administration of their uncultivated lands than they did to their arable – not that they were personally involved in the exploitation of the land, but they sometimes took an active part in the negotiation of leases for grazing rights, which were typically short-term contracts. But even here, the large landowners were likely to have a *mayordomo* represent them. Similarly, when Castilian aristocrats owned flocks and herds, they tended to turn the administration of their livestock business over to stewards, who supervised the herders actually caring for the animals. There were exceptions, to be sure, to this rule of noble non-involvement in the basics of agropastoral production. For example, Abelardo Merino Alvarez wrote (1926: 191–4) that the nobility of sixteenth-century Avila maintained country houses on their estates, the better to supervise their administration. But this was surely not true of all the local nobles, because elsewhere in Castile it seems quite clear that the overwhelming majority of large noble landowners preferred to live in the city. They found village life boring, and thought it unbelievable that anyone would choose to live there. In 1515 this feeling was expressed by a member of the Mendoza family, who wrote a friend that 'the country is a nice place to visit, but not to live in'.[7]

Because many latifundios had been accumulated bit by bit, and because they were usually not directly exploited by the owners, but rented out in small units to peasants, the existence of large estates did not have much of an impact on the appearance of the landscape.

It was rare, in fact, to find well-grouped estates: they were nearly always made up of dispersed parcels. For example, in 1572 a certain councilman of Valladolid died, leaving an estate of 188 *yugadas* of land. This estate was made up of 137 parcels, the largest of which was barely over 8 *yugadas*, and five of the parcels measured less than one-sixth of a *yugada* (Bennassar 1967: 314–15). But the countryside was dominated by small parcels and small units of exploitation even when the latifundios were made up of contiguous blocks of land.

There is evidence that in some places the concentration of land ownership limited the expansion of agriculture. In the 1500s a widespread complaint of Castilian villagers was that there was a dearth of arable land, and the shortage was frequently blamed on the oppressing proximity of large *dehesas* owned by absentee nobles who were primarily interested in cattle raising, rather than arable agriculture. But these complaints can not always be taken at face value. In most cases, the land was probably really available for cultivation, but the villagers were reluctant to pay the rents demanded by the landowner. We can scarcely believe that the typical Castilian noble landowner would deliberately withhold land from cultivation when it must have been quite clear that to put it into production would bring him considerable additional income. There must have been some stubborn pastoralists who would indeed do so, despite the fact that it was contrary to their own economic interests, but the evidence suggests that most owners of large estates were anxious to have as many peasant farmers as possible on their lands, to cultivate them (Ortega Valcárcel 1966: 87–96; Nader 1977; Corchón 1963: 133–4; Jiménez 1952: 539–41). When we do find examples of noble obstruction of agricultural expansion, there are nearly always other factors involved. In the 1570s, for example, the duke of Lorca successfully blocked an irrigation project organized by the city of Lorca (Murcia), but the reason was that the duke thought the proposed project would deprive him of the water he needed for a profitable lumbering operation in the Sierra de Segura (Merino 1915: 282).

Noble obstruction of the normal tendencies of agricultural development was far more likely to occur indirectly, through the municipal governments. Landowning aristocrats were often able to dominate the municipal councils (frequently through purchased offices), where they could influence the making and enforcing of local laws. The result was that the large landowners were sometimes able to control the use of community property, for their own benefit. In Córdoba, for example, the local aristocrats in the 1530s were able to get the city to enforce pasture-protecting anti-plowing laws on the local *tierras baldías*. The reason they wanted this was that they owned large tracts of uncultivated land that they were unable to get peasants to work, because the peasants preferred to farm the *baldíos*, which could be cultivated without paying rent. But when the city enforced the anti-plowing laws on the *baldíos*, the peasants were obliged to rent the aristocrats' lands.[8]

The owners of large estates sometimes defended their property by hiring private guards to keep out intruders. Often they did so in defiance of local customs regarding free hunting, pasture, and other common usages. And the guards were frequently guilty of mistreating transgressors and their animals. The use of private guards was challenged time and again through lawsuits – usually initiated by municipal governments in behalf of their citizens. For instance, in 1551 the council and *vecinos* of the village of Casar de Cáceres brought suit against a group of landowners from the nearby city of Cáceres for illegally hiring private guards to keep animals out of their vineyards. And in 1584 the council and *vecinos* of the village of Santa Inés (Burgos) initiated a suit against Francisco de Bocanegra, a local noble landowner, for hiring guards to keep them from enjoying their traditional rights to hunt and gather firewood in the area. The high costs of litigation must have discouraged most individuals from defending their rights in court; consequently we can probably assume that only the most flagrantly abusive actions of private guards were challenged.[9]

THE NOBLE *LABRADOR* AND HIS PROPERTY

We should remember that not all members of the Castilian nobility were fabulously wealthy titled aristocrats. Most of them, in fact, lived in relatively modest circumstances, and many *hidalgos* were ordinary *labradores* (independent peasant farmers). As such, they usually owned no more land than they could work themselves – a small amount that placed them in exactly the same economic position as that of their commoner fellow-*labradores*. Some *labradores* – whether *hidalgo* or not – however, became quite well-to-do, and hired laborers to work in the fields under their supervision, or even employed *mayordomos* to oversee their agricultural operations. But the *labrador*, by definition, took a personal hand in the running of his farm, regardless of its size.

The town of Monleón (Salamanca) provides an example of the landownership of the lesser Castilian nobility. A census of 1558 listed 93 *vecinos*, of whom five were *hidalgos*. Two of the *hidalgos* owned no property whatever in Monleón. A third, who was the assistant warden (*teniente de alcaide*) of the local fortress, owned 11 *fanegas* of flax fields, two meadows (*prados*), two vineyards, and a garden – which could classify him as at least a part-time *labrador*, but only a minor property owner in the town. A fourth *hidalgo*, who grandly announced that his profession was 'to serve God and the King', owned only a few olive trees and a vineyard in addition to his house, and ranked economically with the more humble commoners of the town. Only one of the five *hidalgos* of Monleón called himself a *labrador*. He owned 60 *fanegas* of land, one meadow, three *cortinas* (enclosed arable fields), the house where he lived, and a rental house. This *hidalgo labrador* farmed with one pair of oxen and owned a dozen cows. He employed two youths to help him in his farm work, and was the only person in the town with hired help. But he was not the wealthiest person in Monleón, for there were several non-*hidalgo labradores* who owned more land and more livestock.[10]

Compare the situation in Monleón with that of La Zarza (now called Zarza de Montánchez), a village in the jurisdiction of the city of Trujillo (Cáceres province). La Zarza was considerably more aristocratic than Monleón: according to a census of 1561 it had 103 *vecinos*, of whom ten were *hidalgos*. Five of these *hidalgos* were listed as *pobres* (poor), who owned only a very small amount of land (if they owned any at all, it was usually in vines) or a few animals. Two *hidalgos* were ranked as having a moderate estate (*de mediana hacienda*), but they did not own much land. The more prosperous of the two had only 14 *peonadas* of vineyard and an unknown quantity of pastureland that brought him 3,000 mrs of rent per year. Three of the La Zarza *hidalgos* were listed as being *ricos* (rich), but these were actually only moderately well-off. The richest was a Pizarro, whose wealth was concentrated in houses, rather than agricultural land. The largest landowner among the *hidalgos* was a 'rich' widow who owned 28 *peonadas* of vineyard, 60 *fanegas* of grainland, one garden-orchard (*huerto*), and one meadow (*alcacer*). But none of the 'rich' *hidalgos* of La Zarza owned as much land, or as many animals, as the wealthy non-noble *labradores*, of whom there were several in the town. I do not know exactly how representative the preceding examples are, but they are consistent with other property-census reports I have seen for other parts of Castile, and my guess is that they are fairly typical.[11]

From the city of Córdoba we have the example of an exceptionally wealthy *hidalgo labrador*, Don Luis de las Infantas, a younger son of a prominent Cordovan family. Infantas had two important advantages: a modest inheritance; and connections in the municipal government. He used both to develop an extensive agricultural operation. In addition to exploiting the land he inherited, Infantas leased hundreds of *fanegas* of grainland at reasonable rents from the city of Córdoba. Besides growing grain, he also had a vineyard and two wine presses, but a financial crisis in 1534 forced him to sell the vineyard. His operation was large and diversified, including a livestock sector with thousands of animals. By the time he died, in 1546, Infantas had accumulated an impressive amount of land, some of which he had purchased, some rented, and some held in perpetual leases (*censos*). But his estate was no more impressive than those of many non-*hidalgo labradores*, and it was meager when compared to the huge holdings of some of the Andalucían aristocrats (Torre 1931b: 188–91).

ECCLESIASTICAL LANDOWNERSHIP

The church was a formidable power in early modern Castile, and like the nobility it owed much of its influence to the wealth it commanded through property ownership. Some of the landholdings of the church had their origins in Roman and Visigothic times, owing to donations by monarchs and the faithful to monasteries and bishoprics. But the most important roots of ecclesiastical landownership seem to lie in the Reconquest, from which both church and nobility emerged as major landowners, thanks to liberal royal grants in recognition of their support for the crusade. The church, like the nobility, was given grants of both land and jurisdiction in the newly won territories, and the distinction between the two types of grants was also frequently vague (Valdeavellano 1968: 133–74). The church also played an active role in resettling the reconquests. For example, the archbishops of Toledo, who were given the site of Alcalá de Henares (Madrid) in 1126, did everything that they could to attract colonists and to make the place into a thriving town. As a result, it became an important medieval communication axis, capitalizing on its location on the road to Zaragoza. Alcalá also attained early prominence for its fairs and markets, and as an agricultural center (García Fernández 1952: 299–308). Episcopal domains such as this, however, were few in number, and were frequently challenged. Most towns under ecclesiastical jurisdiction were *abadengos* – under a church, monastery, or some other churchly institution – so named because they were generally under the titular leadership of an abbot (*abad*). Salomon (1964: 203–6) found that 11.9 percent of the New Castilian villages he studied were *abadengos* in the 1570s. We have no data for the rest of Castile for that period, but extrapolating statistics from the end of the eighteenth century suggests that the percentage of *abadengo* villages was somewhat higher in Extremadura, and much lower in Andalucía (Malefakis 1970: 59).

Seigneurial tribute collected by monasteries and other ecclesiastical lords was light, as it was in the case of noble lords. For example, the entire town of Monteagudo (Cuenca) gave the bishop of Cuenca only two lambs, four kids, and a few partridges or capons every year. And the town of Lupiana (Guadalajara) owed the Hieronymite Monastery only three pairs of hens at certain holidays in the year (Domínguez 1971: 159). As in the case of noble lordship, some ecclesiastical lords continued to receive personal service from their vassals in the sixteenth century. The town of Calabazanos (Palencia), for instance, still supplied the Convent of Santa Clara a specified number of workdays per *vecino* per year. But by 1574 the requirement was in the process of being converted to a monetary payment.[12]

After the Reconquest the church continued to amass property through the bequests of devout individuals. As early as the mid-twelfth century many noble lords began to donate lands and even entire villages to the church. As a result, it became a large land-owner in virtually every part of Castile. Through the centuries the monasteries, parishes, and bishoprics accumulated more and more property through grants, bequests, and through purchase (García de Cortázar 1969: 49–95). In some parts of the country there seems to have been an accentuation of ecclesiastical landownership in the sixteenth century. That was true of Lorca (Murcia), which in that century witnessed a proliferation of convents that attracted many daughters of the wealthiest families of the area. This occasioned frequent donations, contributing to the growth of church-controlled property (Gil 1971: 157–8). In some places, such as Castro del Río (Córdoba), there were ecclesiastical lands called *donarios*, or *donadios* (given in grants), showing that they had been willed to the church by pious individuals.[13] Like noble landownership, ecclesiastical property owning tended to be concentrated near the large cities, and for the same reasons. There were isolated monasteries, of course, that were major local landowners. The Monastery of Guadalupe (Cáceres), for example, held extensive properties in that area, but donations had made it also the owner of property in distant places like Seville (Blanco 1911: 327–8).

Seigneurial jurisdiction in the hands of the church also tended to be concentrated near important cities, but the largest cities did not necessarily provide the nuclei. For instance, Salomon's study (1964: 205–6) of rural villages in New Castile revealed that ecclesiastical lordship tended to be grouped around Talavera de la Reina (Toledo) and Alcalá de Henares (Madrid), rather than the larger cities of Madrid and Toledo. Whereas church property ownership was on the rise during the sixteenth century, the same was not true of ecclesiastical seigneurial jurisdiction. The perennially bankrupt Charles V and Philip II gained papal approval to increase their income by alienating ecclesiastical lordships. This they did, creating new secular jurisdictions out of domains that had formerly been held by bishops, monasteries, and other church-related institutions. The purchasers of these former ecclesiastical lordships were usually foreign merchants or bankers, or members of the higher bureaucracy like the royal secretary Francisco de los Cobos. In return for their lost domains, Philip II gave the various ecclesiastical entities government bonds (*juros*) (Domínguez 1971: 156; López Martínez 1962).

The proportion of ecclesiastical landownership varied, of course, from place to place. It must have been most unusual for a village to have no church-owned land, but it was quite commonplace for the church to be the major landowner, and not at all rare for it to own all the lands of a village, in the *solariego* sense. This sort of variation existed even within given regions. For instance, Brumont (1977: 28, 35–7, table 4A) calculated that the combined noble and ecclesiastical holdings (unfortunately, he did not separate them) in the La Bureba district of the province of Burgos averaged about 49 percent. But it varied from one village to another from a low of 18 percent to a high of 100 percent. In the village of Rubiales, all of the land was the property of the Monastery of Oña, a powerful institution which also owned property in more than fifty other villages. A similar intra-district variation existed in the La Sagra area (Toledo province), where the average church ownership was around 36 percent for the entire district, but where the actual proportion varied from a low of only 15 percent in Villaseca to a high of 84 percent in Azaña (Carrillo 1970: 442–59). The extremes were not that great in the Valdeburón area of the province of León, where the range of church ownership went from 36 percent of the cultivated land of Retuerto, to 11 percent in Burón (Martín Galindo 1961: 193). The proportion of ecclesiastical property was also rather low in the Maragatería district of León province, where it was barely over 25 percent of the total (Martín Galindo 1958: 59–62). It should be remembered that most of these statistics are derived from the mid-eighteenth-century *catastro*. However, most scholars believe that the landowning picture had not changed drastically since the late 1500s. Whatever change there was is thought to have been most certainly in the direction of increased church and noble ownership.

The concentration of landownership in the hands of the church was a source of concern to taxpayers, because the privileged estates were exempt from many forms of taxation, and that meant that the tax burden fell all the more heavily on the non-noble lay citizens of Castile. The inhabitants of the village of Quintanaloranzo (Burgos) were aware of this, and complained that their per capita tax burden was much higher than that of neighboring villagers, and far higher than it should have been, for the reason that many of the best lands of the locality were owned by the Monastery of San Millán de la Cogolla, and the Monastery of Las Huelgas in Burgos.[14]

The Cortes of Castile took notice of the problem early in the sixteenth century, and called repeatedly for measures to limit ecclesiastical landownership. In 1523 the Cortes of Valladolid directed a petition to the monarch and to the pope, asking that churches and monasteries be prohibited from adding any additional land to their existing holdings, whether through purchase, gift, or bequest – lest all the land in Castile soon come to belong to the church. At the time, the monarch seemed receptive to the suggestion, for he informed the Cortes that he had written the pope for confirmation of the principle. But nothing seems to have come of it, and in 1563, when the Cortes presented the question to Philip II, he gave a disheartening reply: it was 'better not to make changes'. The Cortes of 1573–5 again raised the issue, reminding the monarch that the concentration of landownership in ecclesiastical hands worked a hardship on those subjects of the crown who paid royal taxes. Again the Cortes called for a halt to the further acquisition of lands by the church. But again the monarch replied that it was 'better not to make changes'. This discouraging reply, however, did not keep the Cortes of 1579–82 from introducing the question anew, with the warning that ecclesiastical institutions were 'taking up most of the best property of the realm'. This time, the monarch replied that his council was looking into the matter, that the question would be taken up with His Holiness the pope, and that the appropriate measures would be taken. But nothing, in fact, was done. And by 1587 it was so plain that Philip II would take no action on the subject that the Cortes actually voted not to submit the question to him again (*Actas*: I, 254; IV, 460–1; VI, 824–5; IX, 151).

CHARACTERISTICS OF CHURCH-OWNED LANDS

Because of the piecemeal manner in which ecclesiastical institutions normally acquired their property, the estates of the church were typically fragmented into small parcels interspersed among peasant-owned, noble-owned, and municipally-owned lands. But there was a difference, particularly striking in some regions, in the type of land owned. The property of the municipalities was often limited to pasture and woodlands, whereas the church and the peasants tended to own arable land, and the nobility was likely to own both types. In areas where olives were grown, both church and nobility tended to figure highly among grove owners, but vineyards in most places were the property of peasants. As indicated earlier, ecclesiastical property was usually concentrated around large cities, and the monasteries frequently had property in several (or even dozens of) villages. It seems to have been rare, however, for parish churches to own property outside the village territory which they served. There were some monasteries that directly exploited certain of their lands, through work levies from their vassals or leaseholders (Brumont 1977: 35–7; Higueras 1961: 121–2; García de Cortázar 1969: 193–243). But in the sixteenth century, personal service requirements were an anachronism, and were increasingly difficult, or even impossible to enforce. The Monastery of Valbuena de Duero (Valladolid), for example, complained in 1597 that the *vecinos* of the nearby village of Piñel de Abajo no longer worked as they were supposed to in the monastery's vineyards, thus forcing it to hire laborers to perform tasks that had previously been done free.[15] Consequently, by the sixteenth century, the overwhelming majority of church-owned lands were not managed directly by their owners, but rather were given out in small parcels to peasants, typically through *censos enfitéuticos* or through long leases. The church, like the nobility, had found it preferable to enjoy the reliable income of rents and *censos*, rather than to face the uncertainties of direct exploitation (Ortega Valcárcel 1966: 87–96; Fernández y Fernández 1955: 61–3, 92–5). For the same reason, the monasteries and other ecclesiastical establishments preferred the security of a specified rent – whether in kind, or in coin – to a share of the harvest, which would fluctuate from year to year depending on the weather.[16]

Some parish priests owned rural property in addition to that associated with their benefices. It was not at all unusual for a village priest to own a small vineyard or orchard, or some other parcel of land. The amount of property involved was usually modest, even by village standards. For example, the priest of the village of Zarza de Montánchez (Cáceres) in 1561 owned two vineyards – one of ten *peonadas*, and the other of two – and he also kept eight sheep.[17] Some of these rustic clerics rented their property out, to be sure, whereas others worked their plots themselves, or with hired help. But the agricultural activities of these priest-peasants were not always welcomed by their parishioners, particularly in villages with a shortage of land. In the Cortes of 1542 the delegates from Guadalajara complained that many priests who had adequate benefices were competing with their parishioners for shares of public land, which reduced the amount of land available for lay residents of the area, and which was the source of economic hardship for some (*Cortes*: v, 191).

PROPERTY OF THE MILITARY ORDERS

The medieval Iberian Reconquest brought about the organization of Christian knights into Hispanic military orders, similar to the European Knights Templars and the Knights of Malta. The most important of the strictly Hispanic crusading orders were the Knights of Calatrava, Alcántara, and Santiago, all founded on the Christian–Moslem frontier in the mid-twelfth century. These crusading orders played a major role in expanding and defending the frontier. In return, the kings of León and Castile rewarded them generously with land grants in formerly Moslem territories. It was not long until the three largest orders had become exceedingly powerful, the owners of extensive domains, especially in New Castile. Land meant wealth, and the orders' wealth posed a threat to royal authority. That threat was removed when Ferdinand and Isabella managed to gain for the crown the masterships of all three major Hispanic orders. Thus the orders were deprived of their political independence, but although controlled by the crown, they maintained their traditional structures, and continued to exert a powerful influence over rural Castilian society throughout the sixteenth century.

The property of the orders was assigned to the organizations' various dignitaries, often in *encomiendas* (territories entrusted to their care). Each *encomienda* was administered by a *comendador* appointed by the Grand Master of the order, and included specified lands, revenues, and privileges. The income from the *encomienda* was to be used for the support of the local churches and clergy, and for military expenses. But the *comendadores* could pocket the difference between revenues and expenses; consequently, such positions were much coveted, and they were used to reward personal, political, and military favors. Some *encomiendas* were created at the time of the Reconquest, but others came into existence later, to encourage re-settlement of empty spaces, even as late as the sixteenth century (Quirós 1965: 207–9). The military orders played the same kind of role in resettling their lands as the nobility and the church did on theirs. They repopulated most of the pre-Reconquest settlements, and sponsored altogether new ones, apportioning land to individual colonists for grain and for vines, and to newly formed town councils for pasture and for other community purposes. But the orders reserved for themselves the ownership of a large part of the land of their territories, to provide income through rentals and other dispositions for their own benefit. The orders exercised over their territories the same kind of seigneurial jurisdiction enjoyed by the church and the nobility over some of their lands. The territories of the orders were concentrated in New Castile, but Salomon (1964: 203–6) found that only 16.8 percent of the 569 villages he studied were under the seigneurial jurisdiction of military orders, whereas 31.2 percent were *realengos*, 11.9 percent were *abadengos*, and 39.8 percent were *de señorío*. Order villages tended to be more populous than these others, however, and Salomon calculated that they contained 31.9 percent of the total population of the villages he studied.

Map 3 shows the location of the order territories in Castile during the second quarter of the sixteenth century. The concentration of order influence in New Castile is quite clear. However, it should not

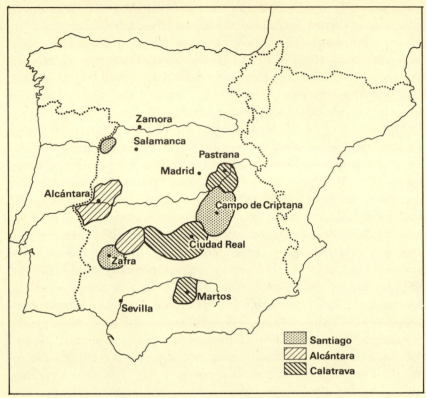

3. Lands of the military orders. Adapted from Phillips, *Ciudad Real*, p. 10

be thought that the orders owned *all* the lands in the areas shown on the map, nor did they even exercise seigneurial jurisdiction over all of those areas. The city of Ciudad Real, for example, located in the middle of a huge territory dominated by the Order of Calatrava, was a royal town, and there were many others within the order areas, originally established by the Castilian monarchs to provide a royal presence to counterbalance the power of the orders. There were, similarly, some *abadengo* and *señorío* villages situated within the areas indicated on the map as belonging to the orders. As stated earlier, the orders had found it necessary to grant landownership to individuals and to towns to encourage colonization. And even after the initial resettlement grants, the *comendadores* followed the practice of granting additional lands as population growth made the original allocations inadequate (Ulloa 1963: 354–6; Phillips 1979: 8–9; Salomon 1964: 316–17). As was the practice in other seigneurial lands, the orders typically reserved for themselves a specified annual tribute, in recognition of their jurisdiction.[18]

After the crown took over the masterships, the orders were administered by the Council of Orders in Madrid. But under this arrangement, although the medieval structures were maintained, the orders could not be supervised as closely as they had been when they were completely autonomous. And this greater laxity was translated into a loss of lands as a result of peasant and other usurpations, and into a gradual loss of revenues and privileges (Quirós 1965: 209–10). These reductions in order property, however, were minor when compared to the losses that came as the result of crown sales. The perpetual financial difficulties of the Habsburgs caused them to be constantly on the search for new revenue-making possibilities. And in 1529 Charles V obtained a bull from Pope Clement VII authorizing him to alienate order property and revenues worth up to 40,000 *ducados* a year. By virtue of that authority, the emperor sold numerous jurisdictions, revenues, and lands, assigning government bonds (*juros*) to the *comendadores* as compensation for their lost property. According to the papal authorization, the funds the crown gained through these were to be used exclusively for building convents and forts in the kingdom of Granada and in Africa, for defense against the Moslems. But the forts and convents, in fact, were never founded. When Charles V abdicated the throne in 1556, he transferred to his son Philip his right to dismember order property up to the 40,000 *ducados* a year. This right, which was confirmed by Pius IV in 1560, was amplified in 1569 by Pius V, who gave Philip another bull authorizing the disposal of an additional 40,000 *ducados* per year. And the 'prudent king' did not hesitate to take full advantage of the opportunity. But he suffered great scruples about the sales, and in his will he ordered Philip III to buy back the alienated property and to restitute it to the orders. But Philip III did not find it possible to do so, and in turn ordered *his* successor to make the restitution. And in the end, despite these royal pangs of conscience, the orders never regained their lost property. Furthermore, it seems that Charles V and Philip II sold more order property than the authorized amount, and when it became difficult for the royal treasury to make payments on the bonds given in return, the crown appropriated additional order revenues to pay them. And it appears that the price the crown allowed the orders for the alienated property was far below its real value (Gómez Centurión 1912: 276–7, 303–5, 314).

Some order lands were sold as *tierras baldías*, in a major fund-raising project developed in the early years of the reign of Philip II (Vassberg 1975). For example, in 1577–80 the crown dispatched two special commissioners to sell the *tierras renteñas* (rental lands) of the Order of Calatrava in the area of Martos (Jaén). These lands were sold to individuals and to municipalities through *censos al quitar* (redeemable mortgages) that yielded payments totalling 7,944,075 mrs per year. But this amount was insufficient for the exigencies of the treasury of Philip II, and in 1580 that monarch sold his rights to the *censo* payments to the German banker Marcus Fugger for the principal sum of 111,217,053 mrs. After that, it was Fugger, rather than the crown, who collected the annual *censo* payments. And in Mohernando (Guadalajara), the *baldíos* sold in the early 1590s were actually lands of the Order of Santiago.[19]

The orders did not directly exploit their lands, but rather gave them out for rental. Arable lands were typically let out to peasants through *censos enfitéuticos*, which might call for the payment of a specified sum each year, or they might require the payment of a share (often one-fifth) of the harvest (Higueras 1961: 122; Quirós 1965: 221–2; Salomon 1964: 32, 137). But some lands were rented for short periods. For example, the Order of Santiago owned certain lands near Seville that it rented out in 1575 for terms of varying length – some for only a year, and others for several years. Each rental contract was different: some provided for cash rent; others for a share of the crop; and still others for a combination of cash and goods. One piece of land, for instance, was rented for 70 *cahizes* of grain, 18 chickens, 1 sheep, 1 hog, 1 calf, 1 *fanega* of chickpeas, 1 *arroba* of cheese, and 3 *ducados* of cash. In some contracts there was a provision that in bad years the renter would be excused from the normal rent, and would pay one-sixth of the harvest, instead. Order lands were rented not only by individuals, but also by town governments, who subcontracted them to their *vecinos* for arable, for pasture, or for both purposes.[20]

But the orders reserved for themselves the best pastures of their vast territories, and these were rented (often at public auction) for use as winter pastures for migratory northern herds, and for summer pasture (*agostadero*) for local animals. The Mesta, of course, claimed the right to pasture its flocks on any lands upon which they had ever grazed, but it had to pay for the privilege. The length and terms of these rental contracts varied, but it was usual to charge a certain amount per animal (Quirós 1965: 221–2). As indicated in chapter 2, the use of acorns was supposed to be common, and free. Nevertheless, there were times when the orders tried to charge a fee for the utilization of the acorns on their lands. In 1491 Ferdinand and Isabella ordered the master of the Order of Alcántara to stop the practice. Nevertheless, in the early 1550s, after the crown had assumed the masterships, the Order of Santiago continued to sell the right to pasture pigs on the acorns of its *dehesas* near Mérida (Badajoz), demonstrating once again that where money was involved, the crown was not consistent in its policies.[21]

5

Private property ownership: the non-privileged

PEASANT LANDOWNERSHIP

Historians who investigate the question of the distribution of land-ownership almost invariably demonstrate a bias in favor of the peasant being the owner of the land he farms. They consider the owner–operator to be vastly preferable to the mere tenant farmer, in both social and economic terms. But as Slicher van Bath has rightly observed (1963: 310–24), this bias is not logical. It can be demonstrated that many peasant owner–operators work lands of inferior quality, which reduces them to a low standard of living. Many peasant tenant farmers, by contrast, work more fertile soils, and are considerably more prosperous. Therefore, landownership is not necessarily tantamount to wealth. In fact, the landowner's annual payment on his debt might be much higher than the tenant's rent to his landlord. As mentioned in chapter 4, the sixteenth-century Castilian peasant who held lands under a *censo enfitéutico* contract was often fortunate indeed, because of the low rates he paid. The question of landownership, then, is not in itself a very useful gauge of peasant wellbeing. If a peasant owned all of his land, but farmed only a small amount, he would be poor; on the other hand, if he rented a large amount of land, he could be quite wealthy, even if he was a non-landowner. If we wish to measure peasant prosperity, then we should be more concerned with the *size* of the peasant's operation than with the question of how much land he owns. Nevertheless, with that caveat in mind, let us proceed to examine the subject of peasant landownership.

There are two origins of peasant landownership in early modern Castile: the property owned by small farmers (both Christian and Moslem) in the pre-Reconquest Iberian Moslem kingdoms; and the private property granted to settlers during the Reconquest through the *fueros* (law codes) and *cartas pueblos* (municipal charters) of the newly reconquered areas. The *fueros* protected the traditions of

Mozarabic property ownership, and encouraged the development of small, peasant-owned property holdings. This was particularly true of New Castile, where the *fueros* of Toledo (1101 and 1118), Madrid (late 1100s?), Cuenca (1177), and others established conditions in which the peasantry could develop free from the encumbrances of servitude that were typical of most of Europe at that time. Peasant property, of course, coexisted with the property of the nobility, the church, the military orders, and the municipalities – they were all part of the same socioeconomic system. And they all profited from the Reconquest. In an earlier chapter we saw that the right of *presura* gave peasants (and others) effective ownership over deserted lands that they occupied and brought into production. The *presura* was sometimes supervised by the monarch himself or by some noble or bishop in the name of the crown, but there was also spontaneous *presura*, both by the powerful and by the weak. The system of *presura* favored the development of small property owners, and from the ninth and tenth centuries there existed in Castile–León a class of free peasants who cultivated small fields (Salomon 1964: 176–80; Nieto 1964: 103–13; Huetz 1967: 171).

During the first centuries of the Reconquest the lands won from the Moslems by the Castilian–Leonese were largely empty, having been depopulated as a result of generations of continual warfare. It was because these territories were practically deserted that the *presura* mode of occupation could be adopted. But beginning with the conquest of Toledo (1085) the Castilian monarchs gained control of lands that contained a sizeable population. According to the principle of Germanic law, and according to the *Siete partidas*, all of the property won from the enemy was at the mercy of the monarch, who could dispose of it at his will. The Castilian monarchs initially followed a policy of allowing the Moslem inhabitants of newly conquered areas to keep their property, whether urban or rural. Later in the Reconquest, the general rule was that the Moslem population of cities that resisted the Christians would lose their property – all they could hope for was to have their lives spared. But the residents of cities that came to terms with the Christians could keep their property, and the new Christian rulers were usually content to receive from them the tribute that had previously gone to Moslem potentates. The most important of the conquered cities were organized as royal towns dependent on the crown, and Christian colonists were allotted lands through *repartimientos* supervised by royally appointed officials. In both Old and New Castile the *repartimientos* established a class of small peasant landowners, often superimposed on the existing Moslem and Mudéjar landowning system. Thus, from the very beginning, a peasant minifundism came to coexist with the latifundism of the privileged estates (Glick 1979: 99–103; Higueras 1961: 112–13; Pérez Díaz 1969: 47).

The *repartimientos* were carried out on the principle that colonists from the same social class should receive allotments of approximately equal value, and toward that end, differences in topography, soil type, vegetation, and improvements were taken into consideration, as well as mere land area. As a result, in the initial distribution of lands, the individual peasant was likely to be allotted several small parcels of land scattered around the territory of the settlement. As time went on, subdivisions due to sale and inheritance would further complicate the picture, as would new allotments made as a response to demographic growth. For example, in Lorca (Murcia) the Reconquest land distributions between 1257 and 1340 left the irrigated plain of the area largely in peasant hands, and in an extremely subdivided state – a situation which prevailed until the seventeenth century, when the Habsburg depression caused a concentration of landownership (Gil 1971: 157).

A like situation emerged in the kingdom of Granada, where peasant minifundios have been important ever since. The proportion of lands allotted to peasants varied from place to place. In Baza (Granada province), for example, 77 percent of the Christian settlers of the 1490s were peasants, but these received only about one-third of the cultivated lands of the area. The other two-thirds went to the privileged estates. In Santa Fe (also in Granada province) the *repartimiento* of the 1490s involved 182 original settlers who were chosen to receive lands in this altogether new town. These settlers, all from the victorious army, were 56 percent non-noble and 44 percent *caballeros*. Each *caballero* was supposed to get twice as much land as an ordinary non-noble colonist. The lots were not all equal, for various reasons, but it seems that the non-nobles, or peasants, were apportioned about 40 percent of the grainlands of the area. The proportion of peasant ownership in other *repartimientos* was higher or lower, depending upon local conditions, and upon the status of the colonists who were involved. And the amount of property received by peasants in the *repartimientos* varied greatly from place to place. In Santa Fe the non-noble colonist received 9.31 *marjales* of *huerta* (land for olives and garden), 45 *marjales* of grainland, and about 5 *marjales* of vineyard. In Almería, by contrast, the commoner peasants of a *repartimiento* of the same period received only 2.13 *marjales* of vineyard, less than half a *marjal* of *huerta*, and 17 *marjales* of irrigated land. They were also allotted thirty olive trees each, but this did not include the ownership of the land upon which the trees were growing (Bosque 1973: 489–90; Garzón 1978: 41–9; Lapresa 1955: 198–234).

In those places where the capitulations with the defeated Moorish rulers permitted the Moslem inhabitants to retain their lands, the *repartimientos* to Christian settlers had to be of *baldíos* or other un-owned lands. The Christians could also acquire property through purchase from Islamic owners, of course. But it was usually not long before they found a pretext to confiscate the property of the Moslems, normally because they had revolted – in response to broken peace agreements or bad treatment. In Lorca (Murcia), for example, the Moslem surrender was in 1243, and in 1257 there was an allotment of unowned lands to Christians. By 1264 there had been a Moslem uprising, which provided the excuse for pushing the Moors into ghettos and giving their best lands to Christians. There was another *repartimiento* in 1272, and new ones in the 1330s, of lots that had been abandoned and of newly conquered lands. Through all of these changes in ownership, the Moorish minifundism was preserved, but gradually was transformed into a Christian minifundism (Gil 1971: 71–5).

In the kingdom of Granada, the transfer from Moslem to Christian ownership followed different rhythms, depending on the region and the time. During the early years of the Reconquest of the area (1481–6), from the taking of Alhama until the capture of Loja, the Christian occupation implied the expulsion of the Islamic population and the confiscation of all their property. This was a continuation of the policy that had been followed during the Reconquest of the Guadalquivir valley (in the mid-1200s), and in the taking of Ante-quera (Málaga province) in 1410. The depopulation of the Moslems affected the entire northeastern part of the present province of Granada, and much of the present province of Málaga. During the second stage of the Reconquest of the kingdom of Granada, begin-ning in 1487, the Moslems were expelled from coastal areas (where they might have maintained contacts with their coreligionists in northern Africa), but they were allowed to retire to the interior regions that had fallen to the Christians, where they could remain as

Mudéjares. The Moslem population of Baza (Granada), which had stubbornly withstood a long siege, were punished by being forced to leave the city and to retire to surrounding villages. But in the remainder of the kingdom, the peace treaties permitted the Islamic inhabitants to stay, maintaining the ownership of their urban and rural property. The treaties gave them the right to continue their customs, language, and religion. Those who preferred not to live under Christian rule could emigrate to northern Africa. The terms of the treaties were soon broken by the Christians, and most of the urban Moslems emigrated, but in rural areas, despite a forced conversion to Christianity, the Moriscos were able to preserve most of their sociocultural–economic traditions. In regions abandoned by the Moslem inhabitants, there was a *repartimiento* of property as soon as possible. The new settlers were allotted lands in accordance with the long-standing rule that *hidalgos* would get at least twice as much as non-nobles. Certain important nobles, of course, received large grants, thus introducing a Christian latifundism into the area. There had been latifundios in the kingdom of Granada even before the Reconquest. The Moslem kings and nobility had been large property owners, as were the mosques, but it seems that most of these large estates had been organized as small units of exploitation held by individual peasants through long-term lease or share-cropping agreements. At the exodus to Africa of the Moslem ruling classes, the property of the Christian crown and upper nobility grew, through purchase or confiscation. But the old customs of landholding tended to survive, and the traditional Islamic system of small, extremely subdivided plots continued (Bosque 1973: 484–91).

After the Reconquest there was a long period of tension between the Christian and Moslem inhabitants of the kingdom of Granada, during which the crown invariably supported the Christians. The Moriscos finally vented their frustrations in a desperate but futile uprising – the Rebellion of the Alpujarras (1568–70), after which they were expelled from the kingdom of Granada and dispersed throughout Castile. Perhaps 100,000 people were thus displaced, leaving large depopulated zones. The Christian population of these areas had been scant, and most of them had been killed during the rebellion. Early in 1571 the crown decreed the confiscation of all the real property of the Moriscos who had participated in the uprising. Those who had not rebelled were also deported, but they were to be recompensed for the loss of their property. Special surveys (*apeos*) of

Morisco property were made, which were the basis for a new *reparti-miento* to Christian settlers from the north. The crown dispatched commissioners to recruit families from Galicia, Asturias, Burgos, León, and Andalucía to come to the kingdom of Granada to farm the lands of the Moriscos. People from mountainous areas were especially sought out, on the grounds that they would adjust more easily to life in the Alpujarra region of Granada. At royal expense 12,524 families were brought in to populate 270 villages, out of some 400 that had existed in Morisco times (Bosque 1973: 493–4).

The number of Christian settlers brought in was less than half of the Morisco population who had previously lived there. Nevertheless, the *repartimiento* resulted in a continuation of the old Morisco mini-fundio system. The lots apportioned to Christian settlers did not normally exceed 2 hectares of irrigated land, or 10 hectares of dry-land. Moreover, these lots were not of single blocks of land, but rather consisted of a number of small, scattered parcels, according to the Morisco pattern. The new Christian colonists were given their property in *censo perpetuo*. The royal treasury was to get the token sum of 1 *real* per house each year, and one-tenth of the annual harvest – except for that from olives and mulberry trees, from which the treasury was to get one-fifth of the first ten years' harvest, and one-third from then and on, in perpetuity. Thus the colonists acquired the effective ownership of former Morisco property, which was eventually transformed into full ownership. Only cultivated lands seem to have been included in the 1571 and 1572 allotments. The hillside and forest lands, which were not assigned to settlers, remained *baldíos* for a time, but eventually became *propios* or commons, in which form they have come down to the second half of the twentieth century. The colonists moving into former Morisco lands had to invest almost no capital to begin exploiting their new farms. They were even provided draft animals, tools, and a quantity of grain to help them get started. Nevertheless, they found life in the Alpujarras to be extremely difficult, and within a few years many of the new colonists had (illegally) transferred their lots to other parties in exchange for an annual payment (Bosque 1971: 81–6; Núñez 1969: 241–71; Sáenz 1974: 336–49, 732–45; Villegas 1972: 249–50). Yet, despite the problems of adaptation, the post-1570 *repartimientos* con-stituted a remarkably long-lived source of Christian minifundio.[1]

We should not forget that in addition to these various royally supervised *repartimientos* there were similar allotments of lands to colonists sponsored by the nobility, the church, and the military orders. And these other small land grants also created an important class of peasant landowners. The municipalities also granted lands to their *vecinos*, using their own authority, quite apart from the royally approved *repartimientos*. Sometimes they did so in collaboration with the local lord. For example, around 1530 the council of Espera (Cádiz) and the duke of Alcalá made grants of *tierras baldías* to the *vecinos* of Espera, who thereafter treated the lands received as their private property. Such grants represented a reduction in the amount of available *baldíos*, which the municipalities usually tried to protect. But under certain circumstances, the granting of *tierras baldías* by a municipality was to the distinct advantage of the local community. The councils making such grants often acted out of a desire to ensure that the possession of those lands would remain with their own *vecinos*. A lively competition often existed between neighboring municipalities over the use of the *tierras baldías* available for their mutual benefit. There were many suits arising from situations where two places claimed the same lands, or where one municipality had usurped the *baldíos* in the sphere of influence of another municipality. Granting the disputed *baldíos* as private property was a way to resolve the difficulties caused by the shared utilization of these public lands, by placing the lands under individual ownership.[2]

The *fueros* of Andújar (Jaén) and Castro del Río (Córdoba) conferred property ownership upon anyone who cultivated a plot in the *baldíos* with plow or hoe, which meant that even poor peasants who owned no draft animals could become landowners. And in the northeastern part of the province of Jaén, several towns in the jurisdiction of Segura de la Sierra followed the practice of holding *repartimientos* of *tierras baldías* to assign them in property to their *vecinos*, as needed. The same thing was true in Estepa (Seville).[3]

But it was not only the *tierras baldías* that the municipalities granted to their *vecinos*. Common property also sometimes entered the private domain in this way. Occasionally this was precipitated by insoluble difficulties in the joint use of inter-municipal commons. For instance, the village of Rus and the city of Baeza (Jaén) had suffered so many costly lawsuits over the use of a certain *cortijo* that in 1538 they reached an agreement whereby the *cortijo* would be assigned to the residents of Rus in a *repartimiento* giving each *vecino* an equal share. The shares (of undisclosed size) would then be the private property of the individual *vecinos* of Rus, with the proviso that they never be sold to a non-*vecino* of the place. In exchange for the exclusive right to the *cortijo*, the council of Rus agreed to pay Baeza a *censo perpetuo* of 8,000 mrs per year, which would come from assessing each shareholder a proportionate amount. But the council of Rus found it impossible to enforce the restriction on subsequent sales of this property, and by the mid-1560s virtually all the shares had been transferred to non-*vecinos*, most of whom were residents of Baeza! We even have one example – highly unusual – of a municipality that abandoned the common system entirely, at least insofar as cultivation was concerned, by granting its common lands in property to the *vecinos* who were using them. This was the town of Cabeza Arados (Ciudad Real), which adopted the system of private ownership in the mid-1550s. The documentary account of this gives no explanation for the change. It might have been to avoid the complications of having to supervise the lottery system to distribute the common arable. In any case, the council of Cabeza Arados continued to exercise control over the rotation schedule of those lands, even after they had become private property.[4]

There is evidence that the town of Sabiote (Jaén) even sold its *vecinos* portions of a *dehesa boyal*. This was in the mid-1500s.[5] The sale or transfer of municipal property into the private sphere must not have been an uncommon occurrence in Castile, because a series of laws were instituted to deal with the phenomenon. In 1329 and 1351 the monarchs Alfonso XI and Pedro I forbade municipal governments to sell or otherwise alienate their property. A law of 1515 reiterated the same principle. And the emperor Charles V repeatedly found it necessary to issue new versions of the law, showing that some municipalities continued to grant public lands to their *vecinos* (*Novísima recopilación*, libro VII, título XXI, Leyes II, VIII, IX). It would be interesting to know what motivated the municipal councils to contribute towards the individualization of landownership in that way. Was it the greed of individual councilmen who coveted public lands? To be sure, much of the land involved went to members of the local elite. But we have many documented examples to prove that peasant landownership also benefitted from the process. Maybe the councils acted in response to expressions of land hunger by the peasantry, for we know that such certainly existed.

Some small property holders received ownership of their lands directly from the crown, in individual grants. This sort of thing must have been rare, but it occurred from time to time, as the crown responded to private petitions. For example, a certain Pedro Ramírez appealed to the crown in 1590, requesting royal recognition of his ownership of 16 *fanegas* of *tierras baldías* in Villarrote (Burgos). Ramírez had been farming the land for several years to support his family, and now he asked for title to the property in recognition of his service to the crown as a soldier in the royal army. He alleged that his most recent service was of eight months spent in finding, collecting, and turning in muskets, arquebuses, and other arms abandoned by soldiers deserting from the Armada stationed at Santander. The crown ordered an investigation, which revealed that Ramírez had indeed served as a soldier, and that the royal treasury owed him 101,750 mrs in back pay. In the end, the veteran was given title to his 16 *fanegas* of land, in lieu of the salary.[6]

PEASANT GARDENS AND VINEYARDS

Much peasant landownership was in the form of small parcels, of gardens (*huertas*) and vineyards. Most of these plots were probably limited to a few trees or vines, perhaps with the space for growing vegetables between the trees. But these tiny garden plots, cultivated with a hoe in most instances, could be highly productive, for they were often irrigated and regularly manured by their owners. In the early Reconquest, when land was plentiful, the arable and pasture lands of many areas were common, and the only inalienable property of the Castilian peasant was his house and garden (Costa 1944: 332–46). The peasant of medieval Castile seems to have come to think that ownership of a garden was essential to his wellbeing. Even noble lords felt obliged to grant their peasants land for orchards and vines. For example, the lords of Valdepusa (Toledo) conferred upon the colonists who settled on their estates not only the ownership of the grainlands they cleared and planted, but also of their gardens, orchards, and vineyards. And the colonists were not required to pay tribute (*terrazgo*) on these small plots of non-grainland. This was an exemption that would certainly have encouraged greater productivity. The garden plots were nearly all situated near the villages (sometimes even within the village itself), typically on the banks of some river or stream, where irrigation was possible. But there were also *huertas* irrigated from wells. In either case, the tiny gardens were frequently irrigated by hand, and were aimed primarily for household or local market needs (Palomeque 1947: 90–127).

128

But in some cases, especially in villages on the periphery of large cities, garden agriculture was geared for the production of fruits and vegetables for the urban market. And this could be a profitable business: according to Ambrosio de Morales (1577: fols. 108v–109v) the small fruit orchards around Córdoba provided their owners with a respectable income. Peasant ownership of *huertas* seems to have been very widespread, but it should not be thought that every Castilian peasant owned his own garden plot, or even that every Castilian village had such plots. The *Relaciones* (Salomon 1964: 87–92) seem to indicate that garden and fruit agriculture represented but a minor element in the rural economy of New Castile. Only 16 out of 81 villages in the province of Toledo mentioned *huertas*; in the province of Madrid it was only 13 of 90; and in Guadalajara it was only 24 of 145. But it seems to me that there should have been a higher proportion than that. It is possible that the *Relaciones* included only market-oriented *huerta* plots, and omitted those geared solely for domestic consumption. Unfortunately, I do not have enough detailed local property lists to make a judgement concerning the proportion of the Castilian peasants who might have owned garden plots, but I do have a few examples. A census of 1586 from Castilblanco (Badajoz) showed that 103 of the 270 *vecinos* of the place were owners of *huertas* or *cercas* (walled plots, usually containing fruit trees). The *vecinos* of Castilblanco included not only peasants, but also individuals with non-agricultural occupations, such as shoemakers, fishermen, and blacksmiths.[7] But even if we make allowances for this, we can not know how representative the sample is. And we can not even be sure that all the plots were included, for some of the smaller ones might have been accidentally or intentionally omitted from the list.

In certain regions it seems to have been the norm for peasants to own a *huerta*. As indicated in an earlier section of this chapter, the *repartimientos* of formerly Moslem lands in the kingdom of Granada included *huertas*, which were assigned to each of the original Christian colonists coming to the area. It might be argued that this represented an abnormal situation, because the *huertas* were already there, having been developed by the Moors, and were now merely exploited by their new owners. But there are many examples of *huertas* being created in a distinctly Christian setting, showing that they were not merely a continuation of existing Moorish institutions. In Lora (Seville), for instance, in the 1530s the town council announced publicly that all the poor of the locality, and anyone else who was interested, could attain free ownership of plots of land (*heredades*) for gardens, orchards, and vineyards. Anyone who had not received a previous grant for that purpose, or anyone who thought that he had been granted too little, could appear before the municipal scrivener to sign up, and each would be given a plot of up to 2 *aranzadas* of land from the local *tierras baldías*. The plot would then become the private property of the individual, on condition that he enclose it with a wall (*tapia* or *vallado*) within a year, and that he have it completely planted with trees or vines within four years. Failure to live up to the conditions could result in repossession by the council, and even if the recipient sold his plot to a third party, the purchaser would also be obliged to live up to the conditions of the grant. Every *vecino* of Lora was eligible to receive an *heredad* in this fashion. To be sure, not everyone would be able to exploit the opportunity, because it would require some capital to do so. But building an adobe or stone wall, and planting trees and vines, probably represented a greater investment of time than of money. Consequently, many must have been able to take advantage of it, by using family members as labor. The plots were very small, seemingly especially designed for peasants with limited means. The council announced, however, that it would grant larger plots to individuals with the resources to properly exploit more land.[8]

Also in the 1530s, the city of Arcos de la Frontera (Cádiz) held a *repartimiento* of some of its *tierras baldías*, so its *vecinos* could plant orchards and vineyards there. The city explained that there was ample grain and pasture land in the area, but a great shortage of vineyards and olive groves. In this case, the recipients of lots were given titles on the condition that they plant them within three years. They were not required to wall their plots, but they were not to plant them with grain, lest the draft animals used to plow grain fields damage adjoining trees and vines. Nevertheless, many recipients of these plots were too poor to clear them of *monte* and plant vines and olives within the specified time. They tried to do so piecemeal, illegally planting grain until they could manage to make their more permanent plantings. The city sympathized with their plight, and passed an ordinance allowing the planting of vegetables, or any other crop except grain, in the transitionary period before the vines and olive trees were established.[9]

Such grants of *huerta* plots from the *baldíos* were quite commonplace, and they resulted in the creation of an important peasant minifundism. The municipal governments liked to encourage the development of *huertas* and vineyards, particularly the latter, because viticulture represented an important source of wealth for the population. Some towns that held *repartimientos* of *baldíos* went so far as to make the planting of vines obligatory. For example, in 1466 the town government of Astorga (León) distributed parcels of land to its *vecinos* with the stipulation that the plots had to be planted to vines within five years, under penalty of a fine of 1 *real* per day. This system gave Astorga an important wine production, it avoided the need for costly importations, and it favored the development of small property ownership and the social egalitarianism that went along with it (Huetz 1967: 595–9). But in some places, such as Badajoz in the mid-1500s, the land assigned for *huertas* and vineyards was not really given in ownership, but merely for use. Here, the vines and trees were the private property of the cultivators, but the land was not, for it reverted back to the municipality as soon as the vineyards or orchards were abandoned.[10]

Huerta and viticulture land had a far more egalitarian distribution than other land. In the early modern period, when the economy was largely geared to local self sufficiency, vineyards and gardens had a far wider importance than they do today. Although there were some parts of Spain that specialized in viticulture, the vine was practically ubiquitous, for local consumption. And almost everywhere vineyards were the property of small peasants. It seems that the reason for this lay in the nature of viticulture: the painstaking work of tending vines did not in most parts of Castile lend itself to large productive units, or to absentee ownership. The small peasant landowner, who could not afford to buy enough land and equipment to keep himself continually occupied with grain farming, was left with a good deal of time on his hands. And he often spent it growing vines – a labor-intensive form of agriculture that required a minimum of capital. Consequently, viticulture in both Old and New Castile was the preserve of the small peasant in the sixteenth century. There seems to have been little specialization in viticulture: the owners of vineyards normally also had cereal lands to exploit. Vine ownership could be widespread because viticulture fitted conveniently into the work schedule of the typical Castilian peasant. It provided him with his own wine, and perhaps with some pocket money as well, if he sold part of his crop (Salomon 1964: 83–6; Brumont 1977: 33–4; Phillips 1979: 41–3, 66).

The typical vineyard was quite small: those in Ciudad Real averaged around 4 *aranzadas* (Phillips 1979: 42–3), but in Morales de Toro (Zamora) they were normally only about 1 *aranzada* in size, and in Valladolid they were often no larger than a half *aranzada*. And it should be remembered that the vines often shared the land with olives and other trees. This kind of intercropping, which was also commonplace in the *huerta* plots, reduced the usefulness of the traditional forms of land measurement. Consequently, in many places sixteenth-century Castilians did not give the surface area of their vineyards. In Monleón (Salamanca) and in Plasenzuela (Cáceres), for example, although the villagers reported the size of their grain fields in *fanegas*, they merely stated that they owned 'a vineyard', or 'a small vineyard', or 'a very small vineyard'. More sensible still was the custom in Castañar de Ibor (Cáceres), where the size of a vineyard was expressed only in the number of vines it contained. Because of the inconsistent measurement practices of the sixteenth century, we have to rely on extrapolations from the mid-eighteenth-century *catastro* to judge what proportion of the lands of a given area was in vineyard. But it seems clear that in most places the proportion of viticulture lands was quite small. Even in Ciudad Real, a leading wine-growing area whose products were famous, only about 20 percent of the territory was devoted to the vine in the mid-1700s, and in the sixteenth century the figure was probably somewhat less.[11]

COMPLANT CONTRACTS

Peasant ownership of vineyards in Spain was given an early start thanks to a special kind of contract called the *complant* (from the Latin *ad complantandum*). The *complant* was by no means a peculiarly Castilian institution. It also existed in early medieval France, and was used in Cataluña at least as early as 860. It seems to have appeared in Castile at about the same time, and became a commonplace contract in Spain throughout the Middle Ages. The principle of the *complant* was very simple: the owner of an uncultivated piece of land gave it to a peasant to plant to vines, and when the vineyard came into production, which was normally between four and eight years, the property was divided equally between the original proprietor and the cultivator. The monasteries, which received important land grants after the Reconquest, regularly used the *complant* to increase the value of their lands. The peasant workers would be left with the ownership of half of the vineyards, but the *complant* was advantageous to the monasteries nevertheless, because vineyards were far more valuable and profitable than open land. Medieval Castilians used several different expressions to describe their *complant* contracts: in some places the custom was called *plantar a fondos tierra*; another widely used phrase was *plantar a medias*, or *ad mediatem*; and *vinea de postura* was also much in use (Valdeavellano 1968: 250, 257; Huetz 1967: 588–603).

The *complant* contract had various applications, and it could be either written or unwritten. In some places, in fact, the half-and-half division was considered to apply automatically to a peasant who spontaneously took it upon himself to plant vines on someone else's land, if the proprietor allowed him to go ahead, and did not lodge a protest at the time of planting. The *complant* could be applied to a small plot worked by a single peasant; but it could also be used for a large piece of land, when the landowner came to an agreement with a group of peasants, or even with an entire village. Sometimes the contract specified the date by which the vines had to be planted, but many contracts allowed a delay of as many as six or seven years before planting. There were some *complants* that required the building of a wall (*tapia*) to protect the young vines. And the peasant viti-culturalist was obliged to tend the vineyard diligently until the time of division. If he failed to do so, he could be fined; and if he did not pay the fine, some contracts specified that he would forfeit his claim to the vineyard. Frequently the peasant who planted the vineyard was allowed to keep for himself whatever fruit the immature vines yielded before the division time. Normally the landowner, or his representative, had the right to make the division, and it was often stipulated that the vineyard was not to be divided into more than two pieces. But sometimes the division never actually took place, because the cultivator continued to work the entire vineyard, giving the proprietor a portion of his half as rent, and keeping the other half wholly for himself (except for the tithe, naturally). As a new land-owner, the cultivator could freely sell or do whatever he wished with his half of the vineyard. However, the original proprietor generally retained an option to purchase at a price equal to that offered by a third party (Huetz 1967: 588–99).

The combination of municipal grants, *presura* acquisitions, *complant* contracts, and various *repartimientos* made it possible even for peasants in modest circumstances to become owners of vineyards and *huerta* plots. In 1569 a resident of Morales de Toro (Zamora) testified that about 100 out of the village's 250 *vecinos* were day laborers (*jornaleros*) who had no grain fields, and owned no property except for a small vineyard or a garden for melons or vegetables. Another villager from Morales reported that most of the *vecinos* of the place owned vineyards, even if they had no other agricultural property. A similar situation prevailed in the village of Castañar de Ibor (Cáceres), where a census of 1586 identified 22 out of 200 *vecinos* as day laborers or 'poor day laborers' (*jornaleros pobres*). Yet all of these owned some property, and 17 of the 22 had vines or *huertas*. One self-identified 'poor laborer' reported that he was the owner of a *huerta* of fruit trees, a mature vineyard of 800 vines, and a newly-planted vineyard of 1,000 vines. He had obviously been able to make good use of the various opportunities to acquire property. It should be said that some of the laborers of Castañar who owned no gardens or vines were probably young people who had not yet had a chance to become established. One, in fact, was identified as a newly-wed. On the other hand a census of 1558 listed only 22 of the 94 *vecinos* of Monleón (Salamanca) as the owners of vines, gardens, or orchards.[12] Thus, there was considerable regional variation in the proportion of ownership of this type of property. And if we had sufficient data, we would undoubtedly find considerable intraregional differences as well.

THE IMPORTANCE OF PEASANT LANDOWNERSHIP

One should remember the caveat of Slicher van Bath (1963: 311) that landownership does not in itself present a true picture of rural society. To truly understand the socioeconomic stratification of the rural population, it is also necessary to consider the size of the population, the demographic development of the area, general economic conditions, and occupational classifications. One should also examine the importance of the size of farms, the amount of capital investment, the number and type of livestock, the size and composition of the family, and the number of employees, if any. In a future work, I plan to examine some of these broader aspects of rural society. But for the moment, let us examine the question of the importance of peasant landownership. As always, generalizations are dangerous, for there was clearly much variation from place to place. The *Relaciones* certainly attest to the existence of peasant landholdings, but they indicate that in New Castile the property of the nobility, the church, and urban investors was predominant. In fact, in many cases the existence of peasant property is almost hidden in the *Relaciones*. This is not at all surprising, because the villagers who prepared them were quite suspicious of these government questionnaires. They were very much aware that reports of affluence might be used as a justification for increased taxes. Consequently, the authors of the *Relaciones* deliberately minimized the extent of their own wealth, whereas they had no corresponding motivation to understate the wealth of outsiders (Salomon 1964: 178–81). The same psychological factor entered into the preparation of the reports (*averiguaciones*) now found in the Expedientes de Hacienda section of the Simancas archive. This section constitutes one of the most important sources for the history of rural society in sixteenth-century Castile, but it should be remembered that it, too, would tend to minimize the extent of peasant landownership.

In one place in his study of the *Relaciones*, Noël Salomon states (1964: 181) that peasant property ownership in New Castile, except for a few unusual cases, was 'minimal', and 'minuscule' when compared to the extensive holdings of the nobility, the clergy, and the bourgeoisie. According to this view, the non-communitarian property of the peasant was usually limited to garden plots of small size and of little value. But three pages later, Salomon reaches quite a different conclusion: he ventures a guess that peasants owned between 25 and 30 percent of the land in New Castile – an estimate based partly on the few *Relaciones* accounts that contain such information, and partly on extrapolating from late-eighteenth-century sources. These extrapolations also suggest that New Castile enjoyed the highest proportion of peasant ownership in Spain, outside of Galicia. I am inclined to agree with Salomon's second appraisal of the situation, because there were many places where peasant ownership of grainlands was quite important, even though it did not normally measure up to the percentage of lands held by the privileged estates and the urban elite.

But there was clearly much regional variation. Francis Brumont has calculated (1977: 28–9) that in the La Bureba district of the province of Burgos an average of about 50 percent of the landownership was in peasant hands in the late 1500s. But within the district the proportion varied considerably from place to place: the highest peasant ownership was 80 percent, in Solas and Galbarros; and the lowest was between 20 and 25 percent, in Buezo, Solduengo, and Movilla; except for one village, Rubiales, where all the land belonged to the Monastery of Oña. Studies from different parts of Castile show the wildest fluctuation in the proportion of peasant landownership. In the La Armuña area of Salamanca, for example, only a few small plots seem to have been peasant-owned, if we can trust extrapolations from the *catastro*. Within this area, the *vecinos* of Palencia de Negrilla owned only about $6\frac{1}{2}$ percent of the land they worked. The remainder was the property of nobles and other absentee proprietors (Cabo 1955: 118). By contrast, Jesús García Fernández tells us (1953: 220–2, 227–8) that the lands of Horche (Guadalajara) were owned almost exclusively by the peasant inhabitants of the place. Horche's egalitarian landowning structure can be explained by the way the town developed. It was a royal town, and was thus spared the usurpations of a greedy lord. As Horche's population grew, the town purchased successive blocks of the surrounding *monte baldío* from the crown. And each time a new block was purchased, the town government held a *repartimiento* in which each *vecino* got a share. The result was that Horche became (and remained, down to the mid-twentieth century), a village overwhelmingly dominated by peasant minifundios. According to García Sanz (1977: 268–9, 375) the province of Segovia was dominated by medium and small peasant farmers who rented much of their land, but it appears that the proportion of peasant ownership ranged from one-fifth to one-third, depending upon the district, if we can trust the contemporary estimates in Simancas.

I have mentioned earlier the development of peasant ownership in several places in southern Spain, and the prevalence of peasant minifundios in Murcia and in the kingdom of Granada. The available data about the proportion of peasant landownership in the sixteenth century is too spotty for a definitive statement, but if I had to hazard a guess based on the statistical information at hand, I would venture that perhaps one-fifth of the arable lands of Castile was owned by peasants. However, in view of the differences that existed from one place to another, even within small districts, I do not know how much such an estimate is worth. But if we accept the estimate of one-fifth, that means that the other four-fifths were owned by the municipalities, the crown, the nobility, the church, and other non-peasant entities. That would indeed make peasant ownership small, if not 'minuscule', by comparison. However, we should remember that in addition to working his own lands, the peasant often held rented lands at long-term leases or *censos* under conditions that in many cases were actually more advantageous than landownership. Furthermore, the peasant in some places had the possibility of the free, or near-free, use of the *tierras baldías* and common lands. Therefore, one should not necessarily deplore the fact that the Castilian peasant did not own more than he did. In fact, in many cases, an increase in the peasant's share of landownership turned out to be detrimental to his wellbeing, as will be seen in chapter 6.

The comparative data compiled by Brumont (1977: 28–33) for La Bureba indicates that the percentage of peasant landownership was likely to be highest in poor mountain villages that lay far from the beaten path. In these places there was a remarkable degree of egalitarianism in life style: virtually everyone was poor. Yet, in many of these villages almost every *vecino* was a landowner. In Arconda, for instance, every family head had cultivated lands except one – and that one was the owner of some vines. Brumont found that the proportion of peasant landownership was lowest in the larger towns situated along trade routes. Here industry or commerce could develop, and a class of urban investors had become interested in the acquisition of rural property.

THE DISTRIBUTION OF PEASANT PROPERTY
OWNERSHIP

The amount of land owned by each peasant varied greatly, even within regions, depending upon geographical and historical conditions. Consider, for example, the situation in the La Bureba area of the province of Burgos in the late 1500s. Here the average amount per *vecino* was smallest in the isolated egalitarian mountain villages, because of their limited supply of arable land (the non-arable land tended to be community-owned). In Rublacedo de Yuso, for instance, it was only 4.8 *fanegas*, whereas the average in Quintanilla and in Zuñeda – lower-lying villages in the same area – was over 40 *fanegas*. Even in places dominated by minifundia there were great differences in the amount owned by individual peasants. In Quintanaélez, two individuals were the proprietors of fully half the peasant-owned lands, while the other 32 peasant landowners divided the remainder. And in La Parte, a single *labrador* owned 45 percent, and the other 25 peasant owners shared the rest. In certain districts of La Bureba, the inequality was much less pronounced, but the normal pattern was for a few peasants to have large holdings, and for a large number to own amounts too small for the support of a family. These last would have found it necessary to supplement their income in some way – perhaps by farming rented land, or by hiring themselves out as day laborers (Brumont 1977: 31–3, and table 6; Ortega Valcárcel 1966: 96–9).

A similar disparity in property ownership existed in the Montes de Toledo. Michael Weisser (1976: 39–42) has analyzed the distribution of landownership in Navalmoral de Toledo, according to a census of 1583. He found that only 108 of the 243 *vecinos* of the village reported owning land. Of these, 11 each claimed ownership of 50 *fanegas* or more of grainland. Another 11 *vecinos* each owned 30 or more *fanegas*. Together, these 22 households owned nearly half of the community's arable lands, although they represented only 9 percent of the population. Just below them in the socioeconomic ladder were 32 families who owned an average of 13.9 *fanegas* of land. And ranking at the bottom of the list of property owners were 54 families whose average ownership was 10.6 *fanegas*.

We have another breakdown of property ownership for Monleón (Salamanca) in the year 1558. This village had a population of 94 *vecinos*, of whom 36 were identified as *labradores*, and 31 others had distinctly non-agricultural professions such as shoemaker, clergyman, weaver, or innkeeper. Only 36 *vecinos* of Monleón, nearly all of whom were *labradores*, reported that they owned grainland. But there were an additional 20 *vecinos* who had no grainfields, but who owned vineyards, orchards, flax fields, or gardens. Among the owners of grainland, three had from 60 to 100 *fanegas*; three from 35 to 45 *fanegas*; ten from 20 to 30 *fanegas*; eighteen from 4 to 15 *fanegas*; and one who reported owning a field of undisclosed (but undoubtedly very small) size. The distribution of property ownership in Monleón thus seems to correspond to the normal pattern for Castile: a few large landholders, and a much larger group of medium-to-small property owners.[13]

Another example is the town of Plasenzuela (Cáceres), for which we have a census from the year 1575. Landownership here was considerably more restricted than it was in Monleón. Only 41 of the 110 *vecinos* of the place reported that they owned grainland. Another 16 did not own that type of property, but did have some vines, gardens, or other small plots. Here, however, as in all cases of property lists drawn up for the use of the government, one suspects that the extent of property ownership was deliberately understated. According to the census, no one in Plasenzuela owned more than 25 *fanegas* of land. Six individuals were listed as having between 20 and 25 *fanegas*; six others between 10 and 15 *fanegas*; sixteen between 4 and 9 *fanegas*; and thirteen owned no more than 2 or 3 *fanegas*. In the case of Plasenzuela there were no substantial landowners at all, and most property owners had pitifully small quantities of land. Most of these, however, also farmed some other fields in addition to those they owned, and there were twenty inhabitants of the town who owned no land, but reported that they planted grain. Some of this additional land was rented, presumably from absentee landowners, but much of it was probably from the *baldíos*.[14]

Peasant landowners were likely for several reasons to be adversely affected by the presence of noble-owned property in the same locality. For one thing, many nobles aggressively sought to extend their holdings, sometimes by encroaching on the lands of their weaker neighbors. For another, since the *hidalgo* was able to escape many forms of taxation, the existence of a large proportion of noble-owned land would cause non-noble property owners to suffer a higher tax burden. Because of these unfavorable aspects of *hidalgo* ownership, some towns tried to limit the extent of non-plebeian property holding. The town of Yebra (Guadalajara) is an extreme example of this attitude. According to a concession granted to Yebra by the Master of the Order of Calatrava in 1396, no *hidalgo* could purchase real estate within its boundaries. And this rule was strictly enforced: the town's *Relaciones* reply indicated that there were no *hidalgos* living there (nor had there ever been any), and all the property in the locality was owned by non-noble *labradores*. Local ordinances forbade the sale of property to *hidalgos*, under penalty of the loss of the purchase price plus a fine; and any *hidalgo* who bought property there ran the risk of seeing it confiscated without compensation by the municipal government. It was hardly surprising, then, that no *hidalgo* had ever come to live there (Salomon 1964: 178, n. 1).

Of course, one should remember that *hidalgos* could also be *labradores* – that is, peasants. In fact, as mentioned in a previous chapter, the population of some parts of Spain was almost exclusively *hidalgo*. This was principally true of the Basque provinces, which lie outside the scope of this work. But there were pockets of *hidalgo* concentration even in the Castilian heartland. One such place was the village of Ruanes (Cáceres), which had a population of fifty-two *vecinos* (not counting two priests) in 1561. All the *vecinos* of Ruanes were identified as *hidalgos*, except one, who was a plebeian *labrador*. It is interesting that the distribution of property ownership in this all-*hidalgo* village was no different from the pattern one would expect to find in a completely non-noble population. The *hidalgos* of Ruanes were peasants. A few were prosperous, some were very poor, but most seem to have led a fairly comfortable existence, according to the standards of the rural world of the time. The overwhelming majority of the *vecinos* of Ruanes were landowners: only 7 of the lay family heads owned no land; and only 19 owned neither a vineyard nor a garden. But here, as elsewhere in Castile, the landowning statistics alone can be misleading. One person who reported that he owned no land at all was nevertheless identified as being moderately well-off (*tiene medianamente*). And the sole non-noble *vecino* was described as well-to-do (*tiene bien*), although he was one of the minor property owners of the village, with only 4 *fanegas* of land. The source of his wealth was not land, but rather livestock: he owned 150 sheep, and a variety of other animals as well. The largest landowner in Ruanes had 150 *fanegas* of land, but there was another individual who owned almost as much – 120 *fanegas*. There were five *vecinos* who owned from 40 to 70 *fanegas*; thirteen who owned from 20 to 30; eight who had from 10 to 12; another eight with from 5 to 8; and nine with less than 5 *fanegas*.[15]

The data we have for the distribution of landownership suggests that the arable land of Castile was very much subdivided into small plots. The statistics I have offered above do not tell the whole story, however, because the typical Castilian peasant landowner of the sixteenth century owned not just one block of land, but several. The origins of peasant ownership, and the prevailing systems of rotation made such subdivisions inevitable. In Menasalbas (Toledo), for instance, it was normal for the peasant *labrador* to have several different plots of varying size, even within a single *pago* (planting district) of the locality. One *vecino* of Menasalbas owned – in one *pago* – no fewer than fifteen different plots, ranging in size from 1 *fanega* to 15 *fanegas*.[16] In La Bureba (Burgos) there was also an extreme parcelization. According to Brumont (1977: 43–5), the average size of cultivated plots varied from place to place, ranging from 0.4 to 1.7 *fanegas*. This type of extreme subdivision might have been expected in the mountain villages of La Bureba. But it also existed on the plains. Bartolomé Bennassar (1967: 314–15) found that in Valladolid parcels of grainland were normally less than a *yugada* (0.72 *fanegas*). And this was true not only of peasant property, but even of the property of the privileged orders, as has been mentioned earlier. The extreme parcelization of land was also a characteristic of the landholding system of Horche (Guadalajara) (García Fernández 1953: 220–2, 227–8). And it was mentioned earlier in this chapter that it was widespread in the formerly Moorish lands of the kingdoms of Murcia and Granada.

Even in the open spaces of La Mancha the size of fields was small, although much larger than the foregoing examples: the typical grainfield in Ciudad Real seems to have measured less than 5 *fanegas* (Phillips 1979: 38). The fragmentation of the land into small parcels had grave consequences: it occasioned the loss of time, as the peasant went from one field to another; and it represented the loss of useful surface, in the uncultivated turnrows and other boundary lines. It is obvious that this type of loss would increase with each decrease in the size of plots. According to Brumont (1977: 45) research has demonstrated that the land loss caused by parcelization would amount to 0.16 percent of the total surface in fields of 100 hectares; 1.6 percent in parcels of 1 hectare; and 16.1 percent in parcels of only 1 are. It seems to me, based on my personal experiences in farming, that this is a conservative estimate, and the actual loss could be even higher. The loss of time caused by the subdivision of plots could be considerable, because the fields of an individual peasant might be scattered not only around the territory of his own village, but of neighboring villages as well, for many peasants had to look beyond their own locality for fertile lands to work (Silva 1967: 31, n. 17).

RICH AND POOR PEASANTS

In the strict sense, there was no well-defined 'peasant' class in sixteenth-century Castilian society. Some inhabitants of rural villages were mere wage-earners; others were sharecroppers or renters; still others were landowners with a family-farm type of operation, or prosperous large-scale farmers or ranchers with many hired workers; and there were even absentee landowners whom we could call 'peasants'. Furthermore, there was considerable overlapping between these categories. The term 'peasant', then, is really too broad to be of much use, except to designate the rural population, or the population directly linked to agropastoral production, either through actual work in the fields, or through property ownership. But since the rural population tended to live in municipalities, and since many individuals connected with agropastoralism lived in large cities, the issue is further confused, as it is also by the social division between noble and non-noble. No one would think to apply the term 'peasant' to a wealthy grandee who lived an urban existence in Madrid or in some other capital, even though he might have been the owner of many rural properties. But what of the noble who lived in a village, and personally supervised the operation of his estate, to say nothing of the modest rural *hidalgo* who did most or all of the work with his own hands?

Because of the imprecise nature of the term 'peasant' (and it should be said that the Spanish word *campesino* has the same difficulties), many writers have undertaken to clarify the situation by distinguishing between the different kinds of peasants. I did so earlier in this work when I introduced the term *labrador*, which I defined as an independent peasant farmer. But the word *labrador* also has some difficulties, because in Golden Age Castile, it was often used in opposition to *hidalgo* to distinguish the noble from the commoner. For example, the 1561 census of the village of Ruanes (cited four paragraphs above) indicated that there was only one *labrador* in the place, whereas the other fifty-one *vecinos* were *hidalgos*. But, in fact, many of these *hidalgos* were in exactly the same occupational and landowning category as the *labrador*. Hence, the two terms should not really be thought of as being incompatible. Domínguez Ortiz tells us (1971: 149) that the term *labrador* was most frequently used to apply to a peasant proprietor in comfortable circumstances. But because sixteenth-century documents often tell of poor *labradores* who are near the starvation level, we should avoid insisting that the *labrador* was well-off. And we should not insist that the *labrador* was a landowner, for many in this category were renters who owned little or no real estate. Today the most commonly accepted definition of the *labrador* is that used by Salomon – that he was the possessor of one or more teams of draft animals, whether or not he was a landowner (1964: 266). It is implicitly understood that the *labrador* was personally connected with working the soil, whether he did so himself, or through laborers whom he supervised. It should be said that there were some places in Castile where the word *labrador* was rarely used. This was true of the La Bureba region of Burgos province. Nevertheless, in his study of the area, Brumont (1977: 43, n. 1) employed the term because he found it useful to distinguish peasants who owned at least one pair of draft animals.

The definition based on the ownership of a team of oxen or mules is certainly a workable one, but I prefer not to use it, because it excludes independent peasant farmers who rented one or both of the animals of their team. And it includes peasant proprietors of teams who farmed little or no land, and who supported themselves primarily by plowing for hire. My own definition – that a *labrador* was simply an independent peasant farmer – is rather loose, but this is intentional, to allow the inclusion of any peasant who supported himself primarily by the growing of crops on his own fields. These fields could be either his own property, or rented. In 1600 the *arbitrista* (reform writer) González de Cellorigo (fols. 26–7) distinguished between the land-owning and the non-landowning *labrador*, but only to indicate that property ownership gave the former a much higher social esteem.

Many writers – both sixteenth-century and recent – have tried to polarize the peasant world between the *labrador,* who farmed his own fields, and the *jornalero* (day laborer) or *trabajador* (worker), who supported himself solely by working for others. But such a bifurcation breaks down under scrutiny, because there were many *jornaleros* who owned their own small fields, vineyards and gardens; and there were many *labradores* who hired themselves out during part of the year, to supplement their income. The distinction between the two was often so fine as to be practically meaningless. In Monleón (Salamanca), for instance, there was a *labrador* who owned a yoke of oxen with which he farmed only a few small plots (*terezuelas,* of unstated size) and some olives. His position must have been considerably worse than that of a certain *jornalero* from Castañar de Ibor (Cáceres), who owned a fruit orchard, a garden, an olive tree, 400 vines, and four bovines with which he farmed 2 *fanegas* of grain.[17] In the absence of a generally accepted sixteenth-century standard, comparisons of the proportion of *labradores* and *jornaleros* are of questionable value. Nevertheless, the distinction may be useful to help us gauge approximately how many were primarily self-employed, and to separate these from peasants who depended primarily on wages for their livelihood.

Noël Salomon calculates (1964: 257–68) that between 25 and 30 percent of the *vecinos* of the *Relaciones* villages of New Castile were *labradores*. But the proportion varied widely within that region. The percentage of *jornaleros* was also greatly variable, but Salomon estimates that at least 60 percent of the rural family heads fell into this category. In other parts of Castile the proportion also fluctuated from place to place. In the village of Cebolla de Trabancos (Avila) 40 percent were *labradores* and only 4 percent were *jornaleros*, and in little Pineda-Trasmonte (Burgos) – a place with only thirty-five *vecinos* – there were no *jornaleros* at all, and the entire active population was *labrador* except for one shepherd and a tailor. It should be said that the selection of my examples was determined partly by chance (blind selection of documents in the archives), and partly by the availability of the proper kind of data. Looking at such random samples elsewhere in Castile, we find that a 1558 census of Monleón (Salamanca) showed 38 percent *labradores* and $7\frac{1}{2}$ percent *jornaleros*. About the same ratio existed in Castilblanco (Badajoz) in 1586: only 7 percent were listed as salaried workers; and although the term *labrador* was not actually used, a property inventory makes it clear that at least 43 percent fell into that category. And in 1595 the *labradores* of the village of Moncalvillo del Huete (Cuenca) outnumbered the local *jornaleros* (here called *braceros*) by around four to one. Turning again to Extremadura, we find that a report for the year 1595 indicates that 40 percent of the 150 *vecinos* of the village of Las Casas de Reina (Badajoz) were *labradores*. In this case there was no indication of the number of *jornaleros*. Twenty-seven percent of the *vecinos* of the village were described as being 'poor' – a designation often applied to mere wage-earners in sixteenth-century Castile, but it is not clear whether that definition is applicable to the example at hand. Even in Andalucía the proportion of *labradores* was often quite high. The newly established Christian towns in the kingdom of Granada, of course, were predominantly inhabited by independent peasant operators. But *labradores* also formed the majority in many older areas. In 1569, for instance, a royal official reported that 800 (57 per cent) of the 1,400 *vecinos* of Quesada (Jaén) were in this class.[18] And finally, Brumont (1977: table 32) has calculated that in the La Bureba villages of Burgos province, an average of 35 percent of the *vecinos* were *labradores*, and only $6\frac{1}{2}$ percent were *jornaleros*. But within that region, the percentages varied widely: for *labradores*, from a low of 6 percent at Oña, to a high of 72 percent at Movilla; and for *jornaleros*, from a low of 2 percent in several villages, to a high of 25 percent in Navas. The foregoing examples demonstrate the danger of making generalizations for the whole of Castile from a limited data base. But they do indicate that a significant percentage of the Castilian peasantry in the 1500s were independent operators in the *labrador* category, and many of them were doing quite well.

The image of the rich *labrador* is prominent in Castilian Golden Age literature. In Cervantes's *Don Quixote* (part I, ch. 28) the beautiful Dorotea is the daughter of an Andalucían *labrador* whose wealth is so great that it almost confers *hidalgo* status. This *labrador* has many servants, both domestic and agricultural, and is involved in grain, wine, olive oil, apiculture, and livestock. Another character in *Don Quixote* (part II, chs. 19–21) is Camacho the Rich, a prosperous Manchegan *labrador*, who demonstrates his affluence by staging an extravagant open-air wedding feast. And in Lope de Vega's *El hombre de bien*, there is the *labrador* Felicio, who gives a list of his assets, including 100 oxen, 2,000 sheep, two or three large grainfields, four fruit orchards, and extensive vineyards and olive groves (Arco 1941: 863). The rich *labrador* was not a mere figment of the writers' imagination – he represented a real historical socioeconomic type. The *Relaciones* show that *labradores* who owned five or six teams of oxen or mules were usually the wealthiest villagers, but there was an aristocracy of non-noble *labradores* who were very wealthy indeed (Salomon 1965: 355, 748–9, 758–9, 779–80). For example, Domín-guez Ortiz cites (1971: 149) a report that some *labradores* in Utrera (Seville) kept 300 oxen for draft animals, and that many sowed 1,500 to 2,000 *fanegas* of wheat, and more. The *Relaciones* value the fortunes of the rich *labradores* of New Castile between 2,000 and 6,000 *ducados*, and according to the *arbitrista* Guillén Barbón y Castañeda (1628: fol. 9), in the late 1500s there were *labradores* in Old Castile with estates of 8,000 and 9,000 *ducados* or more.

'Rich' and 'poor', of course, are subjective or comparative terms. For instance, the most prosperous *labrador* in the village of Zarza de Montánchez (Cáceres), according to a census of 1561, had an estate that was quite modest compared with some of the preceding exam-ples: nevertheless, he was described as 'rich'. This individual owned 2 houses, a mill, a half-interest in an orchard-garden, 6 *peonadas* of vineyard, 11 cows, 110 sheep, 11 hogs, a mule, and 2 yoke of oxen. Apparently he owned no grainland, but undoubtedly he farmed a sizeable area in the local *baldíos*. In the same province, by contrast, in the village of Castañar de Ibor, there lived a *labrador* who appears to have been just as well-off – although he was by no means the wealthiest peasant in the place – but who was *not* identified as being rich. According to a census of 1586, this *labrador* had 3 houses, a fruit orchard, a 1,200-plant vineyard, 2 *fanegas* of grainland, 2 hogs, 100 goats, 3 bovines, 2 beehives, and a mule. In addition to the 2 *fanegas* he owned, he must have farmed at least a dozen *fanegas* of *tierras baldías*, because in 1586 it was reported that he had 7½ *fanegas* of grain sowed. But although the meaning of 'rich' might be vague or changeable, it is beyond question that the wealthy *labradores* constituted a small minority of the peasantry. Most *labradores* led a modest existence, and many were undeniably poor.[19]

Rural poverty was particularly widespread in the mountains of the north – in Soria, Burgos, and León, and the poverty of the entire Cantabrian region was proverbial. In the type of dispersal described by Fernand Braudel (1975: 30–51) large numbers of emigrants fled their mountain villages to seek a better life in the more favored parts of Castile. We should be aware, however, that the inhabitants of these legendary poor regions did nothing to refute the circulating exaggerated accounts of their poverty, realizing that these caused the government to almost forget about them when it made its frequent petitions for new taxes. But their poverty was not just a myth. As mentioned earlier, over half of the peasants of the La Bureba village of the province of Burgos were landowners, but most of them had such minuscule plots that they found it impossible to survive without devoting a significant part of their time to pastoral activities or to non-agricultural pursuits. In La Bureba the average *labrador* farmed with only about one and one-half oxen, and in many villages of the area the average was below one (Brumont 1977: table 10). Remember that this was for *labradores*, who were more prosperous than the average peasant. In 1597 the sole *vecino* from Pinos (a La Bureban village) who was described in a census as being 'rich' had attained that distinction on the basis of the fact that he had a yoke of oxen, and that he farmed his own, rather than rented, land – a meager standard for 'richness' that suggests a generally straitened life style in the area.[20]

But one did not have to go to the mountains to find poor peasants, for they were a fact of life in all parts of Castile. Lope de Vega's Lauro, in *El ejemplo de casados*, represents the stereotype of the humble *labrador*. Lauro owns a small house (*una casilla*), a few diminutive plots of land, a vineyard, twenty goats, and a yoke of oxen (Arco 1941: 867). In the poverty-stricken mountain villages of the north, Lauro might have been considered to be well-off, or even 'rich'; but in the broader Castilian context, his modest estate placed him among the poorer *labradores*. And most *labradores* were in that category. For example, in the village of Las Cases de Reina (Badajoz), which had 150 *vecinos* in 1595, there lived about 60 *labradores*, nearly all of whom worked with one or two yokes of oxen. Only a few owned as many as three pairs of oxen. Thus, the majority of the *labradores* of the place fit into Lauro's category, as did the vast majority of sixteenth-century Castilian *labradores*.[21] Most of them were property owners, even if they had no more than a tiny vineyard or garden. But they normally owned only a part of the grainland they farmed – the remainder being rented, or from the *baldíos* or municipal commons.

THE BOURGEOIS LANDOWNER

The sixteenth century witnessed a growing investment by city dwellers in agricultural property. This was not a peculiarly Castilian phenomenon, but was also true of the rest of Europe, both inside and outside the Mediterranean region. One reason for the investment of urban residents in rural lands was the deepseated conviction that the only real wealth and security lay in land. Furthermore, by the 1500s, landownership was becoming increasingly popular as an attractive investment. The extraordinary demographic growth of the sixteenth century increased the demand, and raised the prices, of agricultural goods. This, plus the social prestige factor, impelled prosperous city dwellers to want to buy land. The potential for profit was not as high as it was in trade, but landownership was far less risky (Delano 1979: 136–7; Braudel 1975: 424–5). And in the second half of the century, some urban investors began to distrust *juros* (government bonds), and turned instead to land. Many bureaucrats, merchants, and artisans invested a portion of their earnings in land, and the *conquistadores* and their families bought rural properties with their loot from America. These urban investors were absentee landowners only up to a point, for they preferred to buy near the city where they lived, so they might have a hand in the management, so they could enjoy fresh agricultural products from their estates, and so they could reap the maximum social prestige from their landownership (Domínguez 1973b: 164–5).

Bourgeois investment in rural property was particularly noticeable around large cities such as Madrid, Toledo, and Valladolid. The village of Vicálvaro is a good example of what could happen to a rural settlement that became caught in the orbit of a large metropolis. Situated just to the east of Madrid, Vicálvaro seems to have had a closed, self-sufficient economy based on its own agropastoral production, until the sixteenth century. Then, as Madrid expanded into an important capital, the *vecinos* of Vicálvaro increasingly took advantage of the city's market and job opportunities. And residents of Madrid became interested in buying land in Vicálvaro. Whereas the village had once been dominated by small and medium land-owners, by 1576 only one-third of the *vecinos* of the place owned any land. But the 'poor' who had sold, or lost, their property were able to support themselves very nicely in the labor and produce markets of Madrid (Pérez-Crespo 1969: 462–5). Another example, an extreme case from the same area, is the village of Ribas de Jarama. According to the *Relaciones* (*Madrid*, p. 528), it had a population of twenty-five *vecinos*, all of whom were *labradores*. But because of the proximity of the capital, the normal landholding patterns did not hold true here, for *all* the lands of the village were owned by residents of Madrid, to whom the *labradores* who worked them had to pay rent (Terrasse 1968: 152).

The phenomenon of urban investment in agricultural property existed also around smaller cities like Guadalajara, Talavera de la Reina, and Ciudad Real (Salomon 1964: 165–76; Phillips 1979: 65–75). And it could be found in all parts of Castile. We have an interesting example of the operation of the process in the Tierra of Plasencia (Cáceres) in the early 1500s. The 1520s were a period of hard times for the *labradores* of the area, and many of them were obliged to sell their lands to provide funds for subsistence. The merchants and officials of the city of Plasencia were quick to exploit the situation, buying up as much rural property as they could at depressed prices during the period of agricultural crisis. By 1531 the rural economy had recovered, but city dwellers now owned a large proportion of the farm lands of Plasencia's villages. The *vecinos* of the villages complained, via a lawsuit lasting from 1531 to 1549, that these new landowners, although commoners, were claiming the tax-exempt status traditionally enjoyed by *hidalgos*. There had always been an important noble investment in the agricultural properties of the area, but bourgeois ownership was something new, and it was resented by the villagers, especially since many of the new urban landowners were *conversos* (Jewish converts to Christianity, and their descendants). We have a somewhat similar example of bourgeois land acquisition in the province of Jaén in the 1560s. The council of the village of Rus lodged suit against a group of *vecinos* of the nearby city of Baeza. The city dwellers had bought up the lands of the deserted settlement of Arquillos, which was illegal, according to Rus, because of a certain agreement forbidding land transfers to outsiders. The Baeza landowners included officials of the city, professional men, and artisans, but only one was an *hidalgo*. Together they owned the *entire* area of the deserted village, which was divided into some thirty-four parcels.[22] But bourgeois ownership was not everywhere important. There were many areas where it was quite inconsequential – places such as La Bureba, whose remoteness from any large urban center made it unattractive as a focus of investment (Brumont 1977: 35, n. 1).

The increasing bourgeois investment in agricultural property had far-reaching consequences. It spurred the development of a market-oriented agriculture, in which vineyards and olive groves played the major role, particularly in Andalucía. It encouraged the concentration of the rural population, and as a result, the depopulation of many small rural settlements. The new urban landowners and the rich *labradores* formed a class that contemporaries called the *poderosos* (powerful). This was a class outside the traditional distinction between nobles and commoners. The rich commoner – whether *labrador* or urban bourgeois investor – was often far more important in his town than some impoverished *hidalgo*. In many places the *poderosos* were able to monopolize the municipal offices, and to use them to consolidate their wealth. They were often quite successful in exploiting the crisis of the late 1500s and the 1600s, to absorb the property of bankrupt small and medium *labradores*. They also were the leaders in the movements for juridical independence (*villazgos*) for their towns, to increase their freedom and power (Domínguez 1973b: 164–6; Salomon 1964: 169). Another consequence of bourgeois land buying was that the funds thus invested were seldom used to foment increased productivity. There was a mere shift in the ownership of part of the land, without any major changes in the methods of production. Fernand Braudel (1975: 729–34) has called this the 'defection ["treason", in the original French] of the bourgeoisie'. By investing in titles of nobility and land, they deserted their 'proper' function. Rather than making true capitalistic investments, in commerce, industry, and banking, they turned instead to

149

the soil, seduced by the prestige value and security of landownership. One should not exaggerate the consequences of this 'treason', especially since it was not peculiar to Spain. But the effects seem to have been especially pernicious in Castile, and this certainly helps explain the prolonged economic depression in the area during the late Habsburg period.

6

Changes in production and ownership

The classical topographical division used for the lands of Mediterranean Europe is the threefold *ager, saltus,* and *silva,* which correspond to an economic classification into arable, pasture, and woodland. The term *ager* refers to all cultivated land; *saltus* includes all lands used for grazing, regardless of botanical composition; and *silva* refers to all *natural* arborescent vegetation (planted groves and orchards are counted as tree-crops on arable land – *ager*). But it should be recognized that *ager, saltus,* and *silva* refer to land use, rather than land potential. Consequently, the spatial extent of each category is variable. A change in one necessarily has repercussions on one or both of the other two. Arable, for example, historically has expanded at the expense of pasture and woodland. In traditional Mediterranean peasant societies there was a close relationship between arable agriculture, stock raising, and the utilization of the woodlands (Delano 1979: 166–7). As early as the first century, the agronomist Columella (Spanish Columela, who was a native of the Roman city Gades – now the Spanish city Cádiz) recognized the desirability of combining cultivation and pastoral activities (1824: 1, 232–3).

As we have seen, in the traditional rural society of Castile, the distinction between arable, pasture, and woodland was often blurred. The *derrota de mieses,* for example, extended grazing into the arable lands; and there could be both cultivation and grazing in the *monte*. Nevertheless, the classical land-use trifurcation is serviceable to measure the changing balance between the different types of economic activity. There is a disagreement among scholars regarding the extent of the ancient forests of Iberia, but they were unquestionably far more widespread in medieval times than in the modern period. But the Middle Ages witnessed a progressive deforestation, and by the late medieval period the forests of Old Castile had already been considerably reduced in area, as the result of cuttings for fuel and lumber, and because of the fire clearings (*rozas*) of both stock raisers and cultivators (Hopfner 1954). Furthermore, eight centuries of Reconquest occasioned the wanton destruction of woodlands by fire and for the construction of stockades. The armies of both sides destroyed forests to desolate the environs of a besieged city, and the inhabitants of a stronghold themselves liked to do away with surrounding forests to avoid surprise attacks from an enemy concealed in the undergrowth (Sánchez-Albornoz 1963: 29). The progressive reduction of the area of woodlands provided ideal geographical conditions for the growth of stock raising. Moreover, during the Reconquest the danger of Moslem raids made mobile property (livestock) a better investment than easily destroyed crops and orchards. These factors promoted the rapid expansion of ranching, in preference to arable agriculture, into the new frontier settlements of the Duero–Tajo region of central Spain. And from the mid-1100s this flourishing Castilian pastoralism was a powerful factor in the Christian expansion into La Mancha and Andalucía. Of course, there was also a development of arable agriculture, but cultivation was clearly of secondary importance in an economy that was overwhelmingly pastoral. The predominance of livestock raising is reflected in the *fueros* of the frontier cities, which gave special protection to the pastoral sector. The creation in the thirteenth century of the powerful royal Mesta, and of the various municipal Mestas, is further evidence of the early strength of the stock industry (Bishko 1963: 49, 54–65; 1978).

As the empty spaces of Castile became populated, and with the decreasing menace of Moorish attack, arable agriculture came to occupy an ever more important position in the economy. As indicated earlier, the *montes* suffered an increasingly widespread damage at the hands of cultivators, stockmen, and city dwellers in search of fuel and timber. And the demographic pressure upon the available land resources not only occasioned the growth of *ager* and *saltus* at the expense of *silva*, but also an increasing antagonism between the first two. During the late Middle Ages, the Castilian bourgeoisie, and some of the aristocracy, became interested in the exportation of wool. And because the crown's chief revenues came from taxes on the wool industry, it is hardly surprising that the laws of the kingdom showed a pastoral bias. This was particularly true during the reign of Ferdinand and Isabella. But despite royal pampering of the stock industry, the demand for grain and other arable crops could not be denied.

The demographic growth of the 1500s made it essential to expand the area under cultivation to feed the swelling population. Furthermore, there was a market for wine, grain, and oil in Spain's overseas territories. Consequently, although Charles V tried to favor (and exploit) the wool industry as his predecessors had done, he continually found himself obliged to grant licenses for the plowing of new lands. As the agropastoral balance shifted in favor of cultivation, the Mesta lost its favored position. But the change was gradual, and there were other factors at work. Charles V, for example, had assigned to the Fuggers the revenues of the lucrative pastures of the military orders, and the bankers pressured him not to permit further usurpations or plowing in their rented pastures. The Mesta also exerted its still formidable influence, and in 1525 the emperor issued a decree to return to pasture all new plowings made during his reign (Gómez Mendoza 1967: 501–2, 508–9). But the effect of this seems to have been minimal, for the plow moved inexorably forward, and it did not halt when the emperor made a new anti-plowing pronouncement in 1551 (Laiglesia 1918–19: II, 360). During the reign of Philip II there was continued resistance to the new plowings by the Mesta and other pastoral interests, which inspired a royal order of 1580 for the restoration to pasture of all lands plowed in the previous twenty years. But the advance of the plow was favored by the increasing difficulties of the royal treasury, which sold the towns licenses to plow their pastures and *montes*. The towns, for their part, were willing to pay for the privilege of expanding the area of arable, because their *vecinos* demanded it, and because in many cases an expanded cultivation was the only way the towns could pay their rising taxes (Domínguez 1973b: 160).

Although the equilibrium in the sixteenth century was plainly shifting toward cultivation, the towns made an effort to maintain a certain balance between pastoral and arable activities (García Sanz 1977: 275; Martín Galindo 1958: 62–3). The weight of tradition, and the needs of a growing population in an era when interregional transportation was cumbersome and expensive explain this concern. What happened in the villages of the Montes de Toledo is a good example of this. As population pressure in the mid-1500s caused a crescendo of demand for more arable land, many former pastures of the area were planted to grain, with the permission of the city of Toledo (the owner of the Montes). But the council of Toledo tried to moderate the effects of the increased cultivation by establishing new pastures to take the place of those lost to the plow (Weisser 1976: 56–62; Jiménez 1965: 98–100).

There was normally a complementary relationship between cultivated agriculture and stock raising in the sixteenth-century Castilian rural economy, but that did not prevent the eruption of squabbles, and even violence between arable and pastoral interests. The reader is referred back to chapter 3 for a discussion of the problems between the royal Mesta and local interests, and for additional considerations about the expansion of arable. Despite the gradual erosion of Mesta influence during the century, the association of livestock owners continued to protest the changing agropastoral balance, and it tried to maintain as many of its old privileges as possible. As indicated above, Charles V and Philip II issued a number of royal pro-pasture orders, and it is generally true to say that the Mesta was able to retain its theoretical predominance. But in practice, especially during the reign of Philip II, the *labradores* and other arable interests gradually got the upper hand. By the 1580s a sort of informal anti-Mesta alliance had been formed, including noble landowners and a number of city governments (particularly from Andalucía and Extremadura). These parties ardently defended agriculture, and vehemently denounced migratory herds as being the cause of all the evils of the period, including high prices, the depopulation of rural villages, and the deforestation of Castile. They argued that the privileges of the Mesta ran counter to the ancient liberties of the towns and cities. These arguments, and the changing economic reality, led the Chancillerías increasingly to hand down decisions favoring the extension of cultivation. These pro-arable court decisions of the mid and late 1500s were symptomatic of the decline of Mesta influence, both at the court, and also in the economy. At the beginning of the seventeenth century, Miguel Caxa de Leruela, a staunch defender of the Mesta, lamented (1631: 3–7) the sixteenth-century expansion of arable, which he regarded as excessive. Caxa blamed the economic ills of Castile on the loss of pastures and the corresponding diminution of the number of livestock. There is indeed ample evidence that the Mesta, and pastoralism in general, had been relegated to an inferior position vis-à-vis arable agriculture. But the Mesta's power, though greatly reduced, was still sufficient to constitute a continuing nuisance to land-hungry, expansion-minded *labradores*. A résumé of *corregidores*' reports from the last years of the reign of Philip II indicates that the activities of Mesta officials were still regarded as a hindrance to agriculture in the provinces of Zamora, Salamanca, Cáceres, Badajoz, Ciudad Real, and Jaén.[1] And the *arbitrista* Barbón y Castañeda, writing in the early 1600s (1628: fol. 10), also named harassment by the Mesta as a continuing cause of the unfortunate plight of the Castilian *labrador*.

It is well known that the population of Castile increased dramatically during the sixteenth century. By the last decade of the 1500s the kingdom as a whole had grown by at least 50 percent, and there were many areas that had experienced a veritable demographic explosion (Ruiz Martín 1967). This population increase had to be accompanied by a corresponding expansion of the food supply. There were three possible ways of effecting this: (1) by raising agricultural productivity through intensive cultivation; (2) by enlarging the area under cultivation; or (3) by combining the first two possibilities. In sixteenth-century Castile, the food supply was augmented primarily through the second possibility – by putting new lands to the plow. It would be tedious to cite all the available sources attesting to the fact that new land was being broken in all parts of the kingdom. All authorities, both contemporary and recent, are in agreement, and this can be amply substantiated by an abundance of documentary evidence in various archives. It is also well known that these new plowings were made primarily at the expense of the pastoral sector, as Caxa de Leruela had correctly observed at the beginning of the seventeenth century (Vassberg 1980).

Much of the expanded cultivation was made possible by taking advantage of the *tierras baldías*. In 1536 a *vecino* of Córdoba gave the principal reason for this. He testified that the advance of the plow in the area had been principally into the *baldíos*, rather than into privately owned lands, because in the former the *labradores* needed to pay no rent, but only the tithe.[2] As indicated in chapter 1, the Castilian *labrador* had the right, albeit ill-defined, to occupy and to exploit unused *tierras baldías*. Due to factors outlined earlier, this occupation tended to become transformed into permanent possession, which perpetuated the effects of the expanded cultivation. Many of the *baldíos* that were the object of this new cultivation were in *monte*. Thus, the increase in arable contributed to the deforestation of Castile.

Map 4 provides a graphic representation of one example of the expansion of arable at the expense of *monte*, and of the gradual transformation of the economy from the pastoral to the arable. The

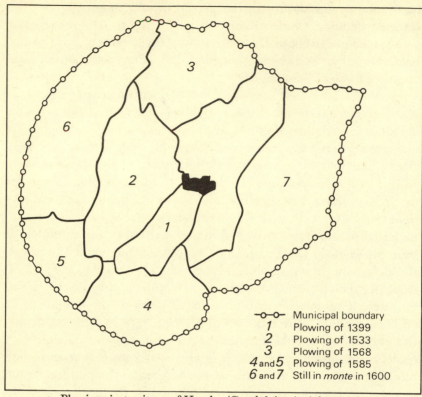

—o—o—	Municipal boundary
1	Plowing of 1399
2	Plowing of 1533
3	Plowing of 1568
4 and *5*	Plowing of 1585
6 and *7*	Still in *monte* in 1600

4. Plowings in territory of Horche (Guadalajara). Adapted from
García Fernández, 'Horche'

example at hand is the town of Horche (Guadalajara). In the 1300s
Horche was a small pastoral village (200 *vecinos* in 1399) in the
montes of Guadalajara. Arable agriculture was a mere subsidiary
activity, and the space dedicated to cultivation was very small, probably limited to the most fertile and level soils near the village itself.
But as the population of Horche grew, it needed more arable lands,
and the town began the plowing of the *monte* which dominated its
territory. Permission to expand cultivation into the *monte* was secured
time and time again through purchase from the crown. The chief
cause of the progressive destruction of the *monte* in the territory of
Horche was demographic pressure. The greater the population, the
more land needed to be plowed. But not all of the population increase was natural: the availability of land in Horche encouraged
immigration from neighboring villages with a shortage of arable.
And this population influx, of course, made it necessary to plow still

more land. By the time of the *Relaciones* (1575) the population had grown to 500 *vecinos*, and by then the arable sector had become undeniably more important than the pastoral. The tithes from olive oil alone, in fact, were twice as much as those from wool-bearing animals. Horche still maintained large flocks of sheep, and there remained an abundance of pasture on which to graze them. But the situation continued to change, with the sustained demographic growth. By 1596 there were 600 *vecinos* in Horche, and the march of the plow had persisted at the expense of the *monte*. The economy had nearly completed its transformation from the pastoral to the arable, and this shift in economic activity was reflected in the town's land use. By 1601 nearly the whole of the territory of Horche was under cultivation. The *vecinos* of the place still grew some livestock, but this had now become an activity very much subsidiary to arable agriculture. And what common *monte* still existed was now nearly all outside the territory of Horche, in lands shared with other towns in the Tierra of Guadalajara (García Fernández 1953: 56–62).

Of course, not all places participated equally in the transformation of the agropastoral balance. In some towns the rhythm of change was faster, or slower, than in the case of Horche. And, due to special circumstances, there were some places where pastoral interests were long successful in resisting the expansion of arable. In 1558, for example, the village of Berrocalejo (Cáceres) reported that it was poorer than ever, because of a shortage of cultivated land. It seems that the area was dominated by *dehesas* owned by absentee nobles who were interested only in livestock, and who refused to permit new plantings on their land (Corchón 1963: 133–4).

As indicated in chapter 3, the sixteenth-century population explosion also encouraged an arable assault upon the especially designated pastures for livestock – such as the *ejidos*, the *dehesas boyales*, and various other areas that were theoretically safe from the plow. The demographic pressure that made it imperative to expand the area of arable, exerted a simultaneous and unbearable strain on the *montes* of Castile, for lumber and firewood. As a result, it seemed that the *montes* fled the cities. In almost every place where there was an important concentration of population, there came to be a wide circle of deforested surrounding lands that were used almost exclusively for cultivation (Hopfner 1954: 423–4). The city of Toro (Zamora), for example, which had once boasted a number of common woodlands, by 1542 found itself with no *montes* at all, and was obliged to rely on roots and vine prunings for fuel.[3] The late-fifteenth-century and early-sixteenth-century development of the Castilian commercial economy in Medina del Campo (Valladolid), Segovia, Toledo, and other centers hastened the destruction of entire forests in a wide radius around these trading cities. And there were some places where industrial activities contributed to deforestation. The requirements of the mines of Almadén (Ciudad Real) and the textile works of Segovia, for example, were partly responsible for denuding the local hillsides (García Sanz 1977: 31–2, 143; Quirós 1965: 224). The consumption of forests for these non-agricultural purposes facilitated the extension of arable, because cutting down the trees made it easier for new areas to be brought into cultivation.

THE CONVERSION FROM OXEN TO MULES

As indicated in the previous section, the increase in agricultural production in sixteenth-century Castile was based primarily upon an extension of the area under cultivation, rather than upon a qualitative transformation of the existing agrarian productive forces. In other words, there was a spatial expansion, rather than real development – a mere increase in the quantity of work, land tilled, and animals used, without altering those elements organically to increase productivity. However, sixteenth-century Castile did witness one important technological change – a change without which the great agrarian expansion would have been difficult, or perhaps even impossible. That change was the gradual substitution of the mule for the ox, as the predominant draft animal. The change was revolutionary in several respects. For centuries the ox had been the traditional draft animal. This was true not only of the entire medieval period, but even back in Roman times. In the first century the Hispano-Roman agronomist Columella (1824: 1, 53–5) had specified the ox for plow power, and according to Ambrosio de Morales (1577: fol. 96) the ox was so closely identified with Roman agriculture that a coin was minted in Roman Spain depicting a yoke of oxen plowing on one side. But during the course of the sixteenth century the ox was displaced: whereas in 1500 the ox was still the normal work animal, by 1600 the mule had become the most widely used agricultural work animal, except in certain isolated or backward areas, mainly in the mountains.

The reason for the switch to the mule was quite simple: expansion

was the order of the day, and a mule could plow nearly twice as much
land as an ox. The mule was also more suitable for use in vineyards
and orchards, where a yoke of horned animals was not only difficult
to maneuver, but also a potential danger to tender vines and
branches. Furthermore, the nucleated Castilian peasant population,
the extreme parcelization of farm land, and the prevalent biennial
system of fallow favored the use of mules, because they could move
from village to field, and from one field to another much faster than
the proverbially slow-footed oxen. This was an important consideration when new lands were being brought into cultivation, because
fields were becoming increasingly dispersed. Moreover, mules could
be used as pack animals, to supplement the peasant's income during
slack periods in the agricultural calendar. This could be an important additional source of income for the peasant with a small amount
of land. Many peasants of the La Bureba villages of Burgos province,
for example, were active as muleteers (*arrieros*) along the Burgos–
Bilbao trade route (Brumont 1977: 45–52). Thus, agricultural considerations were not the only factors involved in the ox–mule
selection.

The use of mules brought many advantages, but there were also
some drawbacks. Although mules worked faster, they usually plowed
shallower furrows, leaving the soil less able to absorb heavy rains.
And it seems that the more superficial work of the mules tended to
produce reduced yields. But more important was the fact that mules
could not be used as draft animals unless they were properly fed.
They needed grain, normally barley, which meant that a significant
proportion (perhaps one-quarter) of the harvest produced through
mule power was consumed by the mules themselves. Oxen, by contrast, could get along perfectly well without grain, sustaining themselves exclusively on the *dehesas*, fallow fields, and other common
pastures that were readily available at no cost locally (Anés 1970:
120–2; Domínguez 1973b: 159).

Strictly speaking, the ox is an adult castrated male bovine. But in
practice, cows were also used as draft animals, and were included in
the 'oxen' category. The cow was not as strong as a true ox, but had
the advantage of being able to produce calves, and could even supply
milk for the peasant's kitchen, although at a greatly diminished
amount when the animal was being used for field work. Mules, being
sterile hybrids, could not reproduce themselves. Therefore, it was
necessary to keep horses and asses as breeding stock for their pro-

duction, with the result that mules were much more expensive than oxen – to raise, to purchase, and to own. A final advantage of oxen over mules was that overage oxen could be slaughtered for beef, whereas Spaniards did not normally consider mule flesh to be suitable for human consumption (García Fernández 1964: 144–5; Gómez Mendoza 1967: 505–7; Brumont 1977: 45–52).

As indicated earlier, during the sixteenth century most Castilian peasants became convinced that it was better for them to use mules rather than oxen. The general switch to mule power caused some contemporary observers to conclude that the two types of animals were incompatible, and could not coexist in the same locality. That was the position of Diego Gutiérrez de Salinas, who suggested (1600: 62–81) that the introduction of mules inevitably led to the disappearance of the local *dehesas boyales*, which were plowed (contrary to the laws of the land) because they were no longer needed. Unfortunately, according to Gutiérrez, after these special pastures were gone, it was impossible to return to the use of oxen, because of the lack of adequate grazing land. This was undoubtedly an exaggeration, but it does seem that the ox had all but disappeared in some parts of Castile by the end of the sixteenth century. Miguel Caxa de Leruela (1631: 142–55) wrote that there were virtually no oxen remaining in the environs of Madrid and Toledo. But Extremadura, and the mountainous parts of Castile, tended to remain loyal to the ox. Brumont (1977: 49–52) describes a sort of 'radicalization' of the ox–mule situation in the La Bureba villages (Burgos) in the late 1500s. In parts of the region, the use of mules became the norm, whereas in other areas mule-use actually regressed, and the local inhabitants went back to plowing with oxen. It seems that there was a tendency for the agriculturalists of each locality to opt overwhelmingly for either the one, or the other animal, depending upon local conditions. But this was not always so. In the province of Segovia, for example, there was a marked increase in the use of mules in the late sixteenth century, but this did not cause the disappearance of oxen, who continued to play a significant role furnishing draft power for the area (García Sanz 1977: 113; Le Flem 1973: 400).

The use of mules in Castilian agriculture was associated with the aggressive expansionism of the century, and with a more progressive approach to production (Maravall 1973: 374–5). For example, in the 1590s, when Castillo de Bobadilla wrote of a hypothetical *labrador* with a large-scale operation (1608: ii, 41), he naturally depicted him farming with mules, rather than oxen. The shift from ox to mule as the primary farm animal might have been new and even revolutionary in sixteenth-century Castile. But the effects of the Castilian conversion were not nearly so far-reaching as the northern European switch from the ox to the horse several centuries earlier. It seems that equine plow power was possible earlier in the north because of the greater productivity of the three-field rotational system that was prevalent there. One might ask why the three-field system was not adopted also in Mediterranean Europe. The answer seems to lie primarily in climate and soils: the greater rainfall and more fertile soils of the north made it far more suitable for conversion to the triennial system. Furthermore, there were overwhelming practical difficulties standing in the way of a drastic rearrangement of property holdings from the biennial system to the triennial. The weight of tradition normally precluded such a radical change. But northern Europe was able to effect the transformation, because the devastation caused by Viking and Magyar raids in the ninth and tenth centuries made widespread reconstruction necessary. And the reorganization of lands and communities could be made according to the superior new technology of crop rotation (White 1964: 57–78). In any case, in Castile the older Mediterranean two-field system continued to be prevalent throughout the sixteenth century, and the conversion to mules simply involved an extension of the existing system into new lands. Unfortunately, in many cases the newly plowed lands were shallow, hillside soils. They were easily eroded, and some were permanently harmed by the planting. After the first year or two, yields fell dramatically, often making continued exploitation uneconomical. The plowing of these marginal lands meant a decline in productivity. The result was to further increase land hunger, and to encourage an even wider use of mules (Domínguez 1973b: 160; Weisser 1976: 56–62).

This, combined with the gradually deteriorating general economic situation during the reign of Philip II, caused many *arbitristas* to conclude that the mule was the major source of the growing agricultural ills of Castile. The first of the anti-mule writers seems to have been Juan Valverde Arrieta, who in 1568 published a work entitled *Despertador que trata de la gran fertilidad, riquesas, baratos, armas y caballos que España solía tener y la causa de los daños y faltas en el remedio suficiente.*[4] This work was an impassioned denunciation of the mule. It enumerated the disadvantages of mule-use, and called for a return to ox-plowing, which in the mind of Arrieta was synonymous with the prosperity and abundance of a bygone era. Arrieta's anti-mule tirade caught the attention of the Cortes, which voted in 1580 (*Actas*: VI, 299–302, 623) to subsidize the publication of a new edition of the work, so the message of the evils of mule-use could be disseminated in the provinces. The following Cortes (1583–5 and 1586–8) continued to press for the restoration of ox-use, but the response from the provinces was disappointing (*Actas*: VII, 613; VIII, 271–546; IX, 30, 55–62, 256, 258, 313, 358). The use of mules was already firmly entrenched, and the peasants of most areas displayed no inclination to go back to the use of oxen. After the reign of Philip II there emerged a generation of *arbitristas* who were influenced by Arrieta's work. In 1599 Juan Escribano (a pseudonym?) wrote that the mule was the principal cause of the decadence of Spain. He recommended that the government encourage the return to oxen, through special subsidies. In 1600 Diego Gutiérrez de Salinas published *Discursos del pan, y del vino del niño Jesús . . .* , which contained (pp. 62–81) a virulently anti-mule section based upon Arieta. Gutiérrez called mules 'adulterous and sterile bastards', and 'corrupt monsters', who should be banished by law from Spain. Another writer was Lope de Deza, whose *Gobierno político de agricultura* (1618) lacked the exaggerations of Arrieta and the passion of Gutiérrez. Deza agreed with these writers that the use of mules was associated with the scarcity, poverty, and inflation in Spain, but he also enumerated various other contributing causes (fols. 19–36). And in the end, Deza was willing to permit each *labrador* to own a pair of mules, so long as the rest of his animals were oxen. Then there was Caxa de Leruela (1631), the defender of the Mesta. Caxa supported Arrieta's anti-mule position because he saw the introduction of mule-use as a major cause of the diminution of Castilian pastures. Another *arbitrista* who damned the mule was Pedro Fernández Navarrete (1626: 283) who advocated a law absolutely forbidding the raising of mules in Spain. Fernández, however, unlike his colleagues, was not a champion of oxen, but rather of horses. He wanted Spain to emulate the northern European countries in the use of the horse for both agriculture and transport.

There had long existed a serious concern in Spain over the effect that mule breeding had on horse raising, because if the best mares were used to produce mules, then the quality of horses inevitably would deteriorate. And this could prove disastrous for the country's military, in an age when horses played such a vital role in warfare.

As far back as the 1300s the Castilian monarchs and Cortes had attempted to limit the number of mules in the country, and to encourage the use of horses in their stead (*Cortes*: I, 275, 375, 377, 397; II, 397, 533–6; v, 126, 143, 299, 455). But this legislation did little to discourage the proliferation of mules, so in 1520 the monarchy instituted a law prohibiting the breeding of mules in Castile. This anti-mule provision continued to be in force during the reign of Philip II. And it provoked constant protests from towns and villages all over Castile. The Cortes took an ambivalent stance: requesting the prohibition of mules on some occasions; but asking that the prohibition be lifted on others (Antón 1865: 23; Weisser 1976: 14–15; *Actas*: xv, 631). The crown, always willing to compromise its principles when there was money at stake, gave special exemptions from the anti-mule laws to certain areas. The kingdom of Toledo, for example, the Tierra of Cuenca, and the villages of the Order of Calatrava were permitted to breed mules despite the general prohibition for the rest of Castile.[5] In the final analysis, the anti-mule legislation could not be rigidly enforced – the continued increase in mule-use is proof of this – but it inhibited the production and use of mules, thus depriving an expansion-minded peasantry of a vital source of draft power. In the *Relaciones*, for example, the town of Socuéllamos (Ciudad Real) complained (p. 473) that there was a serious local shortage of mules for agriculture, and that the region normally had to import the beasts from Old Castile. The anti-mule laws causing this shortage may have been misguided, but they demonstrate that there was great concern in the royal government over the transformation that was occurring in the rural world of Castile during the sixteenth century.

THE IMPACT OF THE INDIES

The establishment of a colonial empire in America had far-reaching consequences for Castilian agriculture. Much additional original research needs to be completed before we can fully understand the changes that occurred, but most scholars accept the general view put forward by Gonzalo Anés in *Las crisis agrarias en la España moderna* (1970: 92–7). According to this view, the increased demand for Spanish agricultural products caused by the new colonial market spurred a rise in commodity prices, and also in the price of land. It should be remembered that native Peninsular demand – the result of natural demographic growth – was also a factor, as was the price inflation triggered by the influx of gold and silver from the New World. In any case, in Andalucía between 1511 and 1559 there was a dizzying rise in the price of agricultural products. During that period the price of wheat doubled; that of olive oil tripled; while the price of wine climbed to nearly eight times its previous level! These high prices encouraged the wholesale planting of new olive groves and vineyards, and the valley of the Guadalquivir was transformed by the new, market-oriented agriculture. In 1549 Pedro de Medina (fol. 19) marveled at the quantities of grain, wine, and olive oil that were annually exported from Andalucía to America, to the Netherlands, and to other Spanish possessions. This caused local shortages, which drove prices up still higher. There was widespread consternation over the effect on Andalucía, and the Cortes of 1573–5 petitioned the crown (*Actas*: IV, 475–6) to restrict the exportation of wheat from the area, lest a serious famine occur. The Cortes of 1579–82 went on to ask the crown (*Actas*: VI, 865) to require a special license for the planting of new vineyards, on the grounds that too much land was being converted to viticulture, which was preferred over grain because it was much more profitable. Although the crown did not accede to the Cortes' requests, they are important nevertheless, as a demonstration of the concern over the changes brought by the overseas markets. In many parts of Castile profits were so high that agriculture became a good investment, attracting capital that otherwise might have gone into trade and manufacturing. This was Braudel's 'treason of the bourgeoisie', motivated not only by profit, but also by a desire to emulate the nobility. In fact, many wealthy commoners were able to purchase titles of nobility and seigneurial jurisdictions, and these new nobles and lords were even more intransigent than the old aristocracy in maintaining the traditional privileges of the medieval system of production and tribute (Braudel 1975: 729–34). Thus, the archaic socioeconomic structures were maintained, and the attitude of the bourgeoisie even stimulated a resurgence of the seigneurial regime.

Landowners tried to increase their production by purchasing as much additional land as possible, to take advantage of the opportunity for high profits. As a result, there seems to have been an increase in latifundism, especially in Andalucía – the region most affected by the American trade. And because there was a strong demand for land, property owners could exact from their tenants higher rents, either in cash or in specie (Anés 1970: 92–100). The export-oriented capitalistic agriculture was most visible in the Guadalquivir valley, but it coexisted with the traditional subsistence economy. The rest of Castile, however, continued to produce primarily for its own needs, with surpluses exported mainly to nearby urban centers. The vitality of the economy of Andalucía in the sixteenth century provided an employment opportunity for the poorer peasants and landless workers of other regions. For example, we know that many peasants of Extremadura made their way south to labor as migrant workers (Herrera 1971: 431–5) in the vineyards of Andalucía.[6]

The great boom period for Andalucían agriculture was the middle third of the sixteenth century. After that, the overseas market gradually diminished, because Mexico and Peru were becoming self-sufficient in grain and other products previously imported from Spain. The effects of the loss of this market will be considered later, in chapter 7.

OLD AND NEW TOWNS (THE *VILLAZGOS*)

In sixteenth-century Castile the crown, always pressed for additional funds, resorted to the widespread sale of municipal charters (*villazgos*) as a revenue-producing device. The villages (*aldeas* and *lugares*) under the jurisdiction of the large municipalities (*villas* and *ciudades*) felt tyrannized by them. They complained bitterly about discriminatory laws, and about the highhanded actions of municipal officials. We could give many examples of this type of treatment. For instance, Talavera de la Reina (Toledo) forced its subject villages to purchase its own wine, until the supply was exhausted, before they were allowed to import wine from other areas. The villagers complained that the wine of Talavera was both too expensive and of poor quality. And the government of Medina del Campo (Valladolid) in 1600 attempted to force its villages to buy large quantities of surplus grain, which was in poor condition and consequently difficult to sell on the open market.[7] Another example of overbearing and discriminatory treatment is the city of Trujillo (Cáceres), which presided over a system marred by gross inequities. For example, Trujillo kept all swine out of its own *dehesa boyal*, 'because they root around and cause so much damage'; yet the city insisted that its *vecinos*' hogs had the right to pasture in the *dehesas boyales* of its towns (Vassberg 1978: 55).

The hostility of Castilian villagers towards the municipal governments ruling over them is reflected in the works of Lope de Vega and other Golden Age dramatists (Salomon 1965: 97).

The villagers chafed under the discriminatory organization and system of tribute imposed by the cities and *villas*. Often they regarded their lot as insupportable, and they looked to emancipation as the solution. The *villazgo* gave them autonomy and the right to an independent territory (*término*), and the right to have their own courts and jails, along with other privileges of the *villa*. The Castilian monarchs were generally willing to grant their emancipation: not only because this generated additional funds for the royal treasury, but also because it helped the crown limit the pretensions of the most powerful cities (Vassberg 1980: 486). In some areas there was a torrent of *villazgos*. According to Planchuelo Portalés, for example (1954: 131–2), by the end of the sixteenth century virtually all of the towns in the Campo de Montiel (Ciudad Real) had purchased their *villa* status. One of these towns was Puebla del Príncipe, which negotiated an *asiento* (contract) with the crown on 15 March 1589 for its *villazgo*. According to the terms of this agreement, the town was to pay the royal treasury 6,000 mrs per *vecino* in exchange for its independence. That was a bargain rate: ten years earlier Poveda de la Sierra (Guadalajara) had been obliged to pay over 16,000 mrs per *vecino*. The crown sold *villazgos* not only to villages in the jurisdiction of larger municipalities, but also to the towns of the military orders. And Philip II obtained from Pope Gregory XIII (1572–85) the right to dismember ecclesiastical properties, including jurisdictions. After that it was not long before the crown was selling towns their exemption from the jurisdiction of bishoprics. In 1575, for example, Monteagudo purchased from the crown its freedom from the bishop of Cuenca for 7,000 *ducados*. The bishop protested mightily, but it was to no avail. However, because the crown was primarily interested in raising funds, rather than in freeing the villages, the municipalities (and other entities) that did not wish to lose their subject villages could pay the royal treasury for the privilege of maintaining their jurisdiction intact. For example, when one of the subject villages of the city of Trujillo (Cáceres) purchased a *villazgo* in 1538, the city at first attempted to get the exemption annulled. When that did not work, the city contracted to pay the emperor Charles V 6,000 *ducados* for a royal promise not to sell any more such exemptions from the city's jurisdiction. But the financial exigencies of Philip II caused him to disregard his father's pledge, and Trujillo continued to lose its towns through *villazgos* (Vassberg 1978: 48–9). Nevertheless, despite clear proof that such royal assurances were not likely to be kept, in 1589 the nearby city of Cáceres was willing to try to maintain its jurisdiction intact by taking an *asiento* for 15,000 *ducados*, in exchange for a crown promise not to free any of its subject villages.[8]

The *villazgos* spawned countless lawsuits between the newly independent towns and their former masters, who were understandably resentful over their diminished authority. The Archives of the Audiencias (Supreme Tribunals) of Granada and Valladolid are full of such suits, over pastures, firewood, boundaries, taxation, law enforcement, and other concerns. Many of these suits dragged on almost interminably. For example, one suit between the city of Trujillo and its former villages lasted from 1552 until at least 1631, and that was but one of many suits that plagued the city.[9] A similar situation existed throughout Castile: wherever there were newly independent towns, there were bound to be squabbles between them and the older municipalities. The resulting litigation was both irksome and expensive. But some municipalities found a solution. In the 1560s, for example, Medina del Campo (Valladolid) gained royal permission to repurchase its authority over three former villages that had bought *villazgos*. The major reason for returning the new *villas* to its jurisdiction, according to Medina, was to avoid the disputes which these towns continually brought up about boundaries and common rights (Rodríguez y Fernández 1903–4: 568–70).

There were socioeconomic factors behind most of the problems between the new *villas* and their former masters. The new towns were nearly always short of land, and required additional territory to permit demographic growth. The need for more land was crucial, for the newly independent towns had a higher birth rate than the older municipalities. This was because they had a more youthful population – many younger sons of the older towns had emigrated to new places to try to improve their economic position. Thus, the population of the newly created municipalities was typically young, vigorous, prolific, and hungry for opportunities to expand. They were often in the vanguard of change in the rural world of sixteenth-century Castile. Because they owned relatively few livestock, they had few scruples about plowing pasture, whether it was legal or not, and whether within or beyond the new town's boundaries. These young, aggressive inhabitants of new *villas* were responsible for many unauthorized plowings of common pastures, *montes*, and *baldíos*. And that was the cause of many a lawsuit with the older municipalities, which tended to be more pastoral, and more dependent upon the common grazing areas. Furthermore, the old towns were jealous of the new, and sought to maintain their traditional control over the *baldíos* and *montes*. Both sides appealed to the crown, offering to pay for royal recognition of their rights. But in the sixteenth century the Castilian crown tended to favor arable agriculture over pastoralism, and to uphold individual rights over the old communal traditions. Thus, the *villazgos* were almost inevitably accompanied by new plowings, and by the erosion of the old communitarian structures (Vassberg 1980: 486–7).

The cost of purchasing the *villazgo* was often a severe financial drain. In fact, in many new towns the difficulty of meeting payments encouraged new plowings (a source of new revenue) and even led to the abridgement of common rights. Melchor Soria y Vera (1633: 38–43) and Miguel Caxa de Leruela (1631: 109) observed this in the early 1600s, and Noël Salomon (1964: 149–50) found in the *Relaciones* several examples of the curtailment of communal privileges as the result of aggressive land-seeking by new towns. Sometimes the plowings and anticommunalism were the result of illegal actions by residents of the new towns, but the crown frequently specifically authorized such procedures, to make it easier for the town governments to make their payments to the royal treasury. For example, in its *asiento* (1589) for the *villazgo* of Puebla del Príncipe (Ciudad Real), the crown not only gave its permission for the new *villa* to levy a special tax (*sisa*) on foodstuffs, but also for it to plow the local *dehesas boyales*, and to sell grazing rights in the local common pastures for a period of ten years. During the same year similar privileges were extended also in *asientos* to Alcuéscar (Cáceres) and to Cáceres. There were also many towns that secured the royal permission to rent or plow their commons after the *villazgo* was already an established fact. In some of these cases the towns insisted that they needed funds to pay the royal treasury, but in others the justification was that increased population made it necessary to augment the area under cultivation. For instance, Horche (Guadalajara), which got its *villazgo* in 1537, received repeated subsequent royal authorizations to expand its arable at the expense of the local *montes* (García Fernández 1953: 196–204). Montánchez (Cáceres) noted in 1592

that the *villazgos* in that part of Extremadura were accompanied by
the destruction of the *monte*. And Adobezo (Soria) and Manchuela
(Jaén) got the crown's permission in the late 1500s to plow in the
baldíos. As Antonio Higueras Arnal observed (1961: 119–20), Charles
V and Philip II were so pressed for money that they were willing to
sell almost anything. Unfortunately, in some places the combination
of changes in land use and new taxes brought on by the *villazgos* had
unfavorable economic repercussions. For instance, in 1586 the council
of Torres de Albánchez (Jaén) wrote that the number of local livestock had diminished to only about 3,000 head, down from a previous
12,000, as a consequence of the excessively heavy taxes levied to pay
for the town's *villazgo*, and other difficulties related to its status as a
newly independent *villa*.[10]

THE CASTILIAN ENCLOSURE MOVEMENT

The crown also experimented, rather briefly and with little success,
with selling privileges of enclosure (*acotamientos*, or *cerramientos*). In
1563 the *corregidores* and other royal officials were instructed to make
investigations in various parts of Castile to determine whether landowners would be willing to pay for the privilege of denying access to
their lands to any animals except their own – in other words, of
abrogating the *derrota de mieses* on those particular lands. The royal
investigators reported that most landowners seemed very much in
favor of the idea, and in the late 1560s and the 1570s the crown sold a
number of enclosure permits. The enclosed areas were called *cotos
redondos* (or merely *cotos*), *términos redondos*, *cerramientos*, or merely
dehesas. The crown discovered that although it was easy enough to
sell enclosure permits, the revenue to be gained from them was
disappointingly small. Furthermore, the enclosures incited strong
resistance from the Cortes, and from other powerful interests. In 1566
the Cortes elicited from Philip II a promise not to grant any more
enclosure permits. The monarch by no means kept his promise, but
after that he did not sell many more licenses to enclose. However, the
crown did continue to sell permits to establish hunting reserves.
These, which constituted a different type of enclosure, were purchased by large landowners who wished to curtail the traditional
communal hunting rights on their lands. The Cortes protested, and
in 1566 the monarch promised not to set up any more hunting
reserves. Notwithstanding this pledge, however, Philip continued to

sell permits to restrict hunting rights, and when taken to task by the Cortes, he insisted lamely that his permits had been issued in a form that could harm no one. But the Cortes thought otherwise. A Cortes petition of 1571 asserted that the holders of hunting reserves not only kept outsiders from hunting on their lands, but also denied them the right to pasture there, on the pretext that the herders would do some hunting in their spare moments. In other words: in practice, the restricted hunting areas became enclosed pastures, which were out of the reach of other livestock owners. The Cortes urged the king to revoke all existing licenses for hunting preserves. Philip did not agree to this, but he again solemnly promised that he would refrain from selling any more hunting-reserve permits in the future. The new promise was worth no more than the first, of course, because when Philip needed money, principles were likely to be forgotten. Nevertheless, because of the strong Castilian tradition of common hunting rights, the crown thenceforth exercised considerable restraint in abridging those rights.[11]

As indicated in chapter 1, the *derrota de mieses* was regarded as one of the irrevocable rights of the Castilian peasant, and as such, it was normally defended by the monarchs. The municipalities also usually upheld the *derrota*, but there were instances where they did not do so. In 1491, for example, Ferdinand and Isabella had to overturn an ordinance of the city of Avila which had permitted any *vecino* of that city to enclose up to half a *yugada* of public land (*Novísima recopilación*, libro VII, título XXV, ley III). And during the sixteenth century, which saw a rising current of economic individualism, many other municipalities took it upon themselves to allow the abrogation of the *derrota de mieses*. Arjona (Jaén) did so in 1537 in an ordinance that noted that it was 'unjust' for animals to be allowed access to a landowner's stubble fields without his consent. And around 1548 the city of Loja (Granada) adopted an ordinance allowing its *labradores* to enclose up to three *fanegas* of land, for the exclusive use of their oxen and hogs. The reader will remember from chapter 1 that many towns allowed a partial abridgement of the *derrota*, permitting landowners to maintain the unshared use of their fields until a specified date after the end of harvest. Another type of municipally authorized enclosure had to do with the flocks of the Mesta. As the stockowners' association weakened in the second half of the sixteenth century, the towns were encouraged to rescind some of the pasture privileges the organization had formerly enjoyed. Some examples of this were cited above, in chapter 3. There were several towns that denied Mesta animals the right to the *derrota de mieses*. Lopera (Jaén) and Santa Cruz de Mudela (Ciudad Real) did so in the 1590s. The Mesta naturally attempted to maintain its prerogatives, but in decisions of 1597 and 1598 the Audiencia of Granada ruled that Santa Cruz de Mudela could exclude the Mesta flocks from the stubble fields of the area for six days after the gathering of the sheaves.[12]

The 'enclosures' heretofore described were theoretical, rather than real. But sixteenth-century Castile also had many real enclosures (*cercas*, or *campos cercados*), formed by walling certain plots that were especially vulnerable to damage by livestock. In the previous chapter we learned that the municipal ordinances in some places required the physical enclosure of garden plots and vineyards. Walled cultivated plots were most likely to be an important part of the landscape in places with a predominantly pastoral economy. In the Tierra of Segovia (a sheep-growing area), for example, the ordinances of 1514 required the construction of a wall (*tapia, vallado,* or *valladar*) of a certain specification around each garden plot. And the ordinances declared that the possessor of an unwalled plot could not require damages of the owner of any animals that harmed his crops. Naturally, that rule provided a great incentive for building walls, and in the Tierra of Segovia it was typical for each village and town to be encircled by a zone of intensively cultivated walled plots. But even in areas such as this, the percentage of arable land that was actually enclosed by walls was minuscule. Consequently, that type of enclosure does not seem to have been the cause of any major problems (García Sanz 1977: 32–3).

There were a great many problems, however, with individual landowners who arrogated themselves the right to declare their lands to be 'enclosed', and not subject to the *derrota de mieses*. Some of these were wealthy nobles eager to increase their power; others were peasant or other non-noble landowners who wished to establish full rights of property ownership for themselves. The evidence that I have seen suggests that wealthy landowners – whether noble or non-noble – were the most likely to take the risk of defying local tradition about the *derrota*. The more modest property owners might have wished to do so, but were more easily cowed by municipal authority. In any case, in all parts of Castile there were individuals who tried to deny *derrota* rights to their fields. For example, around 1540 a couple of wealthy *vecinos* of Seville (one was a physician, and the other a city official) invested in some farm land in the village of La Rinconada, just north of Seville. These new landowners immediately attempted to reserve for themselves, or for their renters, the right of stubble grazing. But this flew in the face of local custom, and when the two city men began molesting and even fining the villagers who tried to pasture their animals on their fields, the council of La Rinconada took them to court. And in 1546 the Audiencia of Granada ruled in favor of the villagers, upholding the custom of the *derrota de mieses*.[13]

Unfortunately, as the century wore on, many municipal governments fell under the domination of wealthy individuals who had purchased permanent council seats from the crown. In many places this enabled those powerful individuals to enclose their lands without fear of reprisal from local officials (Gómez Mendoza 1967: 504–5). In the early 1600s Caxa de Leruela lamented that the enclosures had already substantially diminished the amount of common pasture in Castile, and, as a consequence, had seriously reduced the stock-owning capability of the poor. Caxa even went so far as to suggest that the enclosures posed a danger to the survival of the livestock industry (1631: 126, 139–40). This was a gross exaggeration, to be sure, but the enclosures were undoubtedly a serious problem in many areas.

The enclosures were merely one manifestation of a general erosion of the ancient communal customs in Castile during the sixteenth century. As was mentioned earlier in this chapter, demographic pressure and the new export markets spurred a great expansion of the area under cultivation. Much of this growth was made possible by encroaching into the public domain – into the *montes, baldíos, dehesas, ejidos,* and other commons. All of this was a sign of agricultural development, but it was based upon illegal activities. The laws of the realm had not adjusted quickly enough to permit the changes in the system that were necessary for rapid economic growth. However, many of the usurpations of the public domain were later legalized by the municipalities or by the crown.

THE SALE OF THE *BALDÍOS*

The sixteenth-century enclosures were not nearly so important in disrupting the communal system as was a royal revenue-raising scheme based upon the sale of the *tierras baldías*. This project was conceived during the first years of the reign of Philip II. It began tentatively, in 1557 and 1558, when several municipalities asked the crown to sell them the *tierras baldías* in their jurisdiction that had been illegally plowed. The towns wanted to purchase the lands to legalize their continued cultivation. During the 1560s the crown learned through trial and error how to exploit the *tierras baldías* to the maximum. The Royal treasury sent out land commissioners (*jueces de tierras*) to sell the *baldíos* to those who were occupying (or usurping) them. Initially, the crown was willing to issue a bill of sale for a fraction of the actual market value of the property. But it was not long before the policymakers of the treasury decided to adopt a stricter attitude, in an effort to increase receipts. In 1569 it was announced that if the landholders failed to offer a 'just' price for their lands, the property would be sold to someone else. And eventually the crown devised a type of public auction to ensure that the *baldíos* would be sold at the highest possible price. However, it was the general policy to give preference to municipalities over individuals in those cases where the municipalities could be considered as landholders. For example, a town was given first option to buy the lands it had been using as community property, or it could even buy all the *tierras baldías* within its jurisdiction, even if the individuals using those lands protested.[14]

The crown never adopted a consistent policy regarding exactly what type of *baldíos* (remember the vague definition of this term) could be sold. It often repeated the principle that only *plowed* lands were to be sold – the unplowed *baldíos* would be reserved in perpetuity for public pasture. But in practice, the uncultivated *tierras baldías* were also sold. In fact, many bills of sale specifically authorized *baldío* buyers to clear, plow, and plant previously uncultivated land. The land commissioners were ordered to sell as *baldíos* any property for which the occupants could show no good title. This included lands claimed by the municipalities, for many municipal lands had been originally usurped from the *tierras baldías*. Consequently, many *baldío* sales were to the towns. But the vast majority were small sales, to the individual peasants who were occupying the land. There were also sales of large blocks of *baldíos* to members of the nobility, or to wealthy burghers, but because those individuals had usually claimed the land even before buying it, the *baldío* sales were rarely directly responsible for dispossessing peasants of their lands. During the regime of Philip II there were *baldío* sales in almost every part of Castile, but there were three regions where the sales produced the greatest revenues: Andalucía; the great cereal-growing plains of Zamora and Valladolid; and the three central provinces of Madrid, Toledo, and Guadalajara. Those three areas were the wealthiest parts of Castile at the time: Andalucía because of the stimulation of the overseas markets; the cereal-growing area because of its grain and the fairs of Medina del Campo (Valladolid); and the central provinces because of the growing importance of Madrid as a political and commercial center. The *baldío* sales reached a peak in the 1580s. After that they fell off sharply, partly because the most easily exploitable *baldíos* had already been sold, and partly because of the success of resistance to the sales program, particularly by the Cortes. Nevertheless, receipts from *baldío* sales ranked as a major source of income for Philip II's treasury throughout his reign (Vassberg 1975).

It is difficult to assess the impact of the *baldío* sales on the economy and society of Castile, because of the absence of studies showing the effect on local agricultural communities, but we can make certain tentative judgements based on the limited information currently available. We know that the *baldíos* had been crucially involved in the sixteenth-century expansion of the Castilian agricultural economy. The *baldíos* were favored over other lands because they were often available free for the taking. In the boom period of the Castilian economy, those who held *baldíos* were eager to gain legal ownership to them. And in many cases, the immediate effect of the sales must have been salutary. Legal ownership would have encouraged better care of the soil, and it would have permitted the taking of mortgages to finance improvements and to provide ready cash during financial emergencies. But it seems that most of the long-term consequences of the sales were harmful. Many of the *baldíos* were lands of marginal quality, and yields dropped sharply after a few years of cultivation. After that, any indebtedness on those lands might have made continued use economically futile. And most *baldíos* were bought on the installment plan, with the purchaser offering as security not only the land that was being bought, but all of his other lands as well. It seems that many *baldío* buyers simply could not bear the burden of land and mortgage payments on top of the normal obligations of taxation, tithes, and seigneurial levies. They defaulted on their payments, and lost their land. The impact on the local economy was shattering, because in many villages nearly every *vecino* had purchased some *baldíos*. And in many places a large proportion of the arable land was involved (Vassberg 1975). In the

Tierra of Coca (Segovia), for example, García Sanz tells us (1977: 144) that nearly 28 percent of the cultivated land was sold as *baldíos*. And remember, the buyers of these lands had to mortgage the rest of their lands as well. They might not have lost them all, but the strain would certainly have been great. We have testimony that in Villanueva de los Caballeros (Valladolid), where the *baldíos* were sold in the late 1580s, there was widespread defaulting on the installment payments during a period of poor crops which followed. As a consequence, many landowners fled the village, abandoning their property to their creditors.[15]

Some of the lands lost by these unfortunate *baldío* buyers returned to a wild state, but others found their way into the estates of wealthy burghers and nobles. The buyers themselves, having lost their means for an independent economic existence, must have joined the unhappy ranks of the landless rural laborers or become wandering beggars. The Cortes had fought the *baldío* sales practically from their inception, warning Philip that the effect would be disastrous. But the monarch continued the sales, nevertheless, because he needed the additional funds they brought in. By 1598 (the year of the death of Philip II) it was obvious that the Castilian rural economy was in full decline. In a memorial of that year, the Cortes (*Actas*: xv, 748–55) blamed the ruin of Castilian agriculture on the sale of the *baldíos*. This verdict was shared by the *arbitrista* Barbón y Castañeda, who wrote (1628: fol. 9):

Anyone familiar with Old Castile before the sale of the *baldíos* would have seen a large and rich population, with *labradores* from the poorest hamlets of the kingdom having fortunes of eight and nine thousand *ducados*, and some having more. But men like that are no longer to be found – not even in the larger towns and cities.

Both the sale of *baldíos* and the enclosure movement reflected the expansion of individual ownership at the expense of the old communitarian traditions. The erosion of collective ownership enfeebled the social cohesiveness of the village communities as the councils of *vecinos* lost much of their power to supervise local agrarian exploitation. Underlying all of this was the shift in emphasis from pastoralism to arable agriculture. The movement was seemingly irreversible, and it was certainly not limited to Castile. There was a similar decline of communalism in neighboring France and Italy, but it seems that in those countries it came later (Bloch 1966: 150–96; Nieto 1964: 801–25). The Castilian institutions of collective ownership were by

175

no means completely extinguished during the sixteenth century. Many communal practices survived, and even withstood the central government's disamortizations of the nineteenth century. But as medieval institutions were replaced by modern ones, rural collectivism was increasingly an anachronism. In Castile, as in the rest of the West, the individualization of land ownership was an inseparable aspect of the rise of capitalism, modernization, and industrialization (Vassberg 1980; García Sanz 1977: 269–70).

THE CLASH BETWEEN CHRISTIAN AND MOSLEM AGRICULTURE

In the early medieval period the Iberian peninsula was divided into two distinct agricultural economies. The Christian north had an agrarian system in which cereal crops were dominant; whereas the Islamic south had a more typically Mediterranean agriculture, with cereal grains much less important, and vineyards, olive trees, and irrigation far more important in the landscape. Thomas Glick (1979: 51–109) has given us a splendid description of the diffusion of the two systems, and of the dynamics of the moving frontier separating the two. Glick shows that as the frontier moved south, Christian Spaniards adopted many Islamic crops and technologies (for example, they generally maintained the Islamic irrigation system intact), but they also introduced elements of their northern system, such as an expanded cereal cultivation and an aggressive transhumant herding.

The clash between Christian and Moslem agriculture did not end when Granada fell to Ferdinand and Isabella in 1492. Although most of the elite of Moslem society soon emigrated to northern Africa, the Islamic peasantry remained in the kingdom of Granada, and continued their traditional life style. When the government began a policy of forced conversion to Christianity, the First Rebellion of the Alpujarras broke out (1499–1500), but it was quickly crushed. After that, all the Moors remaining in Spain were officially Christians, but in practice they remained Moslem. Throughout the first half of the sixteenth century an uneasy peace existed between the Morisco 'New Christian' population and the Old Christians from the north, who had moved in with the Reconquest. The Moriscos were protected by the marquises of Mondéjar, who held the captaincy-general of Granada, and for nearly two generations the government refrained from interfering with the traditional Islamic way of life (Elliott 1977: 44–5, 232–7).

Chapters 4 and 5 provided some details about the Christian colonization of the kingdom of Granada. There were numerous incidents growing out of the juxtaposition of the Christian and the Islamic agrarian systems. For example, between 1512 and 1519 there were problems between the Morisco agriculturalists and certain Old Christian livestock owners in Motril (Granada). The Moriscos were troubled by the Christians' large herds (some numbering over 600 head) of hogs, who repeatedly damaged their irrigated sugar cane fields, orchards, and vineyards. The Moslem tradition, of course, had not included hogs, and the Morisco *labradores* were totally unprepared to deal with such large numbers of the beasts. For seven or eight years the porcine depredations went unpunished, because the hog owners had powerful friends. But in 1519 the council of Motril put an end to this inequitable situation by passing an ordinance restricting hog pasture rights in the irrigated fields of Motril to a town hog herd (*porcada*), in which each *vecino* of the place had the right to contribute no more than ten animals. There were many difficulties between Christians and Moriscos over conflicting interpretations of pasture rights. Oftentimes these disputes arose over the Christian custom of the *derrota de mieses*, which the Moors did not always accept. This was true of the Morisco villages of the La Axarquia district of the province of Málaga. The inhabitants of Comares, Cútar, Benamargosa, Machar Alhayate, and Borge declared that local custom had always permitted landowners to maintain exclusive rights to their fields, even after harvest. There was trouble in the mid-1530s when the Christian colonists of nearby Río Gordo insisted that their cattle had the right, according to the rule of the *derrota*, to pasture on the stubble fields of the Morisco villages. In confrontations such as this, the Christians were nearly always victorious, for they had the government on their side, and the legal system was prejudiced in favor of Castilian, rather than Moorish, ways.[16]

Nevertheless, the Moriscos remained generally acquiescent until the second half of the sixteenth century, when their position grew progressively worse. In the 1550s a power struggle at the court undermined the power of the Mondéjar family, who had defended them in the kingdom of Granada. At the same time, the Morisco economy was severely crippled, first by a ban on the export of silk fabric in the 1550s, then by a drastic increase in taxes on the silk industry after

1561. And in the mid-1560s the Inquisition began to press charges against crypto-Moslems. All of these factors awakened a deep feeling of resentment in the Morisco population, and it exploded into violent rebellion in 1568, when the government began to enforce a longstanding prohibition on the use of the Arabic language and the traditional Morisco dress. This Second Rebellion of the Alpujarras (1568–70) was crushed militarily, and after that the Granada Moriscos (estimated to number between 60,000 and 150,000) were forcibly dispersed throughout Castile, where it was hoped that they would become assimilated into Christian society (Garzón 1972; Garrad 1956; Elliott 1977: 44–5, 232–7).

The displacement of the Moriscos from the kingdom of Granada had enormous repercussions for the agricultural economy of the area. The expulsion produced a serious demographic trauma, and the accompanying economic problems prompted the Cortes to plead (in 1570 and 1573) for special tax exemptions from the crown (*Actas*: III, 405; IV, 32–87). As indicated in the preceding chapter, the crown attempted to restore the economy of the area by bringing in Christian colonists from the north, apportioning to them the former property of the Moriscos, which had been confiscated by the government after the rebellion. But despite the generous inducements offered to colonists, the repopulation program was disappointing. Some of the new settlers never really settled down to work their assigned lands. Others became discouraged after a season or two and decided to return to their native villages, or perhaps to move on to more attractive lands in the kingdom of Granada. In any case, many settlements that had existed in Morisco days now completely disappeared. The population of the area became more concentrated, because the settlements most likely to be abandoned were small hamlets dependent on larger villages. But the total population of many rural areas dropped to less than half the former level. In the Lecrín River valley, for example, it fell from 1,362 *vecinos* in 1568 to 646 in 1587 (Villegas 1972: 254–5, 312). And in the area of Andarax, 1,242 Morisco householders were replaced with only 545 new *vecinos* from the north (Sáenz 1974: 742–5). Along with this population loss came a sharp decline in agricultural production, aggravated by unfavorable weather in the late 1500s. By the beginning of the seventeenth century the collection of tithes had fallen off so much that sixty-four parish priests in the Alpujarras–Lecrín valley–Motril–Salobreña area were forced to request financial aid from the government to alleviate their straitened financial situation (Bosque 1971: 75; Garzón 1974: 74).

The post-1570 economic crisis was due in large measure to the difficulties that the Christian colonists experienced in adjusting to conditions in the kingdom of Granada. Many historians have echoed the myth that these difficulties existed because the colonists came from the verdant and dissimilar mountains of Galicia, Asturias, and León. Even some contemporaries believed that this was true. For instance, the Jesuit Father Pedro de León, who visited the Alpujarras in 1589, got the impression (cited in Herrera 1971: 440–60) that most of the new colonists in the area were from the distant northwest. But his impression seems to have been wrong: modern scholarship (Villegas 1972: 244; Bosque 1973: 495) has established that most of the colonists were actually from nearby Andalucía, or from New Castile. Only a minority were from Galicia, Asturias, and León. The difficulties of the colonists were real, but they were not so much related to problems of acclimatization as they were to problems of reconciling the Christian agrarian system with the Islamic system left by the Moriscos. The colonists who moved into former Morisco villages found a man-made landscape constructed around an intensive agriculture – almost a garden-type agriculture – in which fruit orchards and tree crops (such as mulberry, for the silk industry) were of fundamental importance. But the Christian settlers found it extremely difficult to adapt to the requirements of the new environment in which they found themselves. They were accustomed to an extensive agriculture in which dryland cereals were the prime ingredient. Consequently, through ignorance or through lack of interest, they allowed much of the old Morisco arboriculture to deteriorate, or even to wither and die, from lack of proper attention. Small wonder, then, that the new settlers soon found themselves on the edge of starvation, whereas their Moslem predecessors had lived rather well.

The contrast between the former Morisco prosperity and the Christian poverty was striking. The Jesuit Father Pedro de León had contact with both populations, and made some interesting judgements about them. He found the Moriscos to have been more enterprising, more generous, and more honest than the Christians who succeeded them. The Jesuit Father (cited Herrera 1971: 440–60) concluded that if the new settlers had not prospered, it was their own fault, because of their laziness, ignorance, and moral laxity.

In fact, he suggested that many of the new settlers were not really suitable colonists, because they had been socioeconomic undesirables even in their native villages. The Moriscos had proved that there was ample opportunity in Granada to produce crops and to have a good life, but on the same land where three or four Moriscos had lived well, a single Christian settler lived in misery. A royal *cédula* in 1595 (cited Sáenz 1974: 349) reported: 'Many of the colonists' houses are falling down, and others have been mistreated; and many vineyards, fields, gardens, and orchards have been destroyed and poorly cultivated and fertilized; and many of the irrigation ditches have collapsed and are filthy.' The experience in Granada was not an isolated phenomenon, for it was a commonplace that the Moors were far more efficient agriculturalists than Christians. In 1568 Juan Valverde de Arrieta had written (1777: 333) that 'the land where a thousand Moors had lived, cannot sustain five hundred Christians'.

In the previous two chapters we saw that although certain powerful nobles were able to appropriate some Morisco lands for themselves, the old system of Moorish minifundios in the kingdom of Granada was maintained largely intact after the post-1570 re-settlement. Moreover, despite the problems of adaptation experienced by the Christian settlers, there were few abrupt changes in agrarian production, and the same basic (Morisco) crops were continued. Many orchards were abandoned, but the transformation must have been slow, for in the mid-1600s the area was still important as a fruit producer. The gradual retreat of arborescent cultivation was accompanied by an extension of dryland grain cultivation. The post-Morisco settlers brought with them certain agricultural forms that were characteristic of the central plateau: for example, the division of the cultivated land of a municipality into compulsory zones (*hojas*) of cultivation and fallow – a custom that was rare in that part of Spain before 1570. The Christian expansion of cultivation was largely made possible at the expense of the remaining woodlands of the kingdom of Granada. After 1570 the Christians gradually pushed back the ancient oak, live oak, pine, and chestnut forests and replaced them with grain fields, and to a lesser extent with vineyards. This application of the traditional Castilian extensive agriculture involved exploiting hillside slopes at far higher altitudes than those that had been used by the Moslems. Unfortunately, the deforestation and the cultivation of steeper slopes increased the velocity of erosion, producing a movement of topsoil from the mountains to the alluvial deltas on the coast. The erosion was so violent that it destroyed the sites of several towns, and forced others to protect themselves through extensive works. Thus the mountains were denuded, but a new band of light and fertile soils was deposited along the littoral, permitting an increasingly active agricultural life there (Bosque 1971: 61–2, 81–9; Díaz 1963: 77–85; Sermet 1943: 26).

The end of the Reconquest initiated a long period of decadence in sugar cane culture in Spain. The Moslems had introduced the crop into the peninsula, and at one time they cultivated it all along the Costa del Sol, up the east coast as far north as Castellón de la Plana, and even a small area in the lower Guadalquivir. At that point Spain had the most important sugar industry in Europe. But the industry declined rapidly in the 1500s. The fall of the kingdom of Granada and the expulsion of the Moriscos were severe blows, and there was increasing competition from plantations in the Atlantic Islands and in the Antilles. Furthermore, it seems that there was a climatic change, perhaps associated with the near-total deforestation of the Cordillera Penibética, although there is evidence that all of Europe was cooling in the second half of the sixteenth century. In any case, the average annual temperatures dropped several degrees, making sugar cane a marginal crop. Cultivation retrogressed to the point that it was practically restricted to the Vega of Motril (Granada). Whereas in 1492 there had been a dozen sugar mills in Motril alone, by 1592 there were only seven remaining in all of Spain (Bosque 1971: 55–6; Delano 1979: 314).

After the expulsion of the Moriscos, the kingdom of Granada also suffered a decline in its silk industry. But it seems that by 1570 the art of sericulture had been assimilated, to a large degree, by Christian Granadans. Thus, production could be maintained even though the new post-1570 colonists were not experienced in silk growing. And despite the exodus of the Moriscos, in the 1600s there were some three thousand silk looms operating in Granada. The really serious decadence in the industry did not come until the 1700s, and according to Garzón Pareja (1972: 129–32) the most important factor in the ruin of Granadan silk was not the expulsion of the Moriscos, but rather a progressive strangulation by well-intentioned governmental and guild regulations. Furthermore, although the Moriscos were officially expelled from Granada in 1570, there were many who escaped detection and were able to continue to live there. Others were able to remain in the kingdom of Granada because they were slaves of Christians. Domínguez Ortiz (1963: 113–28) reports that there were even cases where Moriscos voluntarily embraced slave-status to avoid deportation. There must have been many such deals between Moriscos and sympathetic Christians, who would later manumit their charges, either spontaneously or in exchange for payment. In that way a number of Moriscos were able to remain in their homeland, even after the general expulsion of 1609–14, eventually becoming absorbed into the Spanish population. Their presence, obviously, made it easier for Old Christian Spaniards to adjust to the exigencies of life in Granada, and to learn some of the techniques of the Moorish system.

Many of the Granadan Moriscos expelled in 1570 were sent to rural areas in Castile, where they were expected to work in agriculture. And in some cases they did. But it seems that only a small minority of the Moriscos in Castile were content to remain in agro-pastoral occupations, and fewer still were active in the typical Castilian field activities. Instead, those who were involved in agriculture found it more profitable to grow fruits and vegetables for urban markets. In Palencia, for instance, in 1591 there were nearly five hundred Moriscos, living together in a certain *barrio* of the city. The immense majority of these were horticulturalists (*hortelanos*), probably continuing to practice skills they had learned in Granada (Domínguez 1963: 121). A census taken in 1595 showed that the Moriscos in Segovia were also overwhelmingly devoted to market gardening. In fact, the terraced plots still visible in the southeastern part of the city are attributed to them. But the enormous majority of the Moriscos followed non-agricultural occupations, undoubtedly because they saw that that was where the greatest economic opportunities lay. There were more traders than agriculturalists, and nearly twice as many artisans as there were agriculturalists. And as time went on, there was an increasing tendency for the Moriscos to desert the countryside to seek jobs in the cities (Le Flem 1965). The Moriscos' disinclination to take seasonal agricultural jobs prompted the *corregidor* of Toro (Zamora) to complain that they were of little help in the local grape harvest (Vincent 1970: 232–6). The *corregidor* of Medina del Campo (Valladolid), writing near the end of the sixteenth century, grumbled that the Moriscos in his district preferred to be muleteers or itinerant merchants rather than agriculturalists, and he recommended that the crown force them into agriculture. And the *corregidor* of Avila found a similar situation, reporting that many Moriscos had abandoned agropastoral activities to become transporters and peddlers of goods.[17] The monetary success of the Moriscos in these non-agrarian enterprises excited the resentment and envy of their Christian neighbors, and produced the climate of opinion (*Actas*: xx, 420) that prompted the crown to order their definitive expulsion from Spain in 1609–14 as an unassimilable minority.

7

The increasing rural malaise

By the beginning of the seventeenth century, it was abundantly clear to almost everyone that rural Castile had fallen on hard times. Through the words of Pedro Crespo, a character in *El Alcalde de Zalamea*, the Golden Age dramatist Lope de Vega (cited Arco 1941: 882) lamented the rural depression and harked back to better times in the past:

> ¡Ay de aquella edad sencilla!
> Agora todo es maldad
> en la más pequeña villa.
>
> (Ah, for that simple time!
> Today everything is bad
> in the smallest town.)

It is worth emphasizing that Lope and his contemporaries not only recognized that Castilian agriculture was in a state of decay; they also looked back to a halcyon earlier period. The previous chapter dealt with a number of changes in the sixteenth-century rural world, many of which played a role in worsening the position of the Castilian peasant. The present chapter will examine certain other aspects of the rural economy that also contributed to the deteriorating rural situation.

PRICES AND MARKETS

The twentieth-century observer is likely to think it quite obvious that the Castilian peasant would have been very much affected by changes in prices and markets. But the truth of the matter is that the typical sixteenth-century peasant producer was far less vulnerable to price fluctuations than we might suspect. Most peasants of the day lived in a subsistence or a semi-subsistence economy. In other words, they lived in an economy based on mere survival. They worked continuously to reap low yields. In fact, they often worked lands that only marginally rewarded the labor put into them, because time lacked value in the mind of the peasant, and above all, because even a minimal yield would help feed his family. The peasant family tried to diversify its production to guarantee the maximum self-sufficiency in food and dress. There were scant surpluses to put on the market, and, as a consequence, there was not much cash with which to purchase goods from the outside world. The typical peasant lived an austere life bordering on poverty. But although the peasant's needs were minimal, in many cases he could not support himself solely with his agropastoral production, and had to seek other sources of income. Many families engaged in domestic industries such as textile production or other artisan-type manufacturing activities. This supplied them with cash to buy what they themselves could not produce for their own needs, and occasionally it yielded a surplus. There were rich peasants and poor peasants, of course. But for most peasants, life was precariously balanced on the edge of subsistence (Ortega Valcárcel 1966: 100–6).

Nevertheless, although the *average* peasant rarely had much to sell in the way of agropastoral commodities, a substantial *minority* of peasants were doing quite well exploiting the possibilities of local, regional, and even international markets. It is well known that there was a large and profitable overseas market for oil, wine, and wheat. This market was served chiefly by producers in Andalucía, through the port city of Seville. There was also a lucrative foreign market, both in the Indies and in northern Europe, for Spanish leather and leather goods, and for woolen, silk, and linen textiles – finished and unfinished.[1] Thus the humbler peasant population, who did not normally have any surplus agricultural products to export, could nevertheless profit from the external market by engaging in light manufacturing or processing. The overseas market cooled in the 1570s, when the American colonies began to produce enough grain for their own needs, but before that there was a period of thirty or forty years of economic boom, based on the high prices of the export market (Gómez Mendoza 1967: 502–3).

The prosperity of Castile was reflected in the great fairs of Medina del Campo (Valladolid), where the leading merchant and banking houses of Europe transacted enormous exchanges of goods and of loans and other financial contracts (Rodríguez y Fernández 1903–4: 667). But the peasants were likely to be only indirectly involved in this. They sold their goods in local and regional markets, and if they participated at all in the international economy, it was almost always through middlemen. Throughout the kingdom there were periodic tax-free fairs (*ferias francas*) in the most important provincial cities. And it was to these fairs that the peasants liked to bring their produce for sale. The inhabitants of a given village might have the choice of several fairs. For example, in 1569 the villagers of Casasola de Arión (Valladolid) reported that they could travel eight leagues to the city of Valladolid, where there was an annual fair; or they could go seven leagues to Medina de Rioseco (also in the province of Valladolid) where there were two yearly fairs; or thirteen leagues to Salamanca; seven leagues to Zamora; or only three leagues to the nearby city of Toro (Zamora province), which had several fairs and tax-free markets throughout the year.

In some cases peasants were willing to travel considerable distances to bring their products to the right fair. This was facilitated, of course, when the commodity to be sold was livestock, because the beasts could be transported on the hoof. The hog-raisers of Trujillo, for example, were able to drive their animals to sell in the fairs of Toledo and La Mancha (Vassberg 1978: 52). The fairs dealt with all types of merchandise, but some fairs came to specialize in certain things. The city of Badajoz, for example, had an important livestock fair on St Mark's Day (25 April). And Arévalo (Avila) in the mid-1500s served as the chief marketplace for Castilian wheat, being well-situated between the cereal-growing plains of the Duero valley and the growing urban market in Madrid. Even within more limited geographical areas, the peasants found that they would do better to market their goods in certain nearby towns rather than others. The *vecinos* of Palomas (Badajoz), for instance, in the mid-1570s reported that they preferred to sell their livestock in Mérida, whereas they seemed more inclined to sell their grain in Zafra.[2]

The great national and regional fairs served an important function, providing an outlet for agropastoral surpluses at appropriate times after harvest. But the week-to-week and day-to-day sales and purchases of the country were transacted in the more humble town markets. It was customary for the towns of each area to hold their weekly markets on different days, to enable buyers and sellers to appear at several markets. For example, in the Adelantamiento of León, there was a market every Monday in Santamaría del Rey (?), and on Tuesday there were markets in Mansilla de las Mulas and in

Villafranca del Bierzo. On Wednesday there was one in Mayorga (?), but it was described as 'dismal' (*ruin*). On Thursday one could choose to go to market in Benavides, Valencia de Don Juan, or Venbilas (?), and on Saturday there was a market at La Baneza, which was particularly good for sales of oxen and other livestock. Looking at market days in a more restricted area: in the Tierra de Campos (Palencia province) there was market day in Vallada on Wednesday, in Carrión de los Condes on Thursday, in Paredes de Nava on Friday, and in Villalón on Saturday. For some reason, perhaps because of its mid-week position, Thursday seems to have been considered an especially good day for market. The city of Trujillo (Cáceres), which served as the commercial center for dozens of subject villages, held its *mercado franco* on Thursday. So did the city of Segovia, which similarly ruled over a large Tierra. Villagers who went to market in these administrative–commercial centers could not only exchange goods, but could also learn the latest news, and they could be apprised of the most recent orders emanating from municipal and other authorities. The news-disseminating function of the market towns was underlined in 1556 by the government of Peñafiel (Valladolid), which had about twenty villages in its Tierra. Peñafiel reported that it had its major (undoubtedly tax-free) market on Thursday, but that various goods and supplies could be bought and sold there on any day of the week. This, to be sure, was true also of other market towns, but on ordinary tax-paying days the market would have been not nearly as well-attended.[3]

The vitality of the local and regional markets fluctuated, of course, depending upon general economic conditions. And there were extraordinary local factors that could drastically affect market conditions. The peasants of Morales de Toro (Zamora) discovered this after 1561, when Philip II moved his court from nearby Valladolid to Madrid, on the other side of the Sierra de Guadarrama. The move occasioned grave financial difficulties for the inhabitants of Morales, because they had come to specialize in the production of wine, which could be profitably transported the short distance to Valladolid, but not to Madrid. Consequently, the wines of Morales now had to be sold in local cities, at a greatly reduced price.[4] On the other hand, the court's move created a new and lucrative market for peasants living in villages in the vicinity of Madrid. The prosperity of rural areas, as this example demonstrates, was linked to the economic wellbeing of the cities that served as markets for their surpluses. Generally speaking, both rural Castile and urban Castile were doing well in the early and mid-1500s, with extraordinary economic and demographic growth. But as the export economy soured in the last third of the century, many Castilian manufacturing and trading cities found their economies deteriorating. At the same time, there were decreasing agricultural surpluses, and even crises of subsistence in some places, because the peasants had been obliged to utilize marginal lands to feed the burgeoning population. Given the primitive agricultural methods of the time, the equilibrium between rural and urban populations had always been precarious, and it began to fail in the last decades of the reign of Philip II. The features of the relationship between urban and rural areas have been ably sketched by Angel García Sanz for Segovia (1977: 58, 79), and by Michael Weisser for Toledo (1971: 1976: 56–62).

Agricultural prices on the local level were subjected to a type of economic control that could be described as municipal mercantilism. Throughout Castile it was considered normal for municipal governments to enact regulations fixing prices and restricting the movement of goods. The Castilian wine-growing centers, for example, adopted a strongly protectionist attitude toward their own vintages. This local protectionism, which began in the Middle Ages, initially consisted merely of a tax on outside wine. But from the end of the twelfth century there began to exist ordinances for the complete exclusion of outside wines. In those places where local production was unable to satisfy all the demand, the ban on outside wine was limited to the period necessary to use up the local vintage. In some places the date was fixed; elsewhere it was flexible, to allow for variable local harvests. But the major wine producing centers tended to impose an absolute ban on introducing outside wines for the entire year. The idea was that there was to be no 'foreign' competition (Huetz 1967: 175; García Sanz 1977: 194–5).

This kind of protectionism caused many complaints, especially in places where the local wines were of poor quality. Local consumers resented having to drink up the bad local product before they could buy more palatable imported vintages. Local merchants also protested, because of the loss of sales, and the royal treasury suffered reduced sales-tax receipts. The protectionism was denounced as a privilege that did not benefit the entire community, but only a few wine producers. But these few usually included the most powerful figures of the place, and they were able to control the municipal government for their own profit. And there were certain officials who were accorded special privileges. For example, we find that in Cieza (Murcia), the ordinances of 1523 forbade the importation of outside wine as long as the *vecinos* of the town still had some of their own to sell. But the *comendador* (commander) of the Order of Santiago was permitted to bring in outside wine from his own harvest at his pleasure, and he could bring in any other wine he wished. He could not sell it, however, without the permission of the town council, which was to establish a 'reasonable' price (Salmerón 1777; 94–5). In the city of Segovia there were also regulations of longstanding to exclude all outside wine until the local product had been exhausted. But these exclusionist regulations were increasingly unpopular, and toward the end of the sixteenth century the municipal government liberalized them somewhat. It authorized three taverns to sell 'fine' wine, mainly from the Duero Valley and from La Mancha, which was not subject to the usual import restrictions. But the municipal authorities set such a high price on this outside wine that only the rich could afford to buy it, and most Segovians had to continue to endure the miserable local stock. It is revealing to note that the special interests responsible for these restrictions were thus able to preserve their privileges in Segovia until the eighteenth century (García Sanz 1977: 194–5).

Municipal mercantilism was not limited to wine, but extended to other agropastoral products as well. The councils of every city, town, and village had the power to fix the price of fruit, vegetables, grain, meat, cheese, oil, or any other merchandise. And they did not shrink from their authority. They granted monopoly rights to tavern keepers, butchers, and other officially designated victualers for the locality. And they established detailed price schedules from which no one could deviate without the special permission of the council. The official prices were in force even on market days, when peasants were permitted to bring in their crops for sale. Such price controls (as always, throughout history) caused problems. The legal price was likely to be too low in the eyes of the producer, because the idea behind municipal price fixing was usually to protect the consumer, rather than the producer. The 1583 ordinances of Los Santos de Maimona (Badajoz) went so far as to require any *vecino* who had fish, game, vegetables, or fruit for sale to offer his wares in the market of the town before removing them from the municipal jurisdiction for sale elsewhere. And the council reserved for itself the right to determine how much could be 'exported'. Moreover, the ordinances of Los Santos made it illegal for anyone to offer anything for sale in the town marketplace without notifying the council a day in advance (Guerra 1952: 520–1).

The Castilian municipalities also undertook to regulate the operation of grain and oil mills, and other processing establishments related to agriculture. For example, the council of Arjona (Jaén) adopted a comprehensive and quite specific set of rules for oil mills. The town tried to regulate everything: milling procedures, working hours, measurements, salaries, and prices. All of this was designed to protect olive growers and olive oil buyers from unscrupulous mill operators. It may have succeeded in that, but it also must have discouraged innovation and experimentation, and by ossifying existing structures and techniques it made it difficult (in fact, actually illegal) to adjust to changing circumstances. It is hardly surprising, then, to discover that such well-intentioned trade-regulating ordinances were often honored in the breach. The market gardeners of Yeste (Albacete), for instance, discovered a loophole in the local ordinances, which fixed low prices for all fruit and vegetables sold in the town marketplace. Instead of bringing their produce to the market square, they simply sold it in their homes and gardens, outside the urban area, where they charged whatever prices the market would bear. This worked for a while, but in 1595 the town government ruled that this was illegal, and that all fruit and vegetables had to be sold in the marketplace, at the official price. The gardeners appealed to the Chancillería (supreme tribunal) of Granada to reverse this local ruling, protesting that they would be ruined by such low prices. The documents in the Chancillería archive do not reveal how the case ended, but one suspects that the gardeners lost their suit. And if they were forced to sell at prices they regarded as too low, they probably reduced, or even abandoned their market gardening.[5]

It is well known that there was also price fixing on the national level. During the Middle Ages there had been crown-dictated legal maximum prices for various commodities in both Islamic and Christian Spain. But Ferdinand and Isabella did not establish maximum prices until 1502, when a *tasa* (legal maximum price) was set for wheat, barley, and rye. The declared purpose of the *tasa* was to protect the poor by fixing a value for grain that would be fair to both buyers and sellers. Severe penalties were prescribed for requesting or accepting more than the *tasa*. And local and royal governmental authorities were empowered to force the possessors of surplus grain to sell it at a price not exceeding the *tasa*, when the grain was needed for local consumption or for transportation to other places in the kingdom where there was a shortage. The grain *tasas* expired in 1512, and after that for nearly thirty years there were no royally imposed price controls on Castilian grain. This long interim of free trade can be explained partly by the realization that the first controls – despite the heavy penalties for non-compliance – had been inefficacious. Furthermore, the market price entered a long period of moderation and stability after 1509, and the political situation was unsettled after the death of Isabella. But in 1539 Charles V restored the *tasa* after a poor harvest sent grain prices sharply upward, and after that the legal maximum grain price became a permanent feature of Castilian economic life. The emperor's *tasa*, like the one imposed by his grandmother, exempted Galicia and the Cantabrian region from the price controls, but the *tasa* was to be enforced in the remainder of the kingdom of Castile. The new maximum prices were intended for points of *origin*, rather than for points of ultimate sale (as in the case of the earlier *tasa*), because the regulations permitted the addition of transportation costs, including a 'reasonable' profit. The emperor's *tasa* fixed lower prices for the province (Reino) of Toledo than for the remainder of Castile, although there seems to have been no good justification for this inequity. Charles's maximum prices, which were about twice as high as those of Isabella, remained in effect until 1558, when Philip II revised them upwards to compensate for inflation. And after that, from time to time they were raised still higher, and various new regulations concerning transportation and sale were added. Among the innovations introduced by Philip II were the exemption of imported grain from *tasa* controls (decreed in 1558), the provision of stiffer penalties for non-compliance (1571), and the appointment of special royal judges (1593) to enforce the various price-fixing regulations. But the activities of these judges elicited such loud and bitter complaints from the cities that the monarch felt obliged to recall them (Hamilton 1965: 243–60).

The *tasa* was the subject of lively and continual controversy – in high political circles, among intellectuals, and to be sure among the peasants and other members of the general public who were affected by the price controls. There were many spirited debates on the subject in the Cortes, and the Cortes often requested that the *tasa* be abolished, or that the price be raised, or that special schedules be established for the different provinces (*Actas*: vols. II–XV). Time and again the *tasa* was blamed for the deteriorating condition of the Castilian peasantry. Several *corregidores*, writing near the end of the reign of Philip II, agreed that the *tasa* should be revoked, because it discouraged cultivation. As early as 1539 the chronicler Florián de Ocampo had observed that the price ceiling was low enough to cause some producers to lose money, and that this eventually led to grain shortages.[6] And some *arbitristas* denounced the *tasa* (e.g. Fernández Navarrete 1626: 274–8), but there were many others who staunchly defended it. Among the latter, Melchor Soria y Vera (1633: 38–50, 87–91) even went so far as to condemn the periodic upward adjustments of the *tasa*, on the grounds that they harmed the poor, and benefitted only the small minority of rich *labradores* who ever had surplus grain to put on the market.

It is difficult to assess the effect of the *tasa* on Castilian agriculture. The pioneering agricultural historian Carmelo Viñas y Mey (1941: 103–10) thought the *tasa* was highly prejudicial. He pointed out that whereas there was a price ceiling on grain, the crop of the *labrador*, there was no similar price ceiling on the cost of tools, labor, seed, draft animals, and other instruments of production needed by grain growers. Viñas y Mey concluded that 'the state of permanent disequilibrium between the government's agricultural price policy and its cost policy, to the detriment of the producer, together with all the other unfavorable influences for agriculture, particularly oppressive taxation, was one of the most effective elements in the process of undermining the farming business – which frequently operated at a loss . . .' The problem with this view is that it flies in the face of an abundance of evidence that there was widespread evasion of the *tasa* regulations. In fact, the increasingly severe penalties decreed for infractions suggest that violations must have been a serious problem.

Because of the nature of illegal dealings, we will never be able to ascertain the exact degree of non-compliance with the *tasa*, but Hamilton surmised that at least half the grain transactions in Andalucía and New Castile were in violation of the law. And many seemingly legal sales may have been influenced by hidden considerations forever obscured to the researcher. Friar Francisco Ortiz Lucio (1600: 1–4), writing near the close of the sixteenth century, deplored the general disregard of the *tasa*. He declared that the *labradores* and others who sold grain at prices in excess of the *tasa* were guilty of mortal sin, because the *tasa* represented a 'just' price. But he noted that violations of the maximum price regulations usually went un-punished, because royal justice officials deliberately overlooked them, and failed to take the appropriate action. Some clergymen, when faced with this kind of wholesale lawbreaking, and lack of enforce-ment, tried to resolve the moral dilemma by adopting a double standard. For example, Soria y Vera reported (1633: 90–1) that the bishop of Jaén from 1579 to 1595 instructed his priests to require rich people who confessed non-compliance to return any illegal profits to the grain buyer. But the priests were instructed to overlook the same offence when committed by poor *labradores*, on the grounds that they needed the extra money to compensate for their scanty harvests.

What do we conclude, then, about the effect of the *tasa*? Antonio Domínguez Ortiz has suggested (1973a: 27) that the black market in grain so vitiated the intent of the law that the practical effect of the *tasa* was almost nil. It seems that in years of normal harvest only the clergy paid any attention to the official price ceiling, and in years of famine, virtually everyone (including the government) completely disregarded it. In years of abundance, of course, the market price fell well below the *tasa* level and the existence of a legal maximum had only a potential importance. According to this view, the royal government maintained the *tasa* mainly out of inertia, and the price ceiling was useful chiefly as a point of reference for calculating the value of rents. Nevertheless, there is evidence that the existence of the *tasa* had a moderating effect on prices. And despite the ease of violating the official price ceiling, contemporary observers asserted that there were many peasants who stopped growing grain as a market crop, and turned instead to wine or other alternative crops (Domínguez 1973b: 157; Hamilton 1965: 258–60). It is quite possible that the threat of punishment for *tasa* violations did indeed discourage grain production to some degree, but in view of the evidence, we cannot think that that factor was very important.

Hamilton clearly demonstrated that the market price of grain fluctuated wildly, despite the *tasa*, and this has been corroborated time and again by more recent research. A good storage system, enabling the surplus of good harvests to be held over to make up for the deficit of bad years, would have stabilized prices. Many large landowners *did* store their grain, sometimes for several years. But they did this not to stabilize prices, but rather to take advantage of the movement in prices, for their own benefit. The great price fluctua-tions encouraged speculative grain storage, despite the likelihood of losses from insect damage and spoilage from improper ventilation. Some of these grain speculators sold everything, and even went into debt to hoard grain, knowing that a year of famine would permit them to make astronomical profits (Domínguez 1973a: 26–32). Obviously, if the *tasa* had been enforced, this kind of activity would have been totally impossible. If there had been a sufficient number of private granaries, the surplus grain they contained might have functioned – despite the intent of their owners – to hold prices down during periods of scarcity. But there were not enough of them to exert a significant downward pressure on the market. There were municipal granaries that were supposed to do so. In fact, these existed in all the major towns and cities, not just in Spain, but throughout the Mediterranean area.

In Castile the municipal granaries were called *alhóndigas* or *pósitos*. They were created to eliminate regrating, to stabilize prices, and to guarantee an adequate supply of grain following catastrophic harvests. The *pósitos* purchased grain at threshing time, and stored it for later sale at reasonable prices for planting seed and for bread making. During famines, many of these municipal granaries operated as charitable enterprises, selling grain to the needy below the purchase price. And the *pósitos* of large cities such as Valladolid distributed grain in this manner not only to local residents, but also to the *vecinos* of surrounding villages. The municipal granaries were of unquestionably great importance. Ideally, they would have been able to end the problem of recurring shortages and wide price fluctuations. Philip II realized this, and ordered all the towns of Castile to establish *pósitos*. But most of these lacked the resources to function adequately (Yun 1980: 71–8, 118–19; Bennassar 1967: 65–9, 77–8; Hamilton 1965: 241). Furthermore, many municipal granaries fell under the control of powerful local figures who used them for their own selfish advantage.[7] And in the final analysis, although the *pósitos* in many places certainly acted as a brake on oscillating prices, and although they were often able to mitigate the effects of crop failure, both problems remained a leitmotiv of the Castilian rural world, and they grew much worse near the end of the sixteenth century.

In the eyes of sixteenth-century Castilians, one of the most disturbing features of the century's price inflation was the steady rise of the cost of labor. Near the end of the reign of Philip II the *corregidor* of Ecija (Sevilla) noted that many fields of the area were no longer planted. And he put a large share of the blame for this on the high cost of labor.[8] Those who fulminated against the *tasa* almost invariably pointed to the unfairness of a situation where there was a maximum price for grain, but not for wages. But actually, although it is true that there was no national wage maximum corresponding to the *tasa* on grain, it was quite commonplace to find wage ceilings on the municipal level. Municipal ordinances, promulgated by the local landowning oligarchy, established low wage rates, which had to be observed under pain of severe penalties. And whereas the national grain *tasa* was largely ineffective, it seems that the municipal wage regulations were generally enforced. In some cases the municipal wage rate ordinances were quite specific, but they could still be flexible enough to account for seasonal changes. For example, in 1588 the council of Cifuentes (Guadalajara) established a wage ceiling of 1 *real* (34 mrs) in February, 57 mrs in March, 60 mrs in April, and 2 *reales* (68 mrs) in May and June, both for plowmen and for pruners (Domínguez 1973b: 166). Some intermunicipal unions also adopted wage regulations. The ordinances of the Tierra of Segovia (1514), for instance, specified that the workday for salaried rural laborers was to commence an hour after sunrise, and it was to last until sundown. The Segovia ordinances also flatly prohibited paying rural workers in kind, lest they benefit from the rising prices of grain and other agricultural commodities (García Sanz 1977: 285).

At harvest time there was a vital need for a supply of reasonably priced field help. And the municipal governments, dominated by large landowners, undertook to ensure favorable labor conditions for local producers. In the province of Jaén, for example, the councils of Villanueva del Arzobispo and Iznatoraf enacted ordinances enabling them to set a *tasa* on wages 'whenever they saw that it was needed'. And they prohibited harvest workers from leaving the area until all the grain of the towns' *vecinos* had been reaped.[9] The harvest-time labor requirements were often so high that they could not be met solely with local workers. Consequently it was necessary to recruit outside workers on a seasonal basis. The procedures for this varied. In La Mancha, which had a low population density, landowners contracted to bring harvest workers in from the north. As early as three months before harvest a contract would be made with one or two men from the workers' locality, and these individuals would then arrange for recruiting the rest of the crew. The contract normally included not only a wage agreement, but also specified that the landowner provide bread, meat, wine, and other things that were customarily given to harvesters in the area. The wage agreement could be either a flat rate paid to the contractor, for a given amount of land, or it could be a fee for each *fanega* of land to be harvested, out of which the contractor was to pay the wages of the crew (Phillips 1979: 39, 151 n. 17).

It was not at all unusual for trouble to break out between migrant harvesters and native residents of the harvest place. In 1566 the council of Alpera (Albacete) wrote that the migrant workers who came to the village at reaping time were a 'mutinous and trouble-some' lot, who were the source of many disturbances (including knifings), both among themselves and with the locals. And the Extremadurans who migrated to Andalucía to work in the vineyards and olive groves had a well-deserved reputation as violent and untrustworthy types (Herrera 1971: 431–5). Many migrant workers were ne'er-do-wells, who led lives of unceasing vagabondage. One would expect their conduct to be disreputable. But others were stable, family types – perfectly respectable peasants who were forced by economic necessity to abandon their homes for several months out of the year to work in distant fields. The council of Palomas (Badajoz) reported in 1575 that the majority of the *vecinos* of the place were poor *labradores*, who had to spend over half the year working in Andalucía to earn enough money to feed themselves and their families. It seems that as the economic situation deteriorated in the last third of the sixteenth century, more and more peasants were forced to become hired laborers, many of them homeless vagabonds.[10]

The lot of the sixteenth-century migrant workers was not a pleasant one. As indicated above, their working conditions and wages were likely to be subject to municipal control, to their distinct disadvantage. But they did not always meekly endure their plight. We have an interesting case of labor unrest in Córdoba in the year 1595. Córdoba had just come out of several penurious years, as the result of bad harvests and other unfavorable circumstances. But the 1595 harvest promised to be good, and everyone looked forward to a return to normalcy. Then, quite unexpectedly, the agricultural workers who were supposed to reap the crop took advantage of the situation to declare a strike. It had all the familiar characteristics of twentieth-century strikes: demands for higher wages and shorter hours, and the use of coercion and violence against workers who would not join the strikers. The harvest was endangered, and the city had to act quickly to put an end to the conflict. The municipal council voted to arrest all 'vagabonds' (read striking workers) in the taverns, streets, or plazas, who refused a wage offer. The 'vagabonds' were to be rounded up each Monday, following the Sunday when they traditionally contracted for a week's work in the fields, and they were to be given four hours in the pillory and a ten-day jail sentence. All muleteers who refused to work were to be accorded the same treatment. These draconian measures worked well: the strike was broken, and the crop was harvested, to the satisfaction of the land-owners and municipal authorities. As for the workers, their condition was certainly worse than before, for they had been defeated, and they received no compensation for their days without work. They would not likely be willing to strike again in the near future, nor would the landowners likely accede to their demands, now that both sides in the dispute knew where the city stood (Torre 1931a).

CROP YIELDS

As the agricultural situation became progressively worse in the last half of the 1500s, there were increasing complaints about low yields. The combination of decreasing yields and a growing population was a dangerous one, because in the best of times there was a precarious balance in Castile between the food supply and the needs of the rural and urban population. In the last two decades of the century, an increasing number of subsistence crises produced a malnourished people who were highly susceptible to the eruption of virulent plagues (García Sanz 1977: 79–82; Bennassar 1969: 51–2, 69–70). Let us look at the subject of crop yields in greater detail, for the subject is quite complex, and most important.

The Castilian peasant, like all of history's agriculturalists, spent much of his time worrying about the weather. It seemed that he was always either praying for rain, or praying that the rains would stop. The climate of Spain has probably not changed much over the last four or five hundred years. Thus, in the 1500s, just as today, most of Spain was rather dry, but the climate was variable, and it was subject to great extremes. However, although the climate has remained substantially unchanged, we must be aware that there have been cycles within the last half millenium, and these cycles have had a drastic effect on certain marginal crops. As mentioned in the pre-vious chapter, a slight change in the average winter lows had a

197

devastating effect on the sugar cane industry. Olive trees and citrus trees in marginal locations undoubtedly suffered a similar fate. And a slight drop in the average rainfall might have resulted in the abandonment of marginal dryland fields in many semi-arid parts of Castile. Throughout the sixteenth century there were wet and dry cycles, and good years and bad. Not all parts of Castile experienced the same conditions, of course, and the rain that was beneficial to one crop might be disastrous for another type of crop, because trees, vines, cereals, and legumes do not have identical seasonal needs. We should remember this in speaking about 'bad' years. Furthermore, even within regions such as Andalucía, there might be drought and crop failure in one place, while there were abundant harvests only a day's ride away. With these caveats, let the reader examine the following chronological list (it is incomplete, to be sure) of severe weather and crop failures during the sixteenth century:

1503	A wet year, with devastating storms in the region of Seville. Flooding of the Esgueva River near Valladolid.
1504–6	A droughty period, with famine in all of Spain in 1504. Andalucía, Murcia, and Old Castile suffer crop failures and epidemics.
1507–9	Drought in Andalucía.
1510–11	Floods in Andalucía in 1510, and in Old Castile in 1511.
1513	Drought and famine in Murcia.
1514	Drought and bad harvests around Seville.
1521–2	Drought in Andalucía, with bad harvests, famine, and riots.
1523	Winter floods in Old Castile.
1527–9	Floods throughout Spain. Killing freezes in April of 1529.
1535–6	Record cold winter in Toledo, causing the Tajo to freeze.
1539–40	Drought in Old Castile and Murcia, and famine in 1540.
1543–4	Drought followed by excessive rainfall in Old Castile, Murcia, and Andalucía.
1548–50	Generally dry weather and poor harvests in Old Castile and in Murcia.
1551	Devastating floods in Murcia.
1554–5	Flooding of the Guadalquivir (1554) and the Duero (1555).
1556	Generally droughty spring and summer, causing poor crops.
1557	Uncommonly cold winter in Valladolid.
1558–9	Crops ruined by heavy rains in Andalucía, Extremadura, and Old Castile. Flooding of the Duero.
1561–2	Drought and scarcity in Seville.
1566–7	Terrible drought in Andalucía, followed by famine, and by plague in 1568.
1571	Droughty spring around Seville.
1573–6	Unusually cold and rainy period. Late freeze, causing widespread damage in New Castile.
1582	Flooding around Valladolid.

1584	Crop failures in Jaén, Granada, and Málaga.
1586	Generally harsh winter throughout Spain.
1589–90	Excessive rainfall in all of Spain, followed by epidemics.
1591–2	Bad harvests in Old Castile.
1593	Droughty spring in Old Castile and in Murcia; rain and floods around Seville; poor crops all over.
1594	Bad harvests in Old Castile.
1597	Floods in Old Castile, causing food shortages.
1598	Late freeze kills vines in New Castile. Disastrous harvests in Toledo, and bad harvests in Old Castile.
1599	Drought in Valladolid area, and probably also in Andalucía.[11]

The foregoing list shows yield-damaging weather, or reports of bad harvests, in fifty-four years, clearly indicating that the Castilian peasant was all too familiar with the specter of crop failure. And capricious weather was not the only menace endangering the peasant's fields. A recurring hazard affecting the harvest of many crops was devastation by plagues of locusts (*la langosta*). Mediterranean Europe had always been subject to locust plagues (Delano 1979: 203), and it was a serious problem, because a major locust invasion could cause a complete crop failure, and could even kill livestock, by contaminating their food and water supply. There was no effective way to control the locust population, although many methods were tried, and from time to time the fields of different parts of Castile were ravaged by these voracious insects (Huetz 1967: 617–19; Bennassar 1967: 49–50; Fernández Duro 1882–3: II, 267). Locust populations increased and decreased, depending upon the life cycle of the insect, but the huge migratory swarms that caused the greatest damage were triggered by unusually hot weather. Hence, drought was often followed by an invasion of locusts. There were such plagues in Andalucía in 1508–9, in Old Castile in 1541, and throughout Spain in 1542–3. Andalucía suffered from locusts again in 1547, and the insects struck New Castile in 1549. Many parts of Old Castile reported locust plagues in 1556, and again in 1573–4. Extremadura was devastated in 1579–80, and also in 1585–6, along with Andalucía and La Mancha. And in 1593–4 Old Castile was hit by locusts once more.[12] It should not be thought that locusts were the only insect pests to attack Castilian crops. A number of others, such as aphids and various worms, were always present; but their effect was never as dramatic as that of the locusts.

It is tempting to blame the proverbial Castilian rural poverty on the extreme variability of the climate, and on the other natural causes that we have just mentioned. No one can deny that these factors were responsible for great fluctuations in production, and that this had a serious effect on the life of the Castilian peasant. But we must agree with Domínguez Ortiz (1973b: 156–64) that it is futile to look here for the real root of the agrarian problem. The real problem of Castilian agriculture was not meteorological or entomological, but rather political and social – that is, human. In other words, the environment was not at fault. The poverty that characterized the system was the product, rather, of man-made institutions that were inefficient, and that did not permit the proper utilization of existing resources.

The most prevalent system of crop rotation in sixteenth-century Castile was the biennial *año y vez*, in which half the land was planted, and the other half left fallow every year. Why did Castilian peasants cling to this inefficient rotational system centuries after their northern European neighbors had adopted the far superior three-field system? The answer lies partly in the difficulty of changing existing institutions. As indicated in the previous chapter, there were peculiar historical circumstances that made it easier for northern Europeans to effect a revolutionary change in their rotational system. Furthermore, the climate in Spain is considerably drier and hotter than in northern Europe, and the durability of the biennial system in Castile seems to be linked to this climatic difference. In theory, the biennial fallow was necessary for the soil to absorb rainfall for the next crop, and to recuperate its fertility. But to give their animals the maximum benefit from stubble grazing, Castilian peasants postponed plowing their stubble until March of the post-harvest year (this was discussed under the *derrota de mieses* in chapter 1). This delay reduced to a bare minimum the time needed for soil regeneration and moisture retention before the next planting, thus largely vitiating the benefits of the fallow year, at least as far as arable agriculture was concerned.

It seems that the primary advantage of the biennial system was that it nurtured the pastoral sector, which was of paramount importance in medieval Spain. But the system was retained, probably out of inertia, long after livestock had declined to secondary importance in most parts of the country. *Año y vez* rotation reflected the Castilian preference for extensive, rather than intensive, agriculture. Some fields, mainly small irrigated plots, were planted year after year, but these represented only a tiny proportion of the total arable area. Far more prevalent than annual cropping was triennial rota-

tion (*de tercer a tercer año*), in which the land was planted only once in
three years. This was the system customarily used on second-class
lands. For third-class lands – with shallow hillside soils, or soils that
had become exhausted – there were even longer fallow periods, some
of eight to ten years, or even more.[13]

The extensive agriculture practiced by most Castilian peasants
produced relatively low yields. The staple crop was grain, and the
most commonly planted grains were wheat, rye, barley, and oats.
The proportion devoted to each varied from place to place, but
wheat was everywhere the major crop. Table 1 shows that normally
two-thirds of the grain produced was wheat. Barley and oats were
fairly drought-resistant crops that might have been more widely
planted, but they were disparaged for human consumption, and were
used principally as animal feed. Although table 1 does not show such
a progression, the proportion of barley and oats planted must have
increased during the sixteenth century, along with the increase in
the use of mules.

Table 1. *Proportion of different cereals produced*

Place	Period	% Wheat	% Barley	% Rye	% Oats
Córdoba province	1502–11	67	N.D.	33	N.D.
Mojados (Valladolid)	1558–63	39	37	23	1
Western Andalucía	1563–1600	67	N.D.	33	N.D.
New Castile	1575–8	67	33	N.D.	N.D.
Castañar de Ibor (Cáceres)	1579–84	90	5*	5*	N.D.
La Bureba district (Burgos)	1579–95	63	32	4	1
Segovia province	1587	61.5	19.5	15.4	3.3
Wamba (Valladolid)	1590–1	66	28	4	1
El Campo (Cáceres)	1590–5	67	18	15	N.D.
Pineda de Gigüela (Cuenca)	1591	64	36	N.D.	N.D.

Note. The data above are from Yun, *Crisis de subsistencias*, p. 64; Bennassar, *Valladolid*,
pp. 308–9; Pierre Ponsot, 'En Andalousie occidentale: les fluctuations de la production
du blé sous l'Ancien Régime', *Etudes rurales*, no. 34 (1969), p. 101; Silva, *Desarrollo
económico*, p. 36; Averiguación de Castañar (1579–84), AGS, EH, 74-11-iii; Brumont, *La
Bureba*, p. 72; García Sanz, *Desarrollo*, p. 108; Averiguación de El Campo (1590–5)
AGS, EH, 189-73; Averiguación de Pineda (Huete) (1597), AGS, EH, 142-14.

* Lumped together in my source. I arbitrarily assigned half to each.

Yields for these grains varied, of course, from year to year, and
from field to field. Table 2 shows samples of typical grain yields in
various places in Castile. The table indicates that the normal yield
for wheat was about 5 *fanegas* for each *fanega* sown. But this does

Table 2. *Sample grain yields*

Place	Period	Unspecified grain	Wheat	Barley	Rye
La Bureba (Burgos)	1579–84	5½–1	5½–1	5½–1	N.D.
New Castile	1575–8	8–1	N.D.	N.D.	N.D.
Cigales (Valladolid)	1549	N.D.	5–1	6½–1	8–1
Jerez de la Frontera (Cádiz)	1590–5	N.D.	5–1	N.D.	N.D.
Hoyales (Burgos)	c. 1580	N.D.	5–1	4–1	6–1
Cuevas de Provanco (Segovia)	c. 1580	N.D.	3.75–1	3–1	2.25–1
Ponseca? (Salamanca)	c. 1573	6–1	N.D.	N.D.	N.D.
New Castile	c. 1563	5½–1	N.D.	N.D.	N.D.
Montilla (Córdoba)	1595–6	N.D.	4.75–1	N.D.	6–1
Eastern Toledo province	c. 1561	7½–1	N.D.	N.D.	N.D.
Western Rioja (Logroño)	1557–1603	N.D.	5.7–1	7.1–1	N.D.

Note. Most of the above are averages, representing several harvests or several types of land. The data are from Brumont, *La Bureba*, pp. 29–56; Salomon, *La campagne*, p. 243; Bennassar, *Valladolid*, p. 240; F. Javier Vela Santamaría and Alberto Marcos Martín, 'Las grandes ciudades campesinas de Andalucía occidental en el siglo XVI: el caso de Jerez de la Frontera', *Actas del I Congreso de Historia de Andalucía (1976)*, (Córdoba: Monte de Piedad y Caja de Ahorros, 1978), 403–17; García Sanz, *Desarrollo*, p. 159; Relación de Domingo Hernández (Ponseca, c. 1573), AGS, CG, 361; *Don Alonso de Córdoba v. Doña María Berrio, de Montilla* (1604–17), ACHGR, 3-639-1; Relación de averiguaciones sobre las tierras realengas (no date, but apparently from 1563), AGS, DC, 47, folio 19; Francis Brumont, 'La rerte de la terre en Rioja occidentale à l'époque moderne', *Mélanges de la Casa de Velázquez*, 16 (1980), 243. I have been unable to locate Ponseca on a map, and I suspect that its name has changed.

not tell the whole story, because not all years were normal. In practice, as I have already indicated, yields fluctuated greatly. For example, table 2 shows the wheat yield in Jerez de la Frontera to be 5 to 1, but the actual year-to-year yields (Vela and Marcos 1978: 416) for the period of reference were:

1590 5.83–1 (somewhat above average)
1591 2.25–1 (a very bad year)
1592 6.33–1 (considerably above average)
1593 4.5–1 (somewhat below average)
1594 6.4–1 (a rather good year)
1595 5.5–1 (about average).

This was for grain harvested from essentially the same lands – subject, to be sure, to the prevailing rotational system. Year in and year out it included both good lands and poor lands. Marginal lands were expected to yield no more than half as much as first-class lands. In Cuevas de Provanco (García Sanz 1977: 159) it was exactly half: wheat was expected to yield 5 to 1 on good land, and only 2½ to 1 on inferior soils; the ratios for barley and for rye were the same. The reader should be apprised that the rye yields reported for Cuevas de Provanco were highly unusual, because rye normally outyielded wheat by a comfortable margin. I should also like the reader to know that the best quality lands normally produced yields far in excess of those listed in table 2. To reach the higher averages listed in table 2 it was necessary for the best lands to have yields of 10 or 12 to 1, and even higher, in exceptionally bountiful years.

The sixteenth-century Castilian grain yields are certainly low compared with yields in the industrialized wheat-producing countries of the twentieth century, where yields regularly reach 30 or 40 to 1 (Quisenberry 1967: 6–9, 144–51). In view of this, it is tempting to bemoan the low Castilian productivity, as many writers have done. But actually, as Frédéric Mauro has correctly observed (1969: 13), the Castilian yields are quite respectable when compared with yields in other countries with similar natural conditions and in a similar stage of development. Later, they would be greatly increased through the adoption of modern methods of plowing, fertilizing, rotation, seed selection, and sowing. But in sixteenth-century Castile the economic incentives were not sufficient to stimulate grain producers to make such improvements.

There is considerable evidence that yields were declining in sixteenth-century Castile, at least in the last decades of the century. Michael Weisser found this to be true in the Montes de Toledo (1976: 64–5), as did Francis Brumont for the La Bureba villages of Burgos province (1977: 72–3), and Angel García Sanz for the province of Segovia (1977: 94). There are several reasons for the declining yields. In the first place, the extension of cultivation that characterized most of the sixteenth century involved putting marginal lands to the plow. Many of these were hillside soils, or rocky soils that were poorly suited for cereals, but this fact may not have been readily apparent at the time. Initial yields on these newly plowed lands might have been quite acceptable, but their fertility was soon exhausted, through a depletion of soil nutrients and through erosion. The unecological plowing of shallow hillside soils often caused permanent damage. Stripped of its natural vegetation, the bare soil was completely exposed to the elements; and in some cases agricultural tillage increased the harmful effects of this. Research has indicated (Delano 1979: 295) that the porosity of a clay soil may be reduced by as much as 18 percent after the first forty years of cultivation, because of the diminishing content of nitrogen and organic matter. That would lead to increased run-off of rainfall, and to an intensified erosion. After a few years of cultivation, some of the worst of the affected lands had to be abandoned for grain, but many of them continued to be cultivated, despite meager yields, because their production was necessary for the subsistence of the cultivators.

Many good-quality lands also suffered from diminishing productivity, as a result of improper agricultural techniques. Deeper plowing would have brought higher yields, but Castile, like the entire Mediterranean area, still used the old Roman plow, which did superficial work. In fact, it seems that the quality of plowing deteriorated as a consequence of the sixteenth-century conversion from oxen to mules. The conversion was made in the interest of extensive agriculture, for at the time it seemed advantageous to plow more land – although shallower, using mules – rather than to plow less land using the plodding, although deeper-plowing traditional oxen.

If more fertilizer had been used, productivity could have been increased, but organic fertilizer was the only type available, and there simply was not enough of it. During the sixteenth century the Castilian pastoral sector declined in importance, while the arable area expanded. As a result, there was a steadily decreasing amount of manure available per unit of cultivated land. Sixteenth-century agriculturalists knew the value of manure, but there was little they could do to alter the existing situation, because additional pastureland for more animals could only be obtained at the expense of arable, and all the arable land was needed to feed the existing human population. The *arbitrista* Caxa de Leruela noted (1631: 107–8) that many peasants had tried to remedy the shortfall in fertilizer by plowing freshly-burned *montes*, where the ashes served as a substitute (albeit of inferior quality, and of limited benefit) for animal manure. This, of course, aggravated the perennial problems of deforestation, soil erosion, and a shortage of pastures.

PEASANT INDEBTEDNESS

The peasant who gathered a poor harvest as the result of unfavorable weather, insect damage, or other adverse conditions was faced with a cruel dilemma. Should he save the normal percentage of the harvest to use as planting seed the following year? If so, the reduced planting acreage would guarantee another short crop the following year. Should he eat up his planting seed, and borrow money to buy more, at high prices, when needed at sowing time? Or should he save enough planting seed for a normal planted area, and borrow money to buy food for himself and his family? Notice that almost whatever the peasant decided to do, he was likely to fall into debt.

Peasant indebtedness was an increasing problem during the sixteenth century. According to Noël Salomon (1964: 245–8) this was true because of the clash between the traditional economy, which was largely self-sufficient, and the new and expanding economy of merchants and financiers, which was founded upon the movement of goods, the money economy, credit, borrowing, mortgages, and speculation. Money, the circulation of which was intensified during the century, became a factor in subjugating the peasantry. In Salomon's view, the commercial and financial contracts of an emerging capitalism became the tools for exploiting the peasants. This view is colored by ideology, to be sure, but there is much truth to it. We know that the Cortes, the *arbitristas*, and the clergy from the pulpit deplored the increasing peasant indebtedness. The Cortes of Madrid (1592–8) declared that the peasants were so burdened with debts that they were unable to make their payments (*Actas*: XIII, 136). Sancho de Moncada (with reckless exaggeration, we must admit) wrote (cited Salomon 1965: 203) 'the countryside is deserted, the *labradores* having fled their poverty, overburdened with debts and foreclosures'. And Fernández Navarrete (1626: 270) compared the peasants' debts to a voracious insect, which devoured everything the *labradores* could produce. These observers were not chasing a chimera: peasant indebtedness was indeed a problem, and it intensified as the century wore on. And it is unquestionably true (Salomon was right) that many clever merchants and financiers were able to exploit the situation to their advantage.

The *arbitristas* and other critics railed constantly about the *censo* as the source of the peasants' woe. The *censo*, which was the principal instrument for agricultural credit in early modern Castile, was a contract involving an annual payment. A considerable amount of confusion has arisen about *censos*, because many writers have assumed that all *censos* were similar transactions, whereas there were really two distinct types. The first of these was the commercial loan or mortgage, called the *censo perpetuo* or the *censo al quitar*. The former was a debt conversion. It had a principal that could not be paid off (it was perpetual, as the name suggests), or that was for the term of several lifetimes. This type of contract seems to have originated in the mid-1300s when creditors discovered that they could convert uncollectable short-term accounts receivable into long-term fixed annual payments. This expedient allowed them to salvage their lost capital on a long-term basis. By the mid-1530s the *censo perpetuo* seems to have been largely superseded by the *censo al quitar*, so-called because the principal was redeemable. The *censo al quitar* was similar to the modern mortgage (Phillips 1979: 61–2). The jurist Tomás de Mercado described it (cited Salomon 1964: 245–7) as follows in his *Suma de tratos y contratos de mercaderes* (first published Salamanca, 1569): 'Its nature and substance consist in giving a person a sum of money on the security of some buildings, or lands, or other possessions, in exchange for a certain annual payment, usually in money, but sometimes in wine, wheat, kermes, or other products.' The mortgage *censo*, then, was a legal instrument through which the owner of real property received a sum of money in exchange for an obligation to pay the lender a stipulated annual income. In case of non-payment, the lender had legal recourse to recover his capital by seizing the property encumbered by the mortgage contract. In an age when there were no public banks, these private contracts played an important role in financing agricultural and industrial expansion, and in providing ready cash in times of emergency. Bartolomé Bennassar (1967: 258–61) found a significant rise in peasant borrowing through *censos al quitar* in the province of Valladolid in the mid-1500s. This increased peasant indebtedness probably reflects in some measure the taking of loans to finance agricultural expansion, by peasants who had discovered a new instrument of credit. But in some cases, it probably signifies the arrival of hard times: after bad harvests such as those of 1574–6 peasants needed to borrow not to expand, but just to eat. In 1534 the royal government imposed a legal maximum of 14,000 *al millar* (that is, 7.14 percent) for *censos al quitar*. But there is evidence that this legal maximum, like the *tasa* for grain, was often exceeded. The Cortes complained in 1538 (*Cortes*: v, 132–3) that many lenders were able to effectively double their interest earnings by requiring payment not in money, but rather in honey, soap, wine, and other products, because in an inflationary age rising commodity prices favored the creditor, in such cases.[14]

The other type of *censo* is the *censo enfitéutico* (described in chapter 4), which functioned as a quitrent, or simple agricultural lease. The confusion between the mortgage *censos* discussed above and the lease *censos* lies in the fact that both contracts featured an annual payment based upon a 'principal'. But whereas in the first case this refers to the borrowed sum, in the second it refers to the appraised value of land on which rent is being paid (Nader 1977). The confusion is understandable, particularly since lease contracts were sometimes called *censos perpetuos enfitéuticos*. But since these had to do with an annual rental, rather than an annual debt service, I will consider them later, along with other rental agreements.

Another type of peasant indebtedness came as the result of credit purchases. In 1548 the Cortes noted (*Cortes*: v, 457) that *labradores* regularly made such purchases. Carla Phillips (1979: 60–1) has found that in the province of Ciudad Real the great majority of simple credit sales involved animals and animal products. Draft animals appeared most often in these transactions, and payment was usually delayed several years to enable the buyer to make a profit with his new animals. The use of credit to finance the tools of production must have benefitted many a peasant. Therefore, we should not necessarily deplore this type of agricultural indebtedness. A more insidious type of credit, however, was the *mohatra*, which was extended by merchants (principally selling fine fabrics, tapestries, and lace) who peddled their wares in the villages of Castile in the sixteenth century. To speed up sales, the merchants began the practice of selling on credit, against the buyer's coming crop. The merchant's prices were often exorbitant, but many peasants were beguiled by the dazzling merchandise, by a skillful sales pitch, and by the apparent ease of the credit purchase. Unfortunately, all too often the peasant's crop was insufficient to pay the amount borrowed on top of rent, taxes, the tithe, and other inescapable obligations. The debt was then extended to the next year's crop, and from year to year it would snowball, in the worst cases transforming the peasant into an economic prisoner of the merchant (Salomon 1964: 249–50; Weisser 1971: 228). And what was worse, many of these merchants used their share of the crop to speculate, collecting grain when it was cheap, and selling it months later, when prices were high (*Actas*: XIII, 136–7; XX, 413–20; XXI, 317–18).

Peasant indebtedness was not ipso facto bad. Prudently used, credit could improve one's standard of living, and could hasten the accumulation of wealth. But there always existed the danger that bad harvests, which arrived with perverse frequency, would make it impossible for the peasant to pay his debts. The consequence could be the loss of his property (and the means of his livelihood) through foreclosure, and even imprisonment. And this was no mere theoretical possibility: it happened often, throughout the sixteenth century, whenever there were harvest failures. For example, Bartolomé Yun Casalilla has described (1980: 127–8) how a prolonged drought affected Córdoba during the first decade of the century. The harvest of 1507 was a disaster: the peasants of some places reported that they did not even recover their seed. The municipal government ordered the encarceration of all those who failed to pay the public granary for the seed-grain they had borrowed, and many were jailed. Others fled to avoid debt imprisonment, leaving their property (if they had not already lost it, which was often the case) to the mercy of their more powerful neighbors. And the Cortes in 1538 observed that many *labradores* lost the work oxen and mules they had purchased on credit, because they were unable to make their payments. Compassion for the suffering peasant caused the royal government to prohibit the seizure of draft animals, except for money owed to the landowner, the lord, or the crown (!), when there was no other property to attach. The Cortes also noted as early as 1548, when Castile was still supposed to be in the flush of prosperity, that indebtedness was already causing peasants to lose their houses, vineyards, lands, and other property (*Cortes*: v, 126, 457). But this was probably unusual at that time. Virtually all scholars agree that until the late 1500s most debtors in Castile experienced little difficulty paying the interest they owed, or even redeeming their *censos*, because of the agricultural boom. This is Viñas y Mey's hypothesis, enunciated in 1941, and seldom challenged, yet never really proven (pp. 32–53). Viñas y Mey believed that small- and medium-sized peasant agriculturalists relied on the extensive use of the *censo al quitar* to finance expansion during the growth period of the economy. As long as the boom continued, they could easily meet their obligations, but when the boom collapsed, they could no longer make their payments, and were ruined.

The durability of the Viñas y Mey hypothesis is remarkable, given the absence of hard documentary evidence to support it. It is a logical hypothesis, and it is in harmony with what we know about the economy in general. Helen Nader recently tested it (1981), using notorial records from villages in the province of Guadalajara, but she found neither the heavy indebtedness nor the mortgage foreclosures that are essential to the Viñas y Mey model. Nor was Bartolomé

Bennassar (1967: 261–5) able to find such proof for the province of Valladolid. But as Nader observed, that does not disprove the Viñas y Mey hypothesis, it simply fails to support it. The documentary proof may turn up elsewhere. Or it may not! It is hard for us to believe, given what we know about agrarian finance today, but in an age when there was still free (or almost free) land available, and when human and animal muscle comprised the major source of power, it may have been possible for the typical agriculturalist to function quite well, and even to expand, with a minimum of indebtedness. Before we can make an accurate judgement about this we will have to learn far more about the economics of rural production in sixteenth-century Castile. We do know that many peasants were in debt, and there is good evidence that some were deeply, or even hopelessly in debt. What we do not know, unfortunately, is how prevalent this was, and what the consequences were. The evidence studied by Nader and Bennassar suggests that creditors were reluctant to foreclose on mortgages, and that even when they tried to do so, it was exceedingly difficult to evict delinquent debtors from their lands. But it is hard for us to believe that this was generally true, because the *arbitristas* unanimously declared the contrary, and so did the Cortes. It is highly improbable that the contemporary observers were all so badly mistaken.

In the early 1600s a councilman from the city of Zamora (cited Fernández Duro 1882–3: II, 553–4) declared that many of the *labradores* of the area had formerly been quite prosperous, but they had fallen into debt, and had lost all their property through foreclosures. And what we know about the identity of moneylenders (Phillips 1979: 62) suggests that seizures of property must not have been rare. Some creditors, to be sure, were the confraternities mentioned by Nader, or other religious corporations such as churches, monasteries, and hospitals. These might well have adopted a compassionate policy toward delinquent debtors. But we know that other mortgage holders were wealthy townspeople: professionals, bureaucrats, and nobles who could not be expected to show much reluctance to foreclose on delinquent debtors. And the fact that these were the very individuals who tended to control the local government would have aided them in the execution of the law. In my opinion, the Cortes memorial of 1598, which denounced the *censos al quitar* for having destroyed the poor *labrador* and increased the wealth and power of the rich, has the ring of truth to it (*Actas*: xv, 752).

In chapter 6 I described the sale of *tierras baldías*, which resulted in a massive transfer of funds from the Castilian peasantry to the crown. Nearly all the sales were credit transactions, the terms of which varied greatly, but normally involved a down payment of around 10 percent, and three or four annual installments. Each buyer was required to sign a note for the amount he owed, and to mortgage to the crown *all* his property (not just the *baldíos* being purchased) to guarantee payment in full. In many villages nearly every *vecino* went into debt in this fashion, to buy land from the crown. And it was normal for the town council also to make a credit purchase of at least a portion of the local *baldíos*, the debt for which, of course, was ultimately borne by the inhabitants of the town. The amount of indebtedness of the typical *baldío*-buying peasant was not great in absolute terms – normally falling in the 1,000–20,000 mrs range (Vassberg 1975). By comparison, Bennassar (1967: 261–3) found the private peasant debts in the province of Valladolid to be usually in the 7,000–42,000 mrs range. As long as harvests were good, the *baldío* buyers normally could make their payments to the crown with little difficulty. But when bad harvests struck, combined with rising taxes and other unfavorable conditions, even these small payments could represent an unsupportable burden. Nevertheless, they had to be paid: the crown was willing to grant special disaster postponements to the inhabitants of localities suffering from crop failure or other unusual circumstances, but eventually the payments had to be made. Otherwise, the crown would dispatch collectors to auction off enough property to insure that the debt was liquidated. The land for which the money was owed was the first item sold, but if receipts did not suffice, other property of delinquent *baldío* debtors would also be seized and sold. In one case, the sale of the property of the principal debtor failed to raise enough money, so a slave, a bed, a mattress, and other household goods belonging to a co-signatory of the note were also seized and sold (Vassberg 1983: ch. 4).

Another type of peasant indebtedness to the crown came as a result of the sale of lands of the military orders (mentioned in chapter 4). In the province of Jaén, for example, the *tierras renteñas* (rental lands) of the Order of Calatrava were sold in 1577–80 to individuals and municipalities through *censos al quitar* providing for annual payments for an indefinite period, so long as the principal was unredeemed. A report made by the *corregidor* of the area around the end of the century named these payments as the cause of economic difficulties for the local peasants.[15]

RENTAL COSTS

I have mentioned earlier (in chapter 5) that historians have tended to favor peasant landownership over peasant tenancy. This preference may not always be justified by the facts, but it is undeniable that rent often absorbed a large share of the peasant's harvest. The subject of rental costs merits our careful attention.

In chapter 5 I stressed the great local variations in landholding patterns, but I estimated that around one-fifth of the arable land of sixteenth-century Castile was owned by peasants. The other four-fifths was owned by the municipalities, the crown, the nobility, the church, and other non-peasant entities. Some of this land – the *baldíos*, for example, and the municipal common lands – could be exploited by the peasant without having to pay rent, but the owners of most of this land demanded some sort of payment in exchange for the right of use. Most peasants must have welcomed the opportunity to rent other lands, in addition to their own small plots. Renting may have had some social disadvantages, but these were almost always outweighed by the economic advantages of increased production (else the peasants would have declined to rent). Even if the cost of renting was high, the additional lands were probably indispensable for subsistence, or for growing surplus crops that could be converted into cash to purchase those things that they could not produce themselves. Therefore, we should not be surprised that peasants, such as the villagers of Tarazona de la Mancha (Cuenca) mentioned in the *Relaciones*, were willing to travel considerable distances – even outside the *término* of their village – to find lands to rent (Silva 1967: 31 n. 17).

Fortunate was the peasant who held lands under a *censo enfitéutico* (rent *censo*), which I described in chapter 4. The annual rental in these agreements was specified in the contract, and could not legally be changed by the landlord.[16] Originally payable in kind, by the early modern period most *censo enfitéutico* payments had been commuted partly or wholly to coin. This gave leaseholders an economic advantage during the sixteenth-century price inflation, which had the effect of dramatically shrinking real rental rates. The contracts gave leaseholders the right to transfer land use to a third party. Consequently, the lands held by peasants in this way tended to remain in the family, being passed from father to son. In the 1400s and early 1500s landowners had liked the *censo enfitéutico* because it gave them a more reliable source of income than working the land themselves. But their attitude changed after the effects of inflation became clear, and in the mid-1500s landowners preferred limited contracts, for example with terms of eight or ten years. It should be obvious that peasants with leaseholds under *censo enfitéutico* contracts, especially those antedating the sixteenth century, were much better off economically than those with other rental agreements. Conversely, of course, the landowners were better off with short-term leases, the terms of which could be periodically adjusted (Salomon 1964: 238–9).

As landowners developed a greater concern for profits, sharecropping (*aparcería*, or partnership) contracts were developed, in which the produce of the land was divided between tenant and landowner. Sharecropping was nothing new – it is one of the oldest forms of tenant farming, and has been by far the most common tenant contract over the centuries in the Mediterranean area (Delano 1979: 78–9). The form it took varied from place to place, and from landlord to landlord. The rental agreement often took into account local physical conditions, and when new land was being broken, the contract might provide for relatively light rental payments during the first five or six years, to compensate the cultivator for the troublesome work of clearing and preparing virgin soil. In Moslem Spain rent payments had been as little as one-tenth of the total crop. These liberal terms were continued in some Christian kingdoms, but when rents were that low, the landlord normally expected other forms of income or service, in addition to the rent. In the eleventh century, the Monastery of Sahagún (León) contracted sharecropping leases with rents varying from one-fifth to one-third of the produce. A little later, in New Castile, the prevalent type of sharecropping was the *quintero* lease, where one-fifth of the crop went to the landowner. In the early modern period, throughout the Mediterranean world a fifth of the harvest seems to have been the norm. In Castile, the Cortes of Madrigal in 1438 spoke of rental rates of up to 30 percent of the harvest, but in the sixteenth century sharecropping rents often rose even higher than that. One-third was quite common, and the landlord's share in many places was as high as one-half of the harvest (Salomon 1964: 238–9). We can be sure that peasants would not be willing to pay half of their crop unless the lands in question were of exceptional quality, or unless there were no other lands available, and they needed the additional harvest for survival.[17]

From the peasant's viewpoint, the great advantage of the sharecropping lease was that the proportion of the harvest paid to the landlord remained constant in good years and bad. That meant that the landlord would get a high rent when there was a bumper crop, but when there was a crop failure he would suffer a diminished income along with the peasant. Because of the climatic and other conditions that I have already mentioned, there were dramatic fluctuations in crop yields. The undependability of rental income from sharecropping leases led many landowners to insist upon leases with fixed annual payments. The terms of these leases varied greatly, in all respects. Some were one-year leases, and there were contracts for periods of ten years or more, but rental agreements for three, four, five, or six years seem to have been the norm. Francis Brumont (1980: 241–2) found that the duration of leases in the western Rioja (Logroño) increased in the second half of the sixteenth century, and this may well have been true of the rest of Castile. Payment was sometimes in cash, more often in kind (usually grain, but often including chickens, wine, animals, cheese, straw, or other things), and sometimes a combination of kind and coin. Some leases specified the payment of a certain amount per unit area (usually the *fanega*), which required measuring the size of the field. Other leases simply established a price for the use of a block of land of undisclosed size, but whose limits were surely known to both lessor and lessee.

Consider, for example, the rental contract executed on 2 February 1552 in Jerez de la Frontera (Cádiz) between landowner Nuño de Avila and renters Diego de Medina and Francisco Martín Barbado – all *vecinos* of Jerez. The lease included a detailed description of the boundaries of the piece of land involved, and it stated that it measured 4 *caballerías* and 10½ *aranzadas* in area. The lease was to run for a period of six years, beginning in the middle of October of 1553. The annual rental was 28 *cahizes* (a *cahiz* was equivalent to about 12 *fanegas*) of wheat, 1 *cahiz* of barley, and 4 cartloads of wheat straw to be delivered to the landlord's residence, or to some other location designated by him, on the day of Santiago (25 July). The contract contained a clause to protect the renter in the event of a poor harvest. In many regions such clauses were normal in fixed-payment leases, but there were many different formulas designed to allow for bad years. In the case at hand, when there was a lean year (*esterilidad*) the renter was required to notify the landlord by 1 May, and after it had been agreed that the crop would indeed be poor, the lessor and lessee were to share equally both the costs and the fruits of the harvest for that year. As one can well imagine, there were many suits between renters and landlords over the question of reduced rents in famine years. Finally, in the Jerez contract, the renter was obliged to allow his successor free access to the land to plow one-third of it between 1 January and 1 May of the final year of the lease, in preparation for fall planting, following the local custom among *labradores*. Although this particular lease did not, many contracts contained clauses requiring the renter to observe other local rotational and fallowing practices.[18]

The amount of rent in fixed-payment leases varied greatly, depending on the quality of the land, and other factors. In the La Bureba villages of Burgos province, the normal rental was 1 *fanega* of grain (half wheat and half barley) per *fanega* of land rented. But rents in the area ranged from a low of $\frac{3}{4}$ *fanega* to a high of $2\frac{1}{2}$ *fanegas* per *fanega* of land. In fixed-payment leases, the crop yield determined the proportionate share of the landowner: when yields were high, his share would be low; and when yields were low, his share would be high in relationship to the share of the renter. Brumont has calculated (1977: 28, 37–41) that rental payments in La Bureba represented at least a third of the harvest, and sometimes as much as a half. But this was in a high-rent area: the Castilian norm seems to have been between a fifth and a quarter. In a hypothetical case where the annual rent payment was 2 *fanegas* per *fanega* of land, and where only half the land was planted (in the prevalent *año y vez* system), at a yield of 6 to 1 the peasant would have the following fixed costs:

Rent	33% of the crop
Seed	16% of the crop
Tithe	10% of the crop
TOTAL	59% of the crop

leaving the peasant with 41 percent of his harvest. But under the same rental conditions, if the yield fell to 4 to 1, the picture becomes quite different:

Rent	50% of the crop
Seed	25% of the crop
Tithe	10% of the crop
TOTAL	85% of the crop

leaving the peasant a mere 15 percent of his harvest. Toward the end of the sixteenth century, as average yields declined, for reasons already discussed, the peasant found himself with a shrinking share of his own annual production.

Rental terms were reached through mutual agreement between landlord and tenant, following established local customs regarding payment. In some places it was the practice for landowners to put their property up for rent to the highest bidder – a procedure that was disliked by renters because it tended to drive prices up.[19]

I have been describing rentals of grainland, but the same general principles applied also to rentals of land for other crops. Rent could be either in cash, or in a share of the harvest, or both. In the villages of Guadalajara, the normal rent on grain, olive, and vine lands was equal to 20 percent of the harvest (Nader 1981), whereas in north-western Castile vineyard owners seem to have received a quarter rent (Huetz 1967: 589). In La Bureba, by contrast, rent for vineyards was as high as half of the crop (Brumont 1977: 37).

Land for pasture was rented in many different ways. Some pasture leases were for short terms of only a few weeks or months. These short-term rentals were primarily for the convenience of owners of migratory animals. For the same reason, in many places summer and winter pasture rights (*el agostadero* and *el invernadero*) were rented separately. But there were also long-term pasture leases for periods of six or seven years. The price of pasture was calculated sometimes according to the resources of the piece of land involved. But this method of reckoning rents could encourage overgrazing, and to avoid that danger many leases assessed the rental payment on a per animal basis. Nevertheless, a prudent landowner would not allow an excessively large number of animals to use his pastures, for fear that they would cause lasting damage to the vegetation. Grazing rental rates varied according to place, season, quality of pasture, and the animals involved. Around Ciudad Rodrigo (Salamanca) the annual pasture fee (for stubble and fallow grazing on land in a triennial rotational schedule) was about 10 *reales* per head of larger animals (cattle and equines) in the late 1560s and early 1570s. By contrast, in the mid-1500s the Order of Santiago had rented its pastures in the Campo de Montiel area (Ciudad Real) to owners of migratory flocks, on a seasonal basis, for only 8 mrs per head, but this rate seems to have been considerably below the market price, because of the influence of powerful stockowners.[20]

Animal owners who could not find enough pasture using a combination of common lands and their own property would be obliged to rent additional grazing grounds. Members of the Mesta regularly had to do this for their migratory flocks and herds, as did many owners of large sedentary flocks. The typical Castilian peasant, however, did not own many animals, and normally was able to graze his beasts without having to resort to the expedient of renting. But in some places there was a shortage of pasturage, and something needed to be done. I have mentioned earlier (chapter 2) that the towns tried to provide adequate common pastures for their *vecinos*, even to the extent of renting pastures for common use. But that was not always feasible, and some modest peasant stockowners were obliged to lease grazing lands for their animals. I do not know how widespread this was, but I have seen evidence that some peasants formed partnerships to rent the pastures they needed. Martín Galindo (1961: 190–1) has described another form of pasture rental that was practiced in the Valdeburón district of the province of León: a peasant who owned too many animals for his own pastures could rent additional grazing land using an adaptation of the *aparcería* system, which in this situation allowed him to use another land-owner's pasture in exchange for half of the young born during the period of agreement. This custom not only provided supplementary grazing land for some individuals, it allowed others who had lost their herds to rebuild them by renting out their pastures in that way. The Mesta, at the height of its power, persuaded Ferdinand and Isabella to forbid the regrating of pasture rentals,[21] and the prohibition was repeated by Charles V (*Actas*: 1, 359), but I have seen no evidence that profiteering by subletting pasture rentals was a major problem.

We could also consider the *pegujalero* agreements of the province of Segovia to be a type of rental contract. According to the 1514 ordinances of Segovia and its Tierra, a *pegujalero* (also called a *yuguero*) was a rural wage earner whose employer assigned him a plot of land (*pegujar*, or *pegujal*) at least 2 or 3 *obradas* in size as a part (or all) of his salary. The harvest from four-fifths of the landowner's property would go to the landowner, and the harvest from the other one-fifth (the *pegujar*) would go to the *pegujalero*, as compensation for his labor (García Sanz 1977: 284–5). There are two ways to look at the *pegujalero*: he can be perceived as a mere laborer who gets a bit of land as compensation for his work (perhaps the fact that the landowner also supplied him with a house supports this view); or he can be seen as a peasant who is given the use of a piece of land for himself, in exchange for laboring in the other fields of the landlord. In any case, the *pegujalero* must have lived a miserable existence, for he had to pay the landowner an overwhelming share of the crops he produced. The *senarero* of Avila province was analogous to the *pegujalero* of Segovia: his employer gave him a plot called a *senara* to work as a part of his salary (Salinero 1970: 38–9). In other parts of Castile – in the La Jara district of Toledo, for example – the word *pegujar* was used, but it referred to tiny plots of arable land that were usually owned by the peasants who worked them (Jiménez 1951: 570).

How much of a burden did land rents represent for the typical Castilian peasant? The answer is not a simple one. We know that there were many complaints about high rents, and that peasants usually preferred to work lands – such as the *baldíos* – for which they did not have to pay a portion of the harvest to a landlord.[22] That leads us to believe that rents were high, and in fact we know they were high in many places. Salomon concluded (1964: 243–5) that land rent represented a greater share of the peasant's production than did the tithe, and that at times it was as high as three or four times greater than the tithe. Oppressive indeed! Brumont (1977: 41) is more cautious in his assessment of the weight of rent payments, but asserts that rent was almost always higher than the tithe. And both Brumont and Salomon agree that rent was generally the heaviest burden – compared to the tithe and to various taxes – that the Castilian peasantry had to bear. Should we not conclude, then, that rents were truly oppressive for the Golden Age peasant, and a major source of his misery? Not necessarily. Although it is unquestionably true that many rents were burdensome, we must keep in mind that the typical peasant rented only a portion of the lands he used. The remainder were his own property or were common lands of various types. Therefore, although his rent payments may have represented a burdensome proportion – perhaps half – of the harvest from the lands he was *renting*, he may have been renting, for example, only a quarter of the lands he worked, in which case his rent payments would have comprised a mere 12 percent of his production. The oppressiveness of a given peasant's rental payments, then, depended not only upon the rental rate, but also upon the proportion of his rented to non-rented land, and this varied greatly from person to person and from place to place, even within regions.

We can get some idea of the extreme variability of the weight of rent payments by examining Brumont's figures for the La Bureba villages (1977: table 5). Using data from 1586 and 1597, Brumont calculated that the average percentage of peasant production going into land rents ranged from a low of 2.9 (in Galbarros, 1586) to a high of 49.3 (in Rubiales, 1586), but the average in a majority of the villages fell between 15 and 30 per cent. Unfortunately, I do not have comparable information for many other places in Castile. But the peasants of Castañar de Ibor (Cáceres) reported that they paid only 2.4 percent of their grain harvest as rent in the period 1579–84, and those of Pineda de Gigüela (Cuenca) reported 5.14 percent in 1591.[23] In Belvis (Toledo), however, the figure was 31.58 percent (Jiménez 1952: 661). But all of these figures – including the estimates made by Salomon and Brumont – are misleading, because they are based exclusively on data about cereal production. Wine, fruit, and garden crops were omitted, causing notable distortions in places where those crops were important, because vineyards, fruit orchards, and garden plots tended to be peasant-owned. Furthermore, animals and animal products were not included in the previously cited rent calculations. Therefore, the rent paid by the peasants of these villages, figured as a percentage of *total* agropastoral production, would be considerably lower than those given. In sum, until we know much more about the economics of peasant production, we should be skeptical of claims that high rents impoverished the rural population of Castile.

As far as the landowner was concerned, agricultural property was a good investment in the sixteenth century so long as it was not bound by low-paying perpetual leases. Land did not permit the spectacular returns that were possible in mercantile activities, but it was a safe investment, and one that provided a dependable income over the long haul, despite periodic crop failures (Nader 1977; 1979: 114). According to Bennassar (1967: 322) the value of rent as a percentage of the price of land around Valladolid was normally between 4 and 7 percent during the early 1530s. After that, in the mid-1500s the rising price of grain may have made higher profits possible for investors in rural property. But by the end of the century profits were down again, and in 1611 Valle de la Cerda (cited Viñas 1941: 110) calculated that the most productive lands would show a profit of only 5 percent, while ordinary or second-class lands would bring a return of no more than 4, 3, or 2 percent.

TAXATION

The Castilian peasant not only had to pay rent, seigneurial and ecclesiastical levies, and the charges of financiers and merchants; he was also forced to bear the brunt of the burden of supporting the vast sixteenth-century Habsburg imperial venture. Gold and silver from Mexico and Peru were a windfall for the royal treasury, but the sums derived by the Spanish crown from the Americas comprised a small proportion of its total revenue, rising from about 11 percent in 1554 to some 20 percent in 1598. Most of the remainder was paid, directly or indirectly, by the Castilian peasant, for Castile was a rural society, with agropastoral production the basis of her wealth (Vassberg 1975: 629). Salomon has called the Castilian peasant farmer of the time a 'marvellous beast of burden', because in large part the splendors of the magnificent Golden Age rested upon his labor (1964: 213). And in fact, the sixteenth-century Castilian peasant was a model of productive labor for the ruling classes of the day. The Spaniards tried to get the American Indians to produce as much as Castilian peasants, but the result was utter failure, for reasons both psychological and physical. The crown did not hesitate to exploit the tax-paying ability of the Castilian peasantry. Between 1494 and 1598 total royal revenue increased over ninefold. However, the effects of this massive tax rise were mitigated by the fact that over the same period the population doubled, and there was a fourfold price increase. Furthermore, the agrarian economy was expanding, along with the general economic boom. Consequently, the average nominal and real taxes in Castile actually declined until about 1575. Then the tax burden was drastically increased (Phillips 1979: 78–9). About the same time there was a slowing of economic growth, undoubtedly aggravated, if not caused, by the increase in tax rates. As a result of an unfortunate combination of circumstances, including higher taxes, economic recession, and lower yields, the limits of the endurance of the Castilian peasant were finally surpassed near the end of the reign of Philip II: the peasant could no longer pay what was expected of him, and a long period of rural decadence began.

Taxation provided an institutional means for transferring agricultural surpluses to the privileged classes of society. Since these were largely urban, taxation can also be seen as the shifting of rural surpluses to the cities. It should be emphasized that the peasants received scant compensation, if any, in return for the taxes they paid.

One of the basic taxes throughout Europe under the *ancien régime* was the tithe. In Castile the tithe was not a strictly ecclesiastical tribute. It was divided by the church and the crown; therefore, it was as much a civil as a religious duty. In theory, the tithe was a universal tax on all production. God's rights had no limits – everything belonged to Him. Therefore, the tithe should consist of one-tenth of everything, including grain, wine, fruit, animals and animal products, and even the salaries of hired laborers. No expenses could be deducted – not even planting seed – and the tithe had to be paid in *good* quality products, not the sick or the inferior. In some places the tithe was even charged on grain that had been damaged by animals before harvest, on the grounds that proper supervision could have saved the crop! In practice, however, the tithe was not collected on everything (not even agricultural goods) that was produced.

The tithe was gathered in special warehouses (*cillas*) where the produce was stored. During the sixteenth century it became more and more common for the collection of the tithe to be farmed out to private individuals called *cilleros*, after the warehouses they supervised. These tithe collectors naturally had a personal interest in collecting as much as possible, because they could keep for themselves everything in excess of the quantity fixed in their contract. Understandably, there were many abuses connected with the office of tithe collector, particularly with speculation in grain and other commodities (Salinero 1970: 41; Garzón 1974: 30–45). The tithe was far more oppressive than the various seigneurial duties that still remained in Golden Age Castile. In fact, Salomon has calculated (1964: 224–5) that the tithe represented a burden from ten to twenty times greater than all the feudal levies paid by peasants in New Castile in the 1570s: whereas the maximum annual seigneurial duties amounted to some 50 mrs, the minimum tithe was nearly 500 mrs plus $7\frac{1}{2}$ *fanegas* of grain (the tithe was often converted to coin, rather than collected in kind).

In addition to the tithe, the peasant was obliged to pay certain supplementary charges such as first fruits (*primicias*), which gave the parish priest a welcome addition to his meager share of the tithe. Only about a third of the tithe went to the parish priests, although they constituted the large majority of the secular clergy. Another third went to the upper clergy, and by the sixteenth century the final third had been assigned to the crown. In fact, as early as 1219 Fernando III was able to secure a papal bull giving the royal treasury the right to two-ninths of the tithe, which was to compensate the monarch for his expenses in the Reconquest. From time to time the pontiffs reminded the Castilian monarchs that the concession was supposed to be temporary, but the crown was able to increase its share, and in 1494 Alexander VI confirmed the *tercias reales* (royal third of the tithe). After that, there came to be such a close identification between church and state in Castile that it is sometimes difficult to distinguish the one from the other. To support the war against the infidel Turks and the heretic Protestants, Pius V granted Philip II the *diezmo del escusado*, the amount of the total tithe paid by the third largest producer of each village. And in 1569 Gregory XIII gave Philip the tithes and first fruits called *novales*, which were paid on newly plowed lands. And in 1571 the pope increased the *escusado* to include not just the third producer, but also the first. This privilege was initially conferred for a five-year period, but it was extended, and finally became a regular feature of the intertwining royal–ecclesiastical financial system (Garzón 1974: 99–100; Salomon 1964: 219–24; García Sanz 1977: 311–13).

The royal treasury had a policy of collecting its taxes in coin, rather than in kind. That policy presupposed the existence of regular agricultural surpluses that would be sold in local and regional markets, because the peasant would have to obtain enough money from somewhere, to pay his taxes. The backbone of the Castilian tax system was the *alcabala*, a sales tax that the crown originally collected indirectly through tax farmers. But the excesses of these financiers caused widespread dissatisfaction, and Isabella and Ferdinand began the practice of allowing municipal councils to pay their taxes directly to the royal treasury in a fixed annual lump sum called the *encabezamiento*. Taxpayers found this method vastly preferable to collection by extortionate tax farmers. And in 1536 Charles V established the *encabezamiento* as a permanent, generalized feature of the tax system. The city or town at the head of each district was responsible for raising the amount of the district *encabezamiento* owed to the crown. These district capitals then fixed the proportionate share to be paid by each village under their jurisdiction. There were many inequities connected with this, because the district capitals often overcharged their villages, and the villages frequently complained about this and other abuses. Each town or village (or occasionally groups of federated villages) then had the task of collecting the *alcabala* from its own *vecinos*. The *encabezamiento* usually lumped the *alcabala* together with the *tercias reales*, the crown's share of the tithe. For collecting these royal taxes, every town council had to draw up a list of *vecinos*, specifying which were *pecheros* (taxpayers) and which were not. The clergy were generally exempt from taxes, but not always. And contrary to what many historians have believed, the *hidalgos* did not automatically have tax-exempt status; in many places – in Extremadura, for example – the cream of the local nobility figured on the tax rolls along with their plebeian neighbors. A committee appointed by each town government had the task of apportioning the local tax burden, based on an estimate of each *vecino*'s wealth, or an estimate of wealth and his sales during the year. For that reason, paupers were not taxed. The individual tax assessments in most places were made after subtracting from the local *encabezamiento* the local council's receipts from the sale of franchises to vendors of meat, fish, wine, and other goods. But small villages with no such franchise buyers had to collect the entire amount of their *encabezamiento* through a direct tax on their *vecinos* (Salomon 1964: 228–31; Le Flem 1967: 263–7; Weisser 1976: 46–8).

Theoretically, the *alcabala* was a tax representing 10 percent of the value of all goods sold or exchanged, but in practice it was much less in its early history, because of collusion between buyers and sellers to defraud the royal treasury. And in reality, it seldom exceeded 4 or 5 percent of the sale price (*Diccionario* 1968–9: 100–2). After the *alcabala* no longer reflected the actual volume of sales, but instead was based upon the *encabezamiento*, it declined to as little as 2 or 3 percent, as inflation depreciated the value of the crown's receipts. But during the reign of Philip II the crown was able to increase the amount of the general *alcabala encabezamiento*. In 1562 it went up by 37 percent, and in 1576 by 300 percent – a dramatic tax increase that came precisely at the moment when Castile was beginning to show signs of economic distress (Phillips 1979: 78–9). The consequences of these increases were severe for rural taxpayers. García Sanz has calculated (1977: 328) that the taxpaying villagers of the Tierra de Sepúlveda (Segovia) experienced a 654 percent increase in their direct contributions for *alcabalas* and *tercias* between 1561 and 1584. The magnitude of the tax rise in this example was due to the fact that there were fewer taxpayers, at the same time that the municipal councils were less able to contribute toward the tax burden. The amount of the tax was not large in absolute terms (only 543 mrs per taxpayer in 1584), but it must have constituted a severe hardship to have to pay that much cash when times were bad. 543 mrs does not seem like much, but it represented the price of sufficient wheat to feed a family of four for about two weeks. In some parts of the country the *alcabala* burden was much higher than that. In 1597, for example, the *vecinos* of El Acebrón (Cuenca) had to pay well over 1,000 mrs. Writing the crown in tones of despair, they reported that the village was becoming depopulated, because the inhabitants simply could not bear the excessive taxation.[24] And under the *encabezamiento* system, when some *vecinos* emigrated from a place, those who remained behind were left with a higher tax burden.

The *alcabala*, as administered by the Habsburgs, was certainly an inequitable tax. Michael Weisser has calculated (1976: 63) that the gross *alcabala* per *vecino* (before deducting any contributions made by the councils) in the villages of the Montes de Toledo in 1590 averaged 857 mrs, which is consistent with our other examples from the period; but for specific villages, it ranged from a low of 219 mrs to a high of 1,695 mrs. As the economy deteriorated in the 1590s, the situation in many places became truly calamitous. There were increasing numbers of paupers who could not contribute toward their town's *alcabala* obligations. In Cáceres, for example, pauperism grew from 25.7 percent of the *vecinos* in 1557 to 42 percent in 1595, placing an ever increasing load on the taxpaying population (Le Flem 1967: 264–5). It seems that the same thing was happening all over Castile, and the situation was exacerbated by the epidemics of the 1590s. In 1597 the council of Tortuero (Guadalajara) sent a pathetic appeal to the crown, requesting a return to the traditional 10 percent *alcabala* tax, because the *encabezamiento* was bankrupting the village. The place had lost a third of its population in the past nine years, and most of the remaining *vecinos* were tenants and day laborers who could barely feed their families. As a result, it was impossible for them to meet the amount of their *encabezamiento*, and they were harassed by officials seeking to confiscate their possessions for nonpayment of taxes.[25] Now, we should not think that this scenario existed in every village in Castile, but it was all too common in the 1590s.

Because the royal treasury's income from the *alcabala* declined in real terms, until the drastic increases made by Philip II, the crown was obliged to rely more heavily upon the *servicio*, which was a special subsidy voted by the Cortes. It was originally regarded as a temporary subsidy granted for emergency purposes, but under Charles V it became institutionalized as a regular and essential part of royal revenues. It became known as the *servicio ordinario*, and it became the rule for the Cortes to give it every three years. But Philip II's foreign policy required additional funds, and the Cortes voted a supplementary *servicio extraordinario*, which it regularly extended every three years, just as it did with the 'ordinary' subsidy. The *servicio* was a personal tax levied on commoners (clergy and *hidalgos* were exempted). The municipal councils assessed each of their commoner *vecinos* a share of the local *servicio* obligation, in accordance with the property he owned. The average annual amount of the *servicio ordinario* and *extraordinario* by the 1590s was around 135 mrs per taxpaying *vecino*. But, as always in the Castilian tax structure of the day, there were considerable regional inequities: in the province of León, for example, the average was only 100 mrs, whereas it was 165 in Córdoba. Generally speaking, the weight of these taxes was three or four times higher than seigneurial duties, but from five to ten times lower than the tithe (Elliott 1977: 199–202; Salomon 1964: 231–4).

Despite massive increases in the *alcabala* and in the *servicios* in 1575, these traditional sources of revenue were inadequate for the crown's needs, and it was necessary to supplement them with a new tax. In 1590 the Cortes approved a new subsidy called the *millones*, because it was reckoned in millions of *ducados* rather than in the traditional *maravedís* (a *ducado* was equal to 375 mrs). Despite opposition from both inside and outside the government, the *millones* subsidy was not only extended, but actually increased in 1596, and thereafter it became a regular feature of Castilian taxation. This new royal tax, coming on top of the tithe, *alcabala*, and *servicios*, represented a crushing burden for the Castilian peasant. Whereas the average combined *servicio* burden was some 135 mrs per *vecino* in 1594, the first *millones* tax represented at least an annual 337 mrs per *vecino*. And after 1596 this amount was increased (Salomon 1964: 321–34). From 1590 until 1596 the municipal governments were left free to improvise ways of raising the funds they needed to pay their share of the *millones* grants (Castillo 1961). And during this period the councils of many towns, reluctant to impose new direct taxes on an already overburdened population, resorted to the expedient of exploiting the various types of municipal property available to them. Under a blanket authorization of the crown, they rented common pastures to the highest bidder for plowing, they sold common forests for firewood, and they speculated with the resources of public granaries.[26] This was unfortunate, because it exhausted a significant part of the capital reserves of the agrarian sector. Furthermore, it reduced the opportunities for poor peasants to use common facilities, thus worsening their economic position, while it provided new openings for the rich. And after the town and village councils had drained their community resources, it was necessary, after all, to resort to direct taxation. When the amount of the *millones* was increased in 1596, a special excise tax (*sisa*) was introduced to gather the necessary sums. This was a universal tax levied on the necessities of life, such as meat, wine, oil, and vinegar. In theory it made the *millones* an equitable tax, because it applied to *hidalgos* and to clergy as well as commoners. But in practice it was the poor who suffered the most, because wealthy landowners could supply themselves with most of the dutiable articles from their own estates (García Sanz 1977: 145, 332).

In addition to the above, there were a number of other royal taxes such as the *almojarifazgo* on the American trade, the *servicio y montazgo* on transhumant livestock, and a silk tax, that did not affect all parts of Castile, although they were certainly significant in some regions and for certain sectors of the population. And we could consider the sale of *tierras baldías*, and the sale of *villazgos* as well, as forms of royal taxation that fell heavily upon the peasantry. Even more oppressive, in many respects, was the billeting of troops. The peasantry was forced to bear the brunt of the burden of lodging and feeding His Majesty's troops when they were in Spain. We tend to forget, when describing the exploits of the great Spanish infantry of the day, that the army was a scourge for the peasants of Castile. When the famous Spanish *tercios* were not ravaging the Netherlands or Italy, they were stationed in the Iberian peninsula, where they behaved much like they did when they were abroad. The unfortunate Castilian *pechero* was obliged to furnish room and board for the officers and men who had a billet for his house. Only the privileged – the *hidalgos* and the clergy – could escape this type of servitude (Salomon 1964: 236–8). But even *they* could not always avoid it: in 1572 the Chancillería of Valladolid ruled that the *hidalgos* of Briones (Logroño) were obliged to share in the billeting of troops when so large an armed force passed through that the *labradores* of the place could not properly lodge them. The *hidalgos* in this case protested bitterly, and went to court to try to avoid hosting soldiers, for the billeting of troops was regarded as terribly oppressive.[27]

The *Relaciones* show that it was an esteemed privilege to be exempt from billeting. The village of Fuenlabrada (*Madrid*: p. 268) received such an exemption from Ferdinand and Isabella for its services in the cavalry, and the council took pains to get the privilege confirmed by Philip II. The presence of royal troops in a village was far from reassuring. In fact, it upset the rural tranquility by introducing a disorderly element. There was no love lost between the soldiers and the villagers, and they frequently came to blows, sometimes with tragic results. For example, the *Relación* of Getafe (*Madrid*: pp. 290–1) tells of an affray that occurred between a group of villagers and some royal archers who were stationed there. One young villager – seemingly an innocent bystander – was killed when he tried to flee, and two others were injured. The royal justice officials were severe with the murderers: they were beheaded.

Fortunately, civilian–military relations did not often deteriorate to that point, but soldiers were notoriously ill-behaved and dishonest. In 1566 the council of Alpera (Albacete) complained to the crown that troops passing through the village stole chickens and lambs, abused the local women, and generally mistreated the villagers. And in the *Relación* of Los Pedroneras (Cuenca) (cited Salomon 1964: 237) the villagers called the royal soldiers a 'plague' that so devastated the place that many inhabitants emigrated rather than continue to live in such a vulnerable location (on the road from Madrid to Murcia). I am sure that one could fill volumes with the protests of the victims of billeting, and of the requisitioning of grain, draft animals, carts, and other supplies (not to mention humans) needed by the military. The victims – usually peasants – were supposed to be paid for the goods and services they provided. But if they were paid at all – which was not always so – it was at unsatisfactory rates prescribed by the procurement officer. That explains why villagers tried desperately to avoid billeting soldiers, even bribing the officers to keep them away, or to hasten their departure. The presence of soldiers was synonymous with abuse and scarcity. Around the end of the sixteenth century the *corregidor* of Martos (Jaén) reported that the peasants of that area were in desperate straits, because of the frequency with which troops were wintered there, three and four months at a time. While the soldiers were there, their peasant hosts dared not leave their homes, for fear of compromising their honor. And the military used up the reserves of the public granaries, which had been painstakingly accumulated for emergencies. The burden of supporting the military impoverished individual peasants, and sometimes even led to increased indebtedness for the entire community. For example, in 1567 the town of Bobadilla del Camino (Palencia) had to secure royal permission to mortgage its *propios* for 1,000 *ducados*, to help it recover from a sixteen-month stay of a company of men-at-arms.[28]

THE CULMINATION OF RURAL MISERY

On top of the increasing tax burdens, the Castilian peasant suffered repeated crop failures of unusual severity in the last decades of the century. The poor harvests, coming at a time when population had reached unprecedented levels, caused widespread shortages and high prices. Famine, or at least the use of poor-quality foods, produced malnutrition, sapping the resistance of the population and rendering it extremely vulnerable to epidemics. Since the mid-1300s the possibility of plague had been a constant worry, for it seemed that the disease was always present somewhere in Spain. There were widespread outbreaks of plague in Spain in 1506–7 and in 1528–30, following periods of famine, but the most generalized and severe plague epidemic for this period began in 1596 and raged through the Iberian peninsula until 1602. It started in the Basque country, and spread gradually into Old Castile and southward. A proverb current in Toledo at the end of the sixteenth century (cited Capmany 1807: 52–3) went:

> Dios te libre de la enfermedad que baxa de Castilla,
> Y de la hambre que sube de Andalucía.
> (God preserve you from the plague that comes down from Castile,
> And from the famine that comes up from Andalucía.)

The consequences of this plague were similar to those of the famous Black Death of the late medieval period. Misery was heaped upon misery: disease and death upon hunger. Economic life was disrupted, production was paralyzed, leading to rising prices, but also to higher salaries of a greatly diminished population. Many historians have written that the plague affected the cities most of all; but Bartolomé Bennassar has demonstrated (1969: 8–11, 20, 49–52, 68–70, 79–80)

227

that this plague devastated the rural villages of Castile with terrible efficiency.

The condition of the peasantry must really have been miserable, because in the 1590s the Cortes, which was dominated by urban gentlemen and nobles, spoke increasingly of the plight of the Castilian *labrador*. And the *arbitristas*, to a man, deplored the impoverished condition of the rural areas. Early in the seventeenth century Fray Benito de Peñalosa y Mondragón (cited Domínguez 1971: 153; Salomon 1965: 53) wrote these often-quoted words:

The *labradores* of Spain are the most wretched and downtrodden of all classes. You would almost think that there was a conspiracy on the part of everyone else to destroy and ruin them. It has come to the point where the very word '*labrador*' has such a bad connotation that it has become a byword for low-class taxpayer, boor, scoundrel, and even worse. It is associated with coarse food, garlic and onions, crumbs and tough salt beef, putrescent meat, barley or rye bread, sandals, ragged coats, ridiculous headgear, rough shirts and collars, crudely-tanned sheepskin jackets and bags, hovels and shanties, houses with dilapidated mud walls, and a few ill-tended fields and scrawny and perpetually famished livestock . . . So why should we be surprised at the pronounced decline in the population of the rural towns, villages, and hamlets? It is a marvel that there is anyone left at all!

Notice that this described the condition of the *labrador*, who represented a sort of elite of the peasantry. What, then, was the lot of less fortunate rural folk? It must have been dismal indeed. We should remember, however, that those who wrote of the misery of the peasantry were often guilty of exaggeration. We can be sure that the agrarian crisis did not impoverish *all labradores*; in fact, the most clever of them must have been able to profit from their neighbors' misfortune, by acquiring their property on advantageous terms. And the idea, repeated by many *arbitristas*, that the crisis caused a depopulation of rural Castile, is not really true. There were undoubtedly many peasants who left their villages to go to the big cities, but that had always been so. The countryside was certainly not deserted (Brumont 1978), even though many places were decimated by plague, and some villages were even abandoned, in favor of others in more convenient or more salubrious locations.

Yet despite these exaggerations, the misery of the Castilian peasantry was no illusion: it was real. It is hardly necessary to belabor the point: by the end of the sixteenth century rural Castile was in a sorry state. All authorities – both contemporary witnesses and recent scholars – are agreed on this. Gone was the optimism of the *Relaciones*, which had reflected the economic and demographic expansion of the previous half-century. The last two decades of the 1500s were full of doom and despair, of crop failures, devastating tax increases, and virulent epidemics. If Salomon is correct, at the end of the sixteenth century over half of the peasant's harvest went to enrich the non-peasant classes of society, through taxes, rents, tithes, and various other payments (1964: 250). Given that crushing burden, in an age of low productivity, it is surprising that the structure held up as long as it did. The society of Habsburg Spain was overwhelmingly agrarian, and could not continue to prosper without a vigorous agropastoral sector. As long as the Castilian peasant could generate healthy surpluses, the empire could maintain its prestige, and could support the hordes of bureaucrats, lawyers, clergymen, soldiers, and other non-producers who symbolized its glory. But when agrarian production flagged, the entire edifice began to crumble. The treasure of the Indies could not save it, for its foundation had been undermined.

Notes

1. The communitarian tradition

1. Suit between Don Juan de Guzmán and the council of Salvaleón (1517–26), ACHGR, 507-1919-1.

2. See a suit between Muñoz and the town of Segura [mislabeled as Hornos on the title page], ACHGR, 3-1884-6.

3. Averiguación de Piedras Albas (1575), AGS, EH, 906.

4. Testimony from the year 1566, AGS, EH, 252; *Plasencia* v. *los lugares de su Tierra* (1531), ACHVA, PC, FA (F), 64.

5. From the 'Privilegio de 1287 al concejo de Hinestrosa', quoted in Joaquín Costa y Martínez, *Colectivismo agrario en España; doctrinas y hechos* (Buenos Aires: Editorial América Lee, 1944), p. 323. First published Madrid: Imprenta de San Francisco de Sales, 1898.

6. Ordenanzas sobre colmenares de Andújar, AGS, EH, 220.

7. The question of *presura* ownership is examined in Luis G. de Valdeavellano, *Curso de historia de las instituciones españolas, de los orígenes al final de la Edad Media* (Madrid: Revista de Occidente, 1968), p. 241; in the *pressura* article of *Diccionario de historia de España*, 2nd edn, rev. and enl. in 3 vols., dir. Germán Bleiberg (Madrid: Revista de Occidente, 1969); and in Costa, *Colectivismo agrario* (1898), pp. 261–2.

8. The quotation is from Relación del Bachiller de la Concha, 30 May 1569, AGS, CJH, 94.

9. The quotation is from Jerónimo Castillo de Bobadilla, *Política para corregidores y señores de vasallos* (1597), given by Noël Salomon, *La campagne de Nouvelle Castille à la fin du XVIe siècle d'après les 'Relaciones topográficas'* (Paris: SEVPEN, 1964), p. 141, n. 1. See also Costa, *Colectivismo agrario* (1944), pp. 371–7; and 'Don Fernando y Doña Isabel en Córdoba a 3 de noviembre de 1490, y en Sevilla a 26 de enero de 1491', *Novísima recopilación de las leyes de España*, 6 vols. (Madrid: J. Viana Razola, 1805–29), libro VII, título XXV, ley II; Luis Morell Terry, *Estudio sobre las causas de la decadencia de la agricultura en la provincia de Granada y medios para remediarla* (Granada: Imprenta de Indalecio Ventura, 1888), pp. 131–2; Alain Huetz de Lemps, *Vignobles et vins du Nord-Oest de l'Espagne*, 2 vols. (Bordeaux: University of Bordeaux, 1967), p. 599.

10. Ordenanzas de Arjona (1537), AGS, EH, 223; *Bartolomé Serrano* v. *Córdoba* (1573–4), ACHGR, 3-1493-9; *Valdetorres* v. *Guareña* (1548–9), ACHGR, 3-1235-3. The Arévalo information is in *Don Yerro* v. *Rapariegos* (1520-38), ACHVA, PC, FA (F), 33.

11. *Algunos criadores y señores de ganados de Loja* v. *la Ciudad de Loja* (1580–92), ACHGR, 3-691-7. See also *Burgo* v. *Villamunyo* (1548), ACHVA, PC, FA (F), 14; *Arnedo* v. *el consejo de la Mesta* (1584), ACHVA, PC, FA (F), 64.

12. A transcription (1554) of the *rastrojo* ordinance of Málaga and its Tierra, apparently adopted during the reign of Ferdinand and Isabella, and still in force, can be found in *Comares y consortes* v. *Francisco de Santa Olalla y consortes* (1553–5), ACHGR, 3-792-6. The Seville-area data, contested by the village of La Rinconada, can be found in *El Jurado Alonso Osorio y el Doctor Lope Rodríguez de Baeza* v. *La Rinconada* (1543–6), ACHGR, 3-1336-4 and 3-1165-12.

13. Examples of suits can be found in ACHGR, 3-1426-9; 512-2353-11; and 508-1945-1; and in *Arnedo* v. *el consejo de la Mesta* (1585), ACHVA, PC, FA (F), 64.

14. Some arguments in favor of the *derrota* can be found in Costa, *Colectivismo agrario* (1944), p. 372; Josefina Gómez Mendoza, 'Las ventas de baldíos y comunales en el siglo XVI: estudio de su proceso en Guadalajara', *Estudios geográficos*, 28, no. 109 (1967), 555; Angel García Sanz, *Desarrollo y crisis del antiguo régimen en Castilla la Vieja; economía y sociedad en tierras de Segovia de 1500 a 1814* (Madrid: Akal Editor, 1977), p. 28; José-Luis Martín Galindo, *Artículos geográficos sobre la provincia de León* (Valladolid: Editorial Miñón, n. d. [apparently in late 1950s]), p. 14.

2. Municipal property

1. The Castillo de Bobadilla assertion is cited in Carmelo Viñas y Mey, *El problema de la tierra en la España de los siglos XVI–XVII* (Madrid: CSIC, 1941), p. 64.

2. Venta al concejo de la ciudad de Arcos, 8 September 1587, AGS, CR–7, 3257; Parada y Rubiales: Venta que el Licenciado Ortiz otorgó a Don Lope de Herrera Enríquez Rojas, 17 October 1584, AGS, CG, 3254.

3. Quoted in Costa, *Colectivismo agrario* (1944), p. 230, n. 1.

4. Documents about Monteagudo (1575) in AGS, EH, 323.

5. The information about Baeza is found in Venta que el Doctor Brizuela hizo a Don Pedro Vázquez de Cuna, 19 August 1586, AGS, CG, 3253; that about Toro in Venta que Pedro Hernández hizo a Juan de Villar, 23 July 1586, AGS, CR–7, 3261.

6. For Castilblanco, see AGS, EH, 74-14-iii.

7. AGS, EH, 240.

8. *Sueros* v. *el Licenciado Guzmán* (1562–3), ACHVA, PC, FA (F), 15; *Cazorla* v. *El Yruela* [sic] (1562–3), ACHGR, 3-1424-11.

9. *Cédula* to Ledanca, 13 December 1586, AGS, CG, 365. Another example is that of Valdeolmos (Madrid), which got royal permission in 1574 to mortgage its *propios* for ten years to help pay the royal treasury for its jurisdictional independence (*villazgo*). In 1584 the town asked for, and received, royal permission to extend the mortgage for an additional ten years. See an *executoria*, 9 December 1591, and a *cédula*, 14 October 1593, both in AGS, CG, 366.

10. Averiguación de Andújar (1552, 1567), AGS, EH, 220.

11. *Valdetorres* v. *Guareña* (1548–9), ACHGR, 2-1235-2.

12. Averiguación de Poveda de Obispalía (1578), AGS, EH, 360; *Luis Alvarez* v. *Vélez Málaga* (1553), ACHGR, 511-2157-2.

13. *Francisco de los Cobos y consortes* v. *Albánchez* (1552), ACHGR, 511-2295-14.

14. Averiguación de Chinchilla (1506), AGS, EH, 219-13.

15. *Aliaguilla* v. *Mesta* (1590–1), ACHGR, 508-2072-4.

16. *Mesta* v. *Pozalmuro* (1556–8), ACHVA, PC, FA (F), 28; Averiguación de Higuera de Martos (1564), AGS, EH, 209.

17. Averiguación de Andújar (1567), AGS, EH, 220; *Aliaguilla* v. *Mesta* (1590–1), ACHGR, 508-2072-4.

18. See *Talavera* v. *Villafranca* (1547), ACHVA, PC, FA (F), 61.

19. The Soria information is in *Mesta* v. *Pozalmuro* (1556–7), ACHVA, PC, FA (F), 28; the Priego information in a bill of sale made to the town by Alonso López de Obregón, 27 March 1590, AGS, CR–7, 3260; and that about Aliaguilla in a suit with the Mesta (1590–1), ACHGR, 508-2072-4.

20. See various bills of sale (1574–8), AAT, 1-3-82.

21. Averiguación de Puebla del Príncipe (1590–5), AGS, EH, 130-19-xiii; *Monroy* v. *Mesta* (1586), ACHGR, 3-947-13.

22. *Gonzalo Jiménez y consortes* v. *El Casar* (1542–43), ACHGR, 3-1627-8.

23. The difficulty of the coexistence of *prados* and arable plots in the mountainous north is discussed in José Luis Martín Galindo, 'Arcaísmo y modernidad en la explotación agraria de Valdeburón (León)', *Estudios geográficos* 22, no. 83 (1961), 175–6.

24. *Santa Munilla* v. *Mesta* (1595), ACHVA, PC, FA (F), 21; *Arnedo* v. *Mesta* (1584), ACHVA, PC, FA (F), 64; *Donhierro* v. *Rapariegos* (1528), ACHVA, PC, FA (F), 33.

25. *Los cavalleros y fijosdalgo de Santa Cruz de la Sierra* v. *el concejo del lugar* (1515–16), ACHGR, 3-398-4; Probanza del concejo de Fuente Obejuna (1531), ACHGR, 3-518-3 (bis).

26. *Monroy* v. *Mesta* (1586), ACHGR, 3-947-13; Venta que Esteban de Gamarra otorgó a Alonso Guirao de una cavallería de tierra en Cehegín, 19 April 1583, AGS, CR–7, 3260.

27. *Magdalena Marchante* v. *Tejadillos* (1536–9), ACHGR, 3-275-2.

28. Averiguación de Andújar (1560s and 1570s), AGS, EH, 220.

29. *La Alberca* v. *Las Majadas* (1531), ACHVA, PC, FA (F), 35; *Don Lope Zerón Valenzuela* v. *Ubeda* (1588), ACHGR, 508-2024-2; *San Sebastián* v. *Alcobendas* (1592), ACHVA, PC, FA (F), 81.

30. Averiguación de Montánchez (1592), AGS, EH, 323.

31. Averiguación de Cáceres (1543–7), AGS, EH, 240.

32. *Valle de Valdeporras* v. *Pedro Gómez de Porras* (1577), ACHVA, PC, FA (F), 81; *Talavera* v. *Villafranca* (1579), ACHVA, PC, FA (F), 61.

33. Archivo de la Mesta, Executorias, Trujillo, 16 December 1521.

34. Averiguación de Andújar (1560s and 1570s), AGS, EH, 220.

35. See Executoria a Gerónimo de Silva, 1 December 1592, AGS, CG, 368; Relación a Rodrigo Vázquez de Arce de Juan Pérez Pumarejo, 14 August 1587, AGS, CJH, 239 ant. (162 mod.); Venta que Licenciado Andrés de Bueras otorgó al concejo de Malaguilla, 5 August 1585, AGS, CG, 373.

36. *Córdoba* v. *Almodóvar del Río* (1536), ACHGR, 3-716-3.

37. See the document cited in the previous note.

38. Representative samples of places with *tierras cadañeras* are Talamanca de Jarama (Madrid), Carmona (Sevilla), Lerma (Burgos), and many places in the region known as the Campo de Montiel of the Order of Santiago (province of Ciudad Real). Documentary references to the above can be found, respectively, in: Diego de Carbajal a Su Magestad (no date but 1569), AGS, CJH, 65 mod. (94 ant.); Comisión al Licenciado Diego López de Orozco, 14 May 1583, AGS, CG, 362; Venta que el Doctor Falconi otorgó a Lucas de Caniego, 17 November 1590, AGS, CG, 373; and an unsigned and undated draft of a *cédula* to Gaspar de Bustamante (in papers from 1569), AGS, CJH, 91 ant. (62 mod.).

39. Letter to crown from Xtobal Pérez and other *vecinos* of Budia (no date but 1571), AGS, CJH, 78 mod. (114 ant.); for the Torres information, see Comisión

a Luis Sánchez, 14 May 1583, AGS, CG, 362; Venta que el Licenciado Andrés de Bueras otorgó al concejo de Malaguilla, 5 August 1585, AGS, CG, 373. The Alcalá information is in a letter to the crown from Diego de Carbajal (no date, but apparently from 1569), AGS, CJH, 65 mod. (94 ant.); and the Belinchón information is in Gómez Mendoza, 'Ventas de baldíos', pp. 524–5; and a letter to the crown from Gaspar de Bustamante, about lands in Belinchón, 10 December 1569, AGS, CJH, 65 mod. (94 ant.).

40. The information for Torres is in Comisión a Luis Sánchez, 14 May 1583, AGS, CG, 362; that for Talamanca from a letter to the crown from Diego de Carbajal (no date but 1569), AGS, CJH, 65 mod. (94 ant.); and that for Valdepeñas, Manzanares, and Moral de Calatrava from an unsigned and undated draft of a *cédula* to Gaspar de Bustamante (in papers from 1569), AGS, CJH, 91 ant. (62 mod.); Venta que Pedro Hérnandez otorgó a los vecinos de San Román de Hornija, 30 January 1589, AGS, CR–7, 3260.

41. The documentary source for the San Román de Hornija registration was cited in the previous note; that about Alcalá is in the letter to the crown from Diego de Carbajal, also cited in the previous note.

42. The quote is from an Averiguación de Montamarta (1585), AGS, EH, 323; and the source for Campo de Criptana and Socuéllamos is from an undated and unsigned *Relación* to the crown (with papers from 1563), AGS, DC, 47, folio 19.

43. In AGS, CG, 372 there are a number of bills of sale by the royal land commissioner Pedro Hernández to *vecinos* of Toro in the year 1586. These contain considerable interesting information about the local communal customs.

44. About Badajoz, see a suit between the city and Juan Andrés and consorts (1551–2), ACHGR, 3-463-5. See also Huetz de Lemps, *Vignobles*, pp. 595–626; and *Hernán Pérez* v. *Trujillo* (1588–89), ACHGR, 3-1298-2.

45. Averiguación de Alaejos (1581), AGS, EH, 209; for Jerez, Venta que Diego de Vega otorgó a Damián de Hinojosa, 31 January 1585, AGS, CG, 3254.

46. Venta que el Licenciado Alonso Ortiz hizo al concejo y vecinos de Brincones, 24 August 1588, AGS, CG, 367; Executoria a Pedro de Guebara, 25 January 1610, AGS, CG, 373; Averiguación de Montánchez (1581, 1584), AGS, EH, 209.

47. See a letter to the crown from Pedro Díaz de Castañeda, 19 March 1585, AGS, CJH, 229; and *Cardenete* v. *Yemeda* (1588–90), ACHGR, 3-1142-3.

48. Venta que el Licenciado Alonso Ortiz hizo al concejo y vecinos de Lumbrales, 17 August 1588, AGS, CR–7, 3261.

49. About Valencia de Alcántara, see Comisión a Gómez de la Rocha, 6 July 1592, AGS, DGT-24, 1486; about Jerez de la Frontera, see Venta que Diego de Vega hizo a Damián de Hinojosa, 31 January 1585, AGS, CG, 363; about Soria, a letter to the crown from Pedro Díaz de Castañeda, 19 March 1585, AGS, CJH, 229.

50. For Carbajosa, see Venta que Pedro Hernández otorgó al Marquez de la Mota, 7 April 1587, AGS, CR–7, 3260; for Almazul, Venta que Juan de Berástegui hizo a Juan Herrero, 28 October 1588, AGS, CG, 367; for Castrogonzalo, see Gómez Mendoza, 'Ventas de baldíos', pp. 526–7; and for Villarramiel, Executoria a Pedro de Guebara, 25 January 1610, AGS, CH, 373.

51. Venta que el Licenciado Alonso Ortiz hizo al concejo de Lumbrales, 17 August 1588, AGS, CR–7, 3261; Venta que Pedro Hernández otorgó a Villalube, 16 February 1589, AGS, CG, 367; and the last document cited in the preceding note.

52. Venta que Pedro Hernández otorgó a Villalube, 16 February 1589, AGS, CG, 367; Venta que el Licenciado Alonso Ortiz hizo a Brincones, 24 August 1588,

AGS, CG 367; Venta que el Licenciado Ortiz hizo a los vecinos de Vermellar, 17 August 1588, AGS, CG, 367.

53. Averiguación de Alaejos (1584), AGS, EH, 209; Averiguación de Montánchez (1589), AGS, EH, 323.

54. Venta que el Licenciado Alonso Ortiz hizo al concejo de Lumbrales, 17 August 1588, AGS, CR–7, 3261.

55. It would be tedious to list all my sources for the utilizations of the *monte*. Some useful ones are: Fernando Jiménez de Gregorio, 'La población en la zona suroccidental de los montes de Toledo', *Estudios geográficos* 26, no. 98 (1965), 103–5; Averiguación de Andújar (1560s–70s), AGS, EH, 220; *San Sebastián* v. *Alcobendas* (1592), ACHVA, PC, FA (F), 81; *monte* ordinances of the two towns in the suit *Castrillo Texeriego* v. *Olivares* (1556), ACHVA, PC, FA (F), 3 Michael R. Weisser, *The Peasants of the Montes; The Roots of Rural Rebellion in Spain* (Chicago: University of Chicago Press, 1976), p. 102; Averiguación de Castro del Río (1564), AGS, EH, 252; Averiguación de Monteagudo (1575), AGS, EH, 323; *Campillo de Altabuey* v. *Paracuellos* (1589–1614), ACHGR, 504-838-1; Ordenanzas de la caza, Puebla de Montalbán (1529), AGS, EH, 400.

56. *Bartolomé de Avila* v. *Jacome Adorno, vecinos de Jerez* (1575–7), ACHGR, 3-1071-1; Venta que el Licenciado Chávez otorgó a Gonzalo Núñez Arica, 22 September 1586, AGS, CR–7, 3256.

57. *La Alberca* v. *Las Majadas* (1542), ACHVA, PC, FA (F), 35; *Mesta* v. *Antonio Collacos* (1555), ACHVA, PC, FA (F), 2; *Alonso Moyano, en nombre del concejo de Hornachuelos,* v. *alcalde mayor de Córdoba* (no date, but apparently from the 1500s), ACHGR, 3-792-3.

58. *Valdeporras* v. *Pedro Gómez de Porras* (1575), ACHVA, PC, FA (F), 69.

3. Other aspects of the communitarian system

1. *Alonso de Tordesillas* v. *Villaconejos* (1543–50), ACHVA, PC, FA (F), 34.
2. *Toro* v. *La Bóveda* (1542), ACHVA, PC, FA (F), 60.
3. *Osma* v. *Berzosa* (1549), ACHVA, PC, FA (F), 67.
4. *Cardenete* v. *Yemeda* (1588–90), ACHGR, 3-1142-3; *Cazorla* v. *La Iruela* (1562–3), ACHGR, 3-1424-11. The map, made for the purpose of requesting a purchase of jurisdictional rights, is undated, but located among documents from the 1500s, and seems to be from that period. The original map can be found in AGS, CJH, 24 ant. (14 mod.).
5. Averiguación de la Tierra del Vino (1558), AGS, EH, 360; for an example of the use of the phrase 'rejas vueltas', see *Cea* v. *Valderaduey* (1545), ACHVA, PC, FA (F), 63; *Campo de Criptana* v. *Alcázar de Consuegra* (1534), ACHGR, 511-2255-2.
6. The quote about Talamanca is in a letter to the crown from Diego de Carbajal (no date but 1569), AGS, CJH, 65 mod. (94 ant.). See also a transcript of a meeting of the council of Trujillo, 22 September 1536, AAT, 1-3-78, no. 1.
7. Averiguación de la Tierra del Vino (1558), AGS, EH, 360; *Daganzo* v. *el Colegio de la Compañía de Jesús de Alcalá* (1591), ACHVA, PC, FA (F), 72; *Trujillo* v. *Don Juan Alonso de Orellana* (1570–1608), ACHGR, 3-443-3. In 1567 the *alcalde mayor* of Andújar (Jaén) said that his city had gained substantially in population thanks to immigration from nearby villages under seigneurial jurisdiction. The attraction of Andújar was its many communal rights. See Averiguación de Andújar (1567), AGS, EH, 220.
8. In Iscar (Valladolid) the *alcaides* (governors, or wardens) of the fortress of the count of Miranda illegally took for themselves the use of several pieces of common land, and the *vecinos* did not resist, out of fear and respect, according to Relación de Diego López de Ayala, 21 August 1584, AGS, CJH, 215. See also

papers relating to a suit brought by Morón de la Frontera against Don Juan Téllez, the count of Viana, and his son Don Pedro Téllez Girón, the duke of Osuna (a copy from 1739 of documents from 1534-52), AHN, Osuna, 82², no. 9.

9. *La marquesa de Villanueva* v. *La Campana* (1576), ACHGR, 3-417-1; Venta que el Licenciado Chávez hizo a Fernando Giles [de tierras en Espera], 11 August 1588, AGS, CR–7, 3258; Relación del Bachiller Juan de la Concha, 28 June 1569, AGS, CJH, 94.

10. Relación de Juan de la Concha (no date, but apparently from 1564), AGS, CJH, 54; Relación de Bernardino de Barros, 9 September 1573, AGS, CJH, 84 mod. (124 ant.).

11. Venta que el Licenciado Garci Pérez de Bazán otorgó a la villa de Cabeza Arados, 3 May 1590, AGS, CR–7, 3260.

12. Ordenanzas de montes de Trujillo (1499) can be found in AM, Executorias, Trujillo, 16 December 1521; those of Andújar in AGS, EH, 220; Ordenanzas de la corta in Averiguación de Puebla de Montalbán (1529), AGS, EH, 400; Ordenanzas de Monte Nuevo de Soria (1518) in *Soria* v. *Francisco de Vinuesa*, ACHVA, PC, FA (F), 44; and the Cáceres information in *Pueblos del Margen* v. *Juez de Residencia* (1572), ACHGR, 508-1945-1. The modification of an inadequate penalty is described in *Plasencia* v. *Diego Nieto* (1564), ACHVA, PC, FA (F), 25.

13. *Trujillo* v. *las villas y lugares de su Tierra* (1552–1631), ACHVA, PC, FA (F), 54.

14. *Salvaleón* v. *Francisco Durán y el Alcalde Mayor del Estado de Feria* (1585-7), ACHGR, 3-269-3; *La Puebla* v. *Antonio Hernández* (1563), ACHVA, PC, FA (F), 67.

15. *Donhierro* v. *Rapariegos* (1528), ACHVA, PC, FA (F), 33; *Toro* v. *La Bóveda* (1526), ACHVA, PC, FA (F), 1; *Rejas* v. *Don Pedro Zapata* (1565), ACHVA, PC, FA (F), 56; *Valdespinoso* v. *Aguilar* (1526), ACHVA, PC, FA (F), 46; *Badajoz* v. *Talavera* (1569), ACHGR, 3-1570-12.

16. Ordenanzas de Arjona (1537), AGS, EH, 223; Ordenanzas de monte nuevo de Soria (1518) in *Soria* v. *Francisco de Vinuesa*, ACHVA, PC, FA (F), 44.

17. *Trujillo* v. *Don Juan Alonso de Orellana* (1570–1608), ACHGR, 3-443-3.

18. *Soria* v. *Francisco de Vinuesa* (1518), ACHVA, PC, FA (F), 44; AM, Executorias, Trujillo, 16 August 1548; Cuentas de propios de Trujillo (1594), AAT, 1-2-66, no. 1; Ordenanzas de Arjona (1537), AGS, EH, 223; Ordenanzas de montes de Sierra Morena (1537, from a copy made in 1575), Averiguación de Andújar, AGS, EH, 220; *Hernán Pérez* v. *Trujillo* (1588–9), ACHGR, 3-1298-2.

19. *Lucas Alonso Cabrera* v. *Arcos* (1548), ACHGR, 507-1863-3; Ordenanzas de Arjona (1537), AGS, EH, 223; *El Burgo* v. *Villamonyo* (1545), ACHVA, PC, FA (F), 14.

20. Averiguación de Molina (1589), AGS, EH, 220; *Mesta* v. *Revilla* (1549), ACHVA, PC, FA (F), 22.

21. *Soria* v. *Francisco de Vinuesa* (1528), ACHVA, PC, FA (F), 44; Ordenanzas de Arjona (1537), AGS, EH, 223.

22. *Santos Hernández* v. *Guardas de Toro* (1537), ACHVA, PC, FA (F), 71; *Luis Alonso Cabrera y consortes* v. *Arcos de la Frontera* (1548), ACHGR, 507-1863-3; *Toro* v. *La Bóveda* (1542), ACHVA, PC, FA (F), 60; *Badajoz* v. *Talavera* (1569), ACHGR, 3-1570-12; *Serradilla* v. *Mesta* (1576), ACHVA, PC, FA (F), 41.

23. Averiguación de Alpera (incl. Chinchilla) (1566), AGS, EH, 219-13; Visita de la ciudad de Trujillo, año de 1585, AAT, 1-3-82, no. 54; Averiguación de Montefrío (1558), AGS, EH, 323; Averiguación de Molina (1589), AGS, EH, 209.

24. *Congosto* v. *Ahumada* (1537), ACHVA, PC, FA (F), 3; Visita de la ciudad de Trujillo, año de 1585, AAT, 1-3-82, no. 54.

25. Información testifical a instancia de la ciudad de Córdoba (1568), ACHGR,

3-1511-10; *Sevilla* v. *La duquesa de Béjar* (1539), ACHGR, 3-1123-4; *Don Lope Sánchez de Valenzuela* v. *Jaén* (1526–39), ACHGR, 3-420-6; *Jerez de la Frontera* v. *diversos vecinos de ella* (1551–3), ACHGR, 3-465-3. And see especially a transcription of a commission to the Juez de Términos Licenciado Juan del Castillo, original dated 8 February 1535, in a suit between Juan Jiménez and Córdoba (1535–7), ACHGR, 508-2083-11.

26. AM, Executorias, Trujillo, 11 July 1504, 16 December 1521, 16 August 1548, 15 December 1589, and 31 July 1591; AM, Relaciones de los alcaldes entregadores, libro 5, folios 242v. ff (1565).

27. *Monroy* v. *Mesta* (1586), ACHGR, 3-947-13; *Navacerrada* v. *Mesta* (1590), ACHVA, PC, FA (F), 5; *Aliaguilla* v. *Mesta* (1590–1), ACHGR, 508-2072-4; *Arnedo* v. *Mesta* (1585), ACHVA, PC, FA (F), 64.

28. Julius Klein, the Mesta historian, was conservative in assessing the impact of Mesta flocks on cultivated fields. See his *The Mesta; A Study in Spanish Economic History, 1273–1836*, Harvard Economic Studies, vol. XXI (Cambridge, Mass.: Harvard University Press, 1920), pp. 336–42. An example of an inflated view of the Mesta's effect on agriculture can be found in Marcelin Defourneaux, *Daily Life in Spain in the Golden Age*, trans. Newton Branch (London: George Allen and Unwin, 1970), p. 101.

29. Venta que el Licenciado Ortiz otorgó a Rodrigo Gallego, de tierras en Castrillo (no date but 1584), AGS, CG, 3254; Venta que el Licenciado Ortiz otorgó a Brincones, 24 August 1588, AGS, CG, 367; letter to the crown from Nicolás Muñoz, for the town of Castroverde (no date but 1584), AGS, CJH, 216; Averiguación de Piedras Albas (1575), AGS, EH, 906; Venta que el Licenciado Josephelaso otorgó a Andrés de Salamanca, por tierras en Teba, 25 June 1584, AGS, CR–7, 3260.

30. See three Relaciones from Bachiller Juan de la Concha about lands in Quesada, dated 30 May and 28 June 1569 (a third is undated, but clearly is also from 1569), AGS, CJH, 94 ant. (65 mod.).

31. An introductory bibliography for Portuguese agri-collectivism can be found in Angel Cabo Alonso, 'El colectivismo agrario en Tierra de Sayago', *Estudios geográficos*, 17, no. 65 (1956), 600–1, especially notes 15 and 16. The bibliography of European agricultural communitarianism is vast, but one can get an idea of the general trends from Jerome Blum, 'The European village as community: origins and functions', *Agricultural History*, 45 (1971), 157–78; Alejandro Nieto, *Bienes comunales*, Serie J, Monografías Prácticas de Derecho Español, vol. XL (Madrid: Revista de Derecho Privado, 1964), pp. 801–40; *Agrarian Life of the Middle Ages*, vol. 1 of *The Cambridge Economic History of Europe*, 2nd edn (Cambridge University Press, 1966); Catherine Delano Smith, *Western Mediterranean Europe; A Historical Geography of Italy, Spain, and Southern France since the Neolithic* (New York: Academic Press, 1979), pp. 34, 36, 88–9, 243–52; and B. H. Slicher van Bath, *The Agrarian History of Western Europe, AD 500–1850*, trans. Olive Ordish (London: Edward Arnold, 1963), pp. 57, 72–4.

4. Private property ownership: the privileged estates

1. *Torremormojón* v. *Alonso Phelipe* (1558), ACHVA, PC, FA (F), 16; *Villanueva de los Caballeros* v. *Don Juan Quixada de Ocampo* (1537), ACHVA, PC, FA (F), 39; *Haza* v. *Conde de Miranda* (1551), ACHVA, PC, FA (F), 31.

2. Averiguación de Menasalbas (1588), AGS, EH, 400; Asiento y transacción tomado entre Don Juan Pacheco (conde de la Puebla de Montalbán) y el Doctor Villagómez, 13 June 1589, AGS, CH, 366.

3. Examples of towns purchasing their release from *señorío* status are Abelgas (León) in 1586, and Adobezo, Gallineros, Lumbreras, and Cervariza (Soria) in 1569, according to *averiguaciones* in AGS, EH, 209 and 220. See also Averiguación de El Acebrón (1597), AGS, EH, 209; and Relación de corregidores, BN, MSS 9372 = Cc. 42, p. 35.

4. [Copy of] *cédula* to Alonso de Mérida, original dated 16 December 1530, in a suit *Gaspar de Villalta* v. *Guadix* (1557–62), ACHGR, 512-2429-29.

5. Averiguación de Castro del Río (1566), AGS, EH, 252.

6. Averiguación de Casasola (1569), AGS, EH, 329.

7. The Mendoza quote is from Helen Nader, *The Mendoza Family in the Spanish Renaissance, 1350 to 1550* (New Brunswick, N.J.: Rutgers University Press, 1979), p. 225, note 23.

8. *Córdoba* v. *Almodóbar del Río* (1536), ACHGR, 3-716-3. For other examples of self-serving noble influences over municipal government, see the suits *Luis de Ricafuente* v. *Jaén* (1534), ACHGR, 3-1451-19; *Lucas Alonso Cabrera y consortes* v. *Arcos de la Frontera* (1548), ACHGR, 507-1863-3; and Angel García Sanz, *Desarrollo y crisis del antiguo régimen en Castilla la Vieja; economía y sociedad en tierras de Segovia de 1500 a 1814* (Madrid: Akal, 1977), pp. 267, 284–5.

9. *Andrés Hernández y consortes* v. *Casar de Cáceres* (1551–68), ACHGR, 3-1189-5; *Vecinos de Santa Inés* v. *Francisco de Bocanegra* (1584), ACHVA, PC, FA (F), 17. See also *Rejas* v. *Pedro Zapata* (1567), ACHVA, PC, FA (F), 58; and AM, Executorias, Trujillo, 16 August 1548.

10. Averiguación de Monleón (1558), AGS, EH, 323.

11. Averiguación de La Zarza (1561), AGS, EH, 189–56.

12. Averiguación de Monteagudo (1575), AGS, EH, 323; Averiguación de Calabazanos (1574), AGS, EH, 240.

13. Averiguación de Castro del Río (1565), AGS, EH, 252.

14. Averiguación de Quintana de Loranca (1566), AGS, EH, 130-18-i.

15. *El Monasterio de Valbuena* v. *Piñal* (1597), ACHVA, PC, FA (F), 35.

16. Examples of *censos enfitéuticos* on ecclesiastical property can be found in the Monasterio de Valbuena suit cited in the previous note; and in *Badajoz* v. *Juan Andrés y consortes* (1551–2), ACHGR, 3-463-5.

17. Averiguación de La Zarza (1561), AGS, EH, 189–56.

18. *Alcolea* v. *Pedro Suárez* (1568), ACHGR, 3-1276-11 and 3-559-12 bis.

19. Informe del corregidor de Martos (no date, but from the end of the reign of Philip II), BN, MSS 9,371, folio 31; Venta a Marcos Fúcar, 14 June 1580, AGS, CH, 3253; Venta a Alfonso Ruiz de la Tendera, 19 September 1576, AGS, EH, 240, pieza 6; Executoria a Gerónimo de Silva, 31 December 1592, AGS, CG, 368.

20. AHN, Ordenes militares, Santiago, Visita de 1575, Libro de manuscritos 1012C, vol. I, pp. 149–50.

21. See an undated document (apparently from the 1550s) about the *dehesas* of the Campo de Montiel, in AGS, CJH, 24 ant. (14 mod.); El Rey y la Reina al Onrado Maestre, 10 March 1491, BN, MSS 430, folios 418v–419; and various papers from the early 1550s in AGS, CJH, 24 ant. (14 mod.).

5. Private property ownership: the non-privileged

1. About the post-1570 settlers in the Alpujarras, see also Pedro Herrera Puga, *Sociedad y delicuencia en el siglo de oro. Aspectos de la vida sevillana en los siglos XVI y XVII* (Granada: Universidad de Granada, 1971), pp. 440–60; and José Oriol Catena, 'La repoblación del Reyno de Granada después de la expulsión de los moriscos', *Boletín de la Universidad de Granada*, 7 (1935), 8 (1936), and 9 (1937).

2. About Espera, see Venta que el Licenciado Nicolás de Chávez otorgó a Fernando Giles, 11 August 1588, AGS, CR–7, 3258. See also a petition to the crown from the *villa* of El Arahal, 12 August 1592, AGS, CG, 365; Relación de Juan de Salas, 27 March 1587, AGS, CG, 3262; and a letter to the crown from Gerónimo Gómez (no date, but apparently from 1585), AGS, CJH, 225.

3. Ley del fuero, Título 33 de la presura raíz, from Ordenanzas sobre colmenares (1567), Averiguación de Andújar, AGS, EH, 220; *El Licenciado Matheo de Morales y consortes* v. *Castro del Río* (1590), ACHGR, 3-1612-13; Relación de Diego de Argote [sobre tierras en Segura de la Sierra y su Partido] (undated, but apparently from August 1583), AGS, CG, 3262. See also *Pedro de Tarifa* v. *Baeza* (1533-9), ACHGR, 3-1123-2; *cédula* to the *alcalde mayor* of Estepa (undated, but seemingly from 1573), AGS, CJH, 124 ant. (84 mod.); and *Los Caballeros de la Sierra de Hornos* v. *Juan Muñoz* (1572), ACHGR, 3-884-6.

4. *Rus* v. *Baeza* (1565-8), ACHGR, 3-426-3; Venta que el Licenciado Garci Pérez de Bazán otorgó a la villa de Cabeza Arados, 3 May 1590, AGS, CR–7, 3260.

5. Venta que el Licenciado Andrés de Bueras otorgó a Francisco Gómez, 15 March 1589, AGS, CG, 373.

6. Venta que el alcalde mayor del Adelantamiento de Castilla hizo a Pedro Ramírez, 15 October 1590, AGS, CG, 373.

7. Averiguación de Castilblanco (1586), AGS, EH, 74-14-iii.

8. *Lora* v. *Gobernador Maldonado* (1536-9), ACHGR, 511-2288-1, part 4.

9. *Lucas Alonso Cabrero y consortes* v. *Arcos* (1548), ACHGR, 507-1863-3.

10. *Badajoz* v. *Juan Andrés y consortes* (1551-2), ACHGR, 3-463-5.

11. Averiguación de Monleón (1558), AGS, EH, 323; Averiguación de Plasenzuela (1575), AGS, EH, 906; Averiguación de Castañar de Ibor (1586), AGS, EH, 74; Averiguación de Morales (1569), AGS, EH, 329.

12. Averiguación de Morales (1569), AGS, EH, 329; Averiguación de Castañar (1586), AGS, EH, 74-11-ii; Averiguación de Monleón (1558), AGS, EH, 323.

13. Averiguación de Monleón (1558), AGS, EH, 323.

14. Averiguación de Plasenzuela (1575), AGS, EH, 906.

15. Averiguación de Ruanes (1561), AGS, EH, 189–56.

16. Averiguación de Menasalbas (1588), AGS, EH, 400.

17. Averiguación de Monleón (1558), AGS, EH, 323; Averiguación de Castañar de Ibor (1586), AGS, EH, 74-11-ii.

18. Averiguación de Cebolla (1561), AGS, EH, 43; Averiguación de Pineda-Trasmonte (1597), AGS, EH, 142-11; Averiguación de Monleón (1558), AGS, EH, 323; Averiguación de Castilblanco (1586), AGS, EH, 74-14-iii; Averiguación de Moncalvillo (1595), AGS, EH, 130–2; Averiguación de Las Casas de Reina (1595), AGS, EH, 74; three Relaciones from Bachiller Juan de la Concha about lands in Quesada, dated 30 May and 28 June (the third is undated, but clearly also from 1569), AGS, CJH, 94 ant. (65 mod.).

19. Averiguación de La Zarza (1561), AGS, EH, 189–56; Averiguación de Castañar (1586), AGS, EH, 74-11-ii.

20. Averiguación de Pino (1597), AGS, EH, 142-15.

21. Averiguación de Las Casas de Reina (1595), AGS, EH, 74.

22. *Plasencia* v. *los lugares de su Tierra* (1531-49), ACHVA, PC, FA (F), 64; *Rus* v. *vecinos de Baeza* (1565-8), ACHGR, 3-426-3.

6. Changes in production and ownership

1. *Relación de corregidores* (undated, but apparently from the last years of the reign of Philip II), BN, MSS, 9.372, folio 31.

2. *Córdoba* v. *Almodóvar del Río* (1536), ACHGR, 3-716-3.

3. *Toro* v. *La Bóveda* (1512–42), ACHVA, PC, FA (F), 60.

4. The Arrieta work was later included in many editions published in the sixteenth through the nineteenth centuries along with Gabriel de Herrera's *Agricultura general*, a standard work on agronomy. The edition I used was published in Madrid: Don Antonio de Sancha, 1777, and the Arrieta section was entitled *Diálogos de la fertilidad y abundancia de España, y la razón porque se ha ido encareciendo, con el remedio para que vuelva todo a los precios pasados, y la verdadera manera de cavar y arar las tierras*.

5. *La Justicia de Santa Cruz de Mudela* v. *el concejo y ciertos vecinos de ella* (1545–63), ACHGR, 3-1631-11; *Yniesta* v. *el gobernador del Marquesado de Villena* (1516–19), ACHGR, 508-2121-8; *Marcos Hernández Galindo y consortes* v. *Lucas de Peralta* (1554–6), ACHGR, 512-2314-10.

6. *Averiguación de Palomas* (Badajoz) (1575), AGS, EH, 906.

7. *Averiguación de Castilblanco* (1555), AGS, EH, 251; *La Seca* v. *Medina del Campo* (1600–3), ACHVA, PC, FA (F), 53.

8. *Averiguación de Puebla del Príncipe* (1589), AGS, EH, 366; *Averiguación de Monteagudo* (1575), AGS, EH, 323; *Averiguación de Cáceres* (1589), AGS, EH, 240. A full copy of the *asiento* of Puebla del Príncipe is included in the document cited above.

9. *Trujillo* v. *las villas y lugares de su tierra* (1552–1631), ACHGR, 3-958-1. For other examples of suits between old and new towns, see *Cazorla* v. *La Iruela* (1562–3), ACHGR, 3-1424-11; *Peñafiel* v. *Quintanilla* (1551–6), ACHVA, PC, FA (F), 59; and Salomon, *La campagne*, pp. 149–50.

10. *Averiguación de Puebla del Príncipe* (1589), AGS, EH, 366; *Averiguaciones de Alcuéscar and Cáceres* (1589), AGS, EH, 240; *Averiguación de Montánchez* (1592), AGS, EH, 323; *Averiguación de Adobezo* (1569–70), AGS, EH, 209; for Manchuela, see *Actas*, XIX, 366; *Averiguación de Torres de Albánchez* (1586), AGS, EH, 189-2.

11. Examples of the 1563 reports can be found in AGS, DC, 47, pieza 30. For the Cortes action, see *Actas*, II, 440; III, 366–7; IV, 101, 126–44, and 433–4.

12. *Averiguación de Arjona* (1537), AGS, EH, 223; *Algunos criadores y señores de ganados de Loja* v. *la ciudad de Loja* (1580–92), ACHGR, 3-691-7; *Lopera* v. *Mesta* (1593), ACHGR, 3-1426-9; *Santa Cruz de Mudela* v. *Mesta* (1595–8), ACHGR, 512-2353-11.

13. *El Jurado Alonso Osorio y el Doctor Lope Rodríguez de Baeza* v. *La Rinconada* (1543–6), ACHGR, 3-1165-12 and 3-1336-4.

14. The *baldío* sales are described in my article 'The Sale of *Tierras Baldías* in Sixteenth-Century Castile', *Journal of Modern History*, 47, no. 4 (1975), 629–54; and in Gómez Mendoza, 'Ventas de baldíos'. It is also the subject of my book *La venta de tierras baldías: el dominio público y la corona en Castilla durante el siglo XVI*, trans. David Pradales Ciprés, Julio Gómez Santa Cruz, Gilbert B. Heartfield, and Gloria Garza-Swan (Madrid: Servicio de Publicaciones, Ministerio de Agricultura, 1983).

15. See papers relating to *baldío* sales in the Tierra de Zamora (which includes the information about Villanueva de los Caballeros), AGS, EH, 323.

16. *Gonzalo de Baena* v. *Motril* (1519), ACHGR, 3-1046-6; *Comares y Cútar y Machar Al Hayate y Borge* v. *Francisco de Santa Olalla y consortes* (1553–5), ACHGR, 3-792-6.

17. Relación de corregidores (undated, but apparently from the last years of the reign of Philip II), BN, MSS, 9.372 = Cc. 42, pp. 32–3.

7. The increasing rural malaise

1. Florián de Ocampo, 'Noticias de lo sucedido por los años 1550 a 1558', BN, MSS. 9.937, folios 65–6.

2. Averiguación de Casasola (juris. of Toro) (1569), AGS, EH, 329; Averiguación de Navalvillar de Pela (Trujillo, 1597), AGS, EH, 189-76; anonymous manuscript volume (including a description of the Badajoz fairs) 'Floresta española' (1607), BN, MSS 5.989, folio 80; and for the Arévalo market, see García Sanz, *Desarrollo*, p. 36. See also Averiguación de Palomas (1575), AGS, EH, 906.

3. Averiguación del Adelantamiento de León (1588), AGS, EH, 209; Averiguación de la Tierra de Campos (1581), AGS, EH, 209; Averiguación de Trujillo (1595), AGS, EH, 189-49; *Segovia* v. *sus lugares* (1588), ACHVA, PC, FA (F), 2; *Peñafiel* v. *Quintanilla* (1556), ACHVA, PC, FA (F), 59.

4. Averiguación de Morales de Toro (1569), AGS, EH, 329.

5. The Expedientes de Hacienda section of Simancas is rich in documents about municipal monopolies and price fixing. See, for example, Ordenanzas de molinos de aceite, Arjona (1537), AGS, EH, 223, folios 493-6. See also the suit *El Bachiller Alonso Ruiz Quevedo y consortes* v. *la Justicia de Yeste* (1595), ACHGR, 512-2156-21.

6. Relación de corregidores (undated, but coming from the latter part of the reign of Philip II), BN, MSS 9.372 = Cc. 42; Florián de Ocampo, 'Noticias de varios sucesos acaecidos desde el año 1521 hasta el 1549', BN, MSS 9.936, folio 63.

7. See p. 36 of the Relación de corregidores cited in note 6 above. There are many suits in the Chancillerías arising out of charges of malfeasance directed against *pósito* officials. For an example, see *Almorox* v. *los regidores y alcaldes de Almorox* (1582-4), ACHVA, PC, FA (F), 36.

8. See p. 35 of the Relación de corregidores cited in note 6 above.

9. *Iznatorafe* [sic] v. *el arzobispo de Toledo* (1568), ACHGR, 321-4328-18.

10. Averiguación de Alpera (Chinchilla) (1566), AGS, EH, 219-13; Averiguación de Tortuero (Uceda) (1586-97), AGS, EH, 189-9 bis.

11. Most of the data in my chronology of severe weather and bad harvests is from Bartolomé Bennassar, *Valladolid au siècle d'or; une ville de Castille et sa campagne au XVIe siècle* (Paris: Mouton, 1967), pp. 49-50; but some is from Antonio Domínguez Ortiz, *El Antiguo Régimen; los Reyes Católicos y los Austrias* (Madrid: Alianza Editorial, 1973), pp. 154-6; *Actas*, VII (1583-5), 415-16; Abelardo Merino Alvarez, *Geografía histórica del territorio de la actual provincia de Murcia desde la Reconquista por D. Jaime I de Aragón hasta la época presente* (Madrid: Imprenta del Patronato de Huérfanos de Intendencia e Intervención Militares, 1915), pp. 356-9; Melchor Soria y Vera, *Tratado de la Iustificación y conveniencia de la tassa de el pan, y de la dispensación que en ella haze su magestad con todos los que siembran* (Toledo: Juan Ruiz de Pereda, 1633), p. 47; Bartolomé Bennassar, *Recherches sur les grandes épidémies dans le nord de l'Espagne à la fin du XVIe siècle* (Paris: SEVPEN, 1969), pp. 51-2; and García Sanz, *Desarrollo*, pp. 79-82.

12. Florián de Ocampo, 'Noticias de varios sucesos acaecidos desde el año 1521 hasta el 1549', BN, MSS 9.936, folios 213-14; Averiguación de Piedras Alvas (Alcántara) (1586), AGS, EH, 142-5; *Don Francisco de Aranda* v. *Francisco Luján* (1586), ACHGR, 3-542-6; Averiguación de Puebla del Príncipe (1586), AGS, EH, 146-4-i.

13. Examples of rental contracts requiring the triennial system can be found in the Libro de Rentas (1567) of the duke of Arcos, AHN, Osuna, 1618; and in the

suit *Don Alonso de Córdoba* v. *Doña María Berria* (copy of a 1590 contract), ACHGR, 3-639-1.

14. An example of a *censo al quitar*, on a vineyard in Trujillo (Cáceres) (15 June 1548), can be found in AAT, 1-3-82, no. 17.

15. See a synopsis of the report of the *corregidor* from Martos (Jaén) (undated, but apparently from near the end of the reign of Philip II), BN, MSS 9.372, folio 31.

16. Copies of *censos enfitéuticos* can be found in *Badajoz* v. *Juan Andrés y consortes* (1551), ACHGR, 3-463-5; *El condestable de Castilla* v. *Salinas de Rosío* (1513), ACHVA, PC, FA (F), 59; *Herrín* v. *Ybán de Escobar* (1504), ACHVA, PC, FA (F), 5.

17. Documents concerning sharecropping can be found in *Baeza* v. *Francisco de Jesús* (1540–2), ACHGR, 3-1059-8; Cartas de Bezerra, Antonio de Lahoz Cartera (?) (no date, but apparently from c. 1563), AGS, DC-47, fol. 11; Averiguación de Palomas (Mérida) (1575), AGS, EH, 906.

18. The example is from *Jerez de la Frontera* v. *diversos vecinos della* (1551–3), ACHGR, 3-465-3. Other examples of fixed-payment rentals can be found in Averiguación de Biniegra (Avila) (1550–6), AGS, EH, 240; Averiguación de Monteagudo (1575), AGS, EH, 323; Averiguación de Calabazanos (1574), AGS, EH, 240; *Luzón* v. *el duque de Medinaceli* (1592), ACHVA, PC, FA (F), 80; *Don Alonso de Córdoba* v. *Doña María Berria* (1590), ACHGR, 3-639-1; Visita de 1575, Ordenes militares: Santiago, AHN, Libro de Manuscritos 1012c, vol. I, pp. 149–50; Venta que Alonso López de Obregón otorgó a la villa de Priego, 27 March 1590, AGS, CR-7, 3260; Libro de Rentas, duque de Arcos (1567), AHN, Osuna, 1618. For problems arising from allegations of *esterilidad*, see *Actas*, v, 130, 213; and the suit *Don Alonso de Córdoba* v. *Doña María Berria*, cited above in this note.

19. *Luzón* v. *el duque de Medinaceli* (1592), ACHVA, PC, FA (F), 80; Relación de Juan de Salas, 25 June 1583, AGS, CJH, 204.

20. The Ciudad Rodrigo rental rate is from a Relación de Domingo Hernández for land in Ponseca (undated, but from around 1573), in AGS, CG, 361; that about the Campo de Montiel is in an unsigned and undated document among order papers from the early 1500s in AGS, CJH, 24 ant. (14 mod.). Additional information about pasture rentals can be found in Averiguación de Montealegre (1561), AGS, EH, 323; Averiguación de Andújar (1567), AGS, EH, 240; *Catalina y Diego de Pizarro* v. *Diego de Obando* (1557–8), ACHGR, 3-756-15.

21. *Mesta* v. *Diego de San Pedro* (1503–37), ACHVA, PC, FA (F), 31.

22. For the cultivation of *baldíos* to avoid high rents, see *Córdoba* v. *Almodóvar del Río* (1536), ACHGR, 3-716-3; Averiguación de Montamarta (1585), AGS, EH, 323.

23. Averiguación de Castañar (1579–84), AGS, EH, 74-11-iii; Averiguación de Pineda (1591), AGS, EH, 142-14.

24. Averiguación de El Acebrón (1597), AGS, EH, 209.

25. Averiguación de Tortuero (Uceda) (1597), AGS, EH, 189-9 bis.

26. Specific examples of municipal efforts to use public property to help pay the *millones* tax can be found in *San Sebastián* v. *Alcobendas* (1591), ACHVA, PC, FA (F), 81; Averiguación de Herguijuela (1600), AGS, EH, 360; and *Mesta* v. *Valdemoro* (1598), ACHVA, PC, FA (F), 70. See also *Actas*, XI, 472–6.

27. *Briones* v. *los hijosdalgo della* (1571–4), ACHVA, PC, FA (F), 24.

28. Averiguación de Alpera (Chinchilla) (1566), AGS, EH, 219-13; Ocampo, 'Noticias', BN, MSS 9.937, folios 64–5; Relación de corregidores, BN, MSS 9.372-Cc. 42; *Alonso de Port y sus menores* v. *Bobadilla del Camino* (1567), ACHVA, PC, FA (F), 29.

Bibliography

I. Primary sources

Manuscripts

Archivo del Ayuntamiento de Trujillo
Archivo de la Chancillería de Granada
Archivo de la Chancillería de Valladolid
Archivo General de Simancas
Archivo Histórico Nacional (Madrid)
Archivo de la Mesta (Madrid)
Biblioteca Nacional (Madrid)

Published documents and contemporary writings

Actas de las Cortes de Castilla. 1869–1918. 45 vols. Madrid: Imprenta Nacional, *et al.*

Arrieta (See Valverde [de] Arrieta)

Barbón y Castañeda, Guillén. 1628. *Provechosos arbitrios al consumo del vellón, conservación de plata, población de España y relación de avisos importantes a las cosas que en ellas nececitan de remedio, compuesto por el capitán . . .* Madrid: Andrés de Parra

Bergua, José, ed. 1968. *Refranero español; colección de ocho mil refranes populares ordenados, concordados y explicados, precedida del Libro de los proverbios morales de Alonso de Barros.* 7th edn Madrid: Ediciones Ibéricas

Castillo de Bobadilla, Jerónimo. 1608. *Política para corregidores y señores de vasallos en tiempo de paz y de guerra.* 2 vols. Medina del Campo: Christóval Lasso y Francisco García. First published 1597

Caxa de Leruela, Miguel. 1631. *Restauración de la antigua abundancia de España, o prestantíssimo único y fácil reparo de su carestía presente.* Naples: Lazaro Scoregio

Columela, Lucio Junio Moderato. 1824. *Los doce libros de agricultura que escribió en latín.* 2 vols. Trans. Juan María Alvarez de Sotomayor y Rubio. Madrid: Don Miguel de Burgos. First published in 1st century A.D.

Cortes de los antiguos Reinos de León y Castilla. 1861–1903. 7 vols. Madrid: Real Academia de la Historia

Deza, Lope de. 1618. *Gobierno político de agricultura.* Madrid: Viuda de Alonso Martín de Balboa

Escribano, Juan. 1816. Reflexiones sobre la utilidad de los bueyes y perjuicios de labrar con mulas, escritas en Madrid, año 1599. In Fray Manuel Blasco, *El amante de los labradores, o tratado de las grandes ventajas que los labradores en particular, y el Estado en general, pueden sacar del ganado vacuno; y de los gravísimos daños y perjuicios que se siguen de la cría del mular a la del caballar y a la Agricultura,* pp. 142–7. Barcelona: Dorca

Fabila, Manuel, ed. 1941. *Cinco siglos de legislación agraria en México (1493–1940)*. Mexico: Banco Nacional de Credito Agrícola

Fernández Navarrete, Pedro. 1626. *Conservación de Monarquías; Discursos políticos sobre la gran consulta que el Consejo hizo al Senor Rey don Felipe tercero*. Madrid: Imprenta Real

González de Cellorigo, Martín. 1600. *Memorial de la política necesaria, y útil restauración a la República de España, y estados de ella, y del desempeño universal de estos Reynos*. Valladolid: Juan de Bostillo

Guerra, Arcadio, ed. 1952. Ordenanzas municipales de Felipe II a Los Santos de Maimona. *Revista de estudios extremeños*, 8: 495–534

Gutiérrez de Salinas, Diego. 1600. *Discursos del pan, y del vino del niño Jesús*. Alcalá de Henares: Justo Sánchez Crespo

Herrera, Alonso de, *et al*. 1777. *Agricultura general, que trata de la labranza del Campo, y sus particularidades, crianza de animales, propiedades de las plantas que en ella se contienen, y virtudes provechosas a la salud humana*. Madrid: Don Antonio de Sancha. First published in Logroño, 1513

Medina, Pedro de. 1549. *Libro de grandezas y cosas memorables de España*. Seville: Doménico d'Robertis

Morales, Ambrosio de. 1577. *Las antigüedades de las ciudades de España*. Alcalá de Henares: no publisher

Novísima recopilación de las leyes de España. 1805–29. 6 vols. Madrid: J. Viana Razola

Ortiz Lucio, Fray Francisco. 1600? *República christiana y espejo de los que la rigen; con advertencias de algunas cosas, que conviene se remedien en las repúblicas, especialmente en lo que toca al trigo y cebada*. Madrid: Juan Flamenco

Relaciones (see Viñas y Mey)

Soria y Vera, Melchor. 1633. *Tratado de la Iustificación y conveniencia de la tassa de el pan, y de la dispensación que en ella haze su magestad con todos los que siembran*. Toledo: Juan Ruiz de Pereda

Valverde [de] Arrieta, Juan [de]. 1777. *Despertador que trata de la gran fertilidad, riquezas, baratos, armas y caballos que España solía tener y la causa de los daños y faltas en el remedio suficiente*. Included in Herrera, *Agricultura general* (above). Madrid: Don Antonio de Sancha. The Valverde work was first published in 1568

Viñas y Mey, Carmelo, and Paz, Ramón, eds. 1949–71. *Relaciones histórico-geográfico-estadísticas de los pueblos de España hecho por iniciativa de Felipe II; Provincia de Madrid; Reino de Toledo; Ciudad Real*. Madrid: CSIC

II. Secondary sources

Alvarez de Cienfuegos Campos, Isabel. 1963. Notas para el estudio de la formación de las haciendas municipales. In *Homenaje a don Ramón Carande*. 2 vols. Madrid: Sociedad de Estudios y Publicaciones. Vol. 2, pp. 3–19

Anés Alvarez, Gonzalo. 1970. *Las crisis agrarias en la España moderna*. Madrid: Taurus

Antón Ramírez, Braulio. 1865. *Diccionario de bibliografía agronómica y de toda clase de escritos relacionados con la agricultura*. Madrid: Rivadeneyra

Arco y Garay, Ricardo del. 1941. *La sociedad española en las obras dramáticas de Lope de Vega*. Madrid: Real Academia Española

Barcia, Roque. 1902. *Primer diccionario general etimológico de la lengua española*. 5 vols. Barcelona: F. Seiz

Beneyto Pérez, Juan. 1932. Notas sobre el origen de los usos comunales. *Anuario de la Historia del Derecho Español*, 9: 33–102

Bennassar, Bartolomé. 1967. *Valladolid au siècle d'or; une ville de Castille et sa campagne au XVIe siècle*. Paris: Mouton

　1969. *Recherches sur les grandes épidémies dans le nord de l'Espagne à la fin du XVIe siècle*. Paris: SEVPEN

Bishko, Charles Julian. 1963. The Castilian as plainsman: the medieval ranching frontier in La Mancha and Extremadura. In *The New World Looks at its History*, ed. Archibald R. Lewis and Thomas F. McGann, pp. 47–69. Austin: The University of Texas Press

　1978. The Andalusian municipal Mestas in the 14th–16th centuries: administrative and social aspects. In *Actas del I Congreso de Historia de Andalucía (diciembre de 1976); Andalucía Medieval*, pp. 347–74. Córdoba: Monte de Piedad y Caja de Ahorros de Córdoba

Blanco Sánchez, Rufino. 1911. Para la historia del Monasterio de Guadalupe: noticias de un códice interesante. *Guadalupe*, 5, no. 107: 326–30

Blázquez, Antonio. 1905. *La Mancha en tiempo de Cervantes; conferencia leída el día 3 de mayo de 1905 en la velada que la Real Sociedad Geográfica dedicó a conmemorar la publicación del Quijote de la Mancha*. Madrid: Imprenta de Artillería

Bloch, Marc. 1966. *French Rural History; An Essay on its Basic Characteristics*. Trans. Janet Sondheimer. Berkeley: University of California Press

Blum, Jerome. 1971. The European village as community: origins and functions. *Agricultural History*, 45: 157–78

Bosque Maurel, Joaquín. 1971. *Granada, la tierra y sus hombres*. Granada: Organización Sindical, Consejo Económico Sindical Provincial

　1973. Latifundio y minifundio en Andalucía oriental. *Estudios geográficos*, 34, nos. 132–3: 457–500

Braudel, Fernand. 1975. *The Mediterranean and the Mediterranean World in the Age of Philip II*. 2 vols. Trans. Siân Reynolds. New York: Harper & Row

Brumont, Francis. 1977. *La Bureba à l'époque de Philippe II*. Dissertations in European Economic History. New York: Arno

　1978. L'évolution de la population rurale durant le règne de Philippe II: l'exemple du nord-ouest de la Vieille-Castille. *Mélanges de la Casa de Velázquez*, 14: 249–68

　1980. La rente de la terre en Rioja occidentale à l'époque moderne. *Mélanges de la Casa de Velázquez*, 16: 237–72

Cabo Alonso, Angel. 1955. La Armuña y su evolución económica. *Estudios geográficos*, 16, no. 58: 73–136, and no. 59: 367–427

　1956. El colectivismo agrario en Tierra de Sayago. *Estudios geográficos*, 17, no. 65: 593–658

Capmany y de Montpalau, Antonio de. 1807. *Quéstiones críticas sobre varios puntos de historia económica, política y militar*. Madrid: Imprenta Real

Cárdenas, Francisco de. 1873. *Ensayo de historia de la propiedad territorial en España*. 2 vols. Madrid: J. Noguera

Carrillo, Isabel. 1970. La población y la propiedad en la Sagra de Toledo del siglo XVII al XVIII. *Estudios geográficos*, 31, no. 120: 441–64

Casco Arias, Juan. 1961. *Geobiografía e historia de Quintana de la Serena*. Madrid: Prensa Española

Castillo Pintado, Alvaro. 1961. El «Servicio de Millones» y la población del Reino de Granada en 1591. *Saibati* (Valencia), 11: 61–91

Clavero, Bartolomé. 1974. *Mayorazgo; propiedad feudal en Castilla, 1369–1836*. Madrid: Siglo Veintiuno

Concha, Ignacio de la. 1951. Consecuencias jurídicas, sociales y económicas de la reconquista y repoblación. In *La reconquista española y la repoblación del país*, pp. 207–22. Zaragoza: CSIC

Corchón García, Justo. 1963. *El Campo de Arañuelo (Estudio geográfico de una comarca extremeña)*. Madrid: Dirección General de Enseñanza Media

Corominas, José. 1954. *Diccionario crítico etimológico de la lengua castellana*. 4 vols. Madrid: Gredos

Costa y Martínez, Joaquín. 1944. *Colectivismo agrario en España; doctrinas y hechos*. Buenos Aires: América Lee. First published Madrid: Imprenta de San Francisco de Sales, 1898

Defourneaux, Marcelin. 1970. *Daily Life in Spain in the Golden Age*. Trans. Newton Branch. London: George Allen and Unwin

Delano Smith, Catherine. 1979. *Western Mediterranean Europe; A Historical Geography of Italy, Spain, and Southern France since the Neolithic*. New York: Academic Press

Díaz Aparicio, Purificación. 1963. El municipio de Pinos Genil. Memoria de Licenciatura, University of Granada

Diccionario de historia de España. 1968–9. 2nd edn, rev. and enl. in 3 vols. Directed by Germán Bleiberg. Madrid: Revista de Occidente

Domínguez Ortiz, Antonio. 1963. Los moriscos granadinos antes de su definitiva expulsión. *Miscelánea de estudios árabes y hebraicos* (Granada), 12–13, fascículo 1: 113–28

   1971. *The Golden Age of Spain, 1516–1659*. Trans. James Casey. New York: Basic Books

   1973a. *Alteraciones andaluzas*. Madrid: Narcea

   1973b. *El Antiguo Régimen; los Reyes Católicos y los Austrias*. Madrid: Alianza Editorial

Elliott, J. H. 1977. *Imperial Spain, 1469–1716*. New York: New American Library

Fernández Duro, Cesáreo. 1882–3. *Memorias históricas de la ciudad de Zamora*. 4 vols. Madrid: Sucesores de Rivadeneyra

Fernández Martín, Luis, S. J., and Fernández Martín, Pedro. 1955. *Villarramiel de Campos; datos para su historia*. Palencia: Diario-Día

Ferreras, Casildo. 1971. La Aldea del Puente: estudio geográfico de una localidad leonesa de la ribera alta del Esla. *Estudios geográficos*, 32, no. 125: 673–750

Freeman, Susan Tax. 1981. From present to past: the genealogical approach to local history. A paper presented to the Twelfth Annual Conference of the Society for Spanish and Portuguese Historical Studies. Toronto, 24–5 April 1981

García de Cortazar [y Ruiz de Aguirre], José Angel. 1969. *El dominio del Monasterio de San Millán de la Cogolla (siglos X a XIII)*. Salamanca: University of Salamanca

García Fernández, Jesús. 1952. Alcalá de Henares: estudio de geografía urbana. *Estudios geográficos*, 13, no. 47: 299–355

   1953. Horche (Guadalajara): estudio de structura agraria. *Estudios geográficos*, 14, no. 51: 193–239

   1964?. Los sistemas de cultivo de Castilla la Vieja. In *Aportación española al XX Congreso Geográfico Internacional*, Madrid: CSIC

   1965. Champs ouverts et champs clôturés en Vieille Castille. Trans. P. X. Despilho. *Annales, Economies, Sociétés, Civilisations*, 20, no. 4: 692–718

   1967. Organización y evolución de cultivos en la España del sur. Reproduced typescript. Valladolid: Dept. of Geography, University of Valladolid

   1970. *Sobre la 'agricultura de grupo' en Castilla la Vieja; el caso de un pueblo organizado en régimen cooperativo*. Valladolid: CSIC

García Sanz, Angel. 1977. *Desarrollo y crisis del antiguo régimen en Castilla la Vieja; economía y sociedad en tierras de Segovia de 1500 a 1814*. Madrid: Akal

García Terrel, Ana María. 1958. *Salduero; estudio de un municipio de los pinares sorianos del Alto Duero*. Zaragoza: Departamento de Geografía Aplicada del Instituto Elcano

G[arcía] de Valdeavellano, Luis. 1968. *Curso de historia de las instituciones españolas, de los orígenes al final de la Edad Media*. Madrid: Revista de Occidente

Garrad, K. 1956. La industria sedera granadina en el siglo XVI y su conexión con el levantamiento de las Alpujarras (1568–1571). *Miscelánea de estudios árabes y hebraicos*, 5: 73–104

Garzón Pareja, Manuel. 1972. *La industria sedera en España; el arte de la seda de Granada*. Granada: Gráficas del Sur

1974. *Diezmos y tributos del clero de Granada*. Granada: Archivo de la Real Chancillería

1978. Estructura campesina y señoríos de Granada. In *Actas del I Congreso de Historia de Andalucía (diciembre de 1976); Andalucía Moderna (Siglos XVI–XVII)*, pp. 41–49. Córdoba: Monte de Piedad y Caja de Ahorros de Córdoba

Gerbet, Marie-Claude. 1972. Les guerres et l'accès à la noblesse en Espagne de 1465 à 1592. *Mélanges de la Casa de Velázquez*, 8: 295–326

Gil Olcina, Antonio. 1971. *El Campo de Lorca; estudio de geografía agraria*. Valencia, CSIC

Glick, Thomas F. 1979. *Islamic and Christian Spain in the Early Middle Ages*. Princeton: Princeton University Press

Gómez Centurión, José. 1912. Jovellanos y las órdenes militares. *Boletín de la Real Academia de la Historia*, 60: 322–64, 379–426, 468–96; 61: 20–101, 233–314, 370–431

Gómez Mendoza, Josefina. 1967. Las ventas de baldíos y comunales en el siglo XVI: estudio de su proceso en Guadalajara. *Estudios geográficos*, 28, no. 109: 499–559

Guarnido Olmedo, Victoriano. n.d. (1969?). El repartimiento de Huétor-Tájar y su evolución posterior. Memoria de Licenciatura, University of Granada

Hamilton, Earl J. 1965. *American Treasure and the Price Revolution in Spain, 1501–1650*. Reprint edition New York: Octagon. First published Harvard University Press, 1934

Herrera Puga, Pedro. 1971. *Sociedad y delicuencia en el siglo de oro. Aspectos de la vida sevillana en los siglos XVI y XVII*. Granada: University of Granada

Higueras Arnal, Antonio. 1961. *El Alto Guadalquivir; estudio geográfico*. Zaragoza: Departamento de Geografía Aplicada del Instituto Juan Sebastián Elcano

Hopfner, Hellmuth. 1954. La evolución de los bosques en Castilla a Vieja. *Estudios geográficos*, 15, no. 56: 415–30. A translation by M. de Terán of an article originally published in *Romanistisches Jahrbuch* (Hamburg), 3 (1950): 233–53

Hoyos Sáinz, Luis de. 1947. Sociología agrícola tradicional: Avance folklórico etnográfico. *Revista internacional de sociología*, 5, no. 19: 109–131

Huetz de Lemps, Alain. 1967. *Vignobles et vins du Nord-Ouest de l'Espagne*. 2 vols. Bordeaux: University of Bordeaux

Jiménez de Gregorio, Fernando. 1950–2. La población en la Jara toledana. *Estudios geográficos*, 11, no. 39 (1950): 201–50; 12, no. 44 (1951): 527–81; 13, no. 48 (1952): 489–588

1952. El pasado económico-social de Belvis de la Jara, lugar de la Tierra de Talavera. *Estudios de Historia Social de España*, 2 (Madrid): 613–739

1964–6. La población en la zona suroccidental de los montes de Toledo. *Estudios geográficos*, 25, no. 94 (1964): 31–50; 26, no. 98 (1965): 85–125; 27, no. 104 (1966): 451–94

1971. La población en el señorío de Valdepusa (Toledo). *Estudios geográficos*, 32, no. 122: 75–112

Klein, Julius. 1920. *The Mesta; A Study in Spanish Economic History, 1273–1836.* Harvard Economic Studies, vol. XXI. Cambridge, Mass.: Harvard University Press

Laiglesia y Auset, Francisco de. 1918–19. *Estudios históricos (1515–1555).* 2 vols. Madrid: Imprenta del Asilo de Huérfanos del S. C. de Jesús

Lapresa Molina, Eladio de. 1955. Santafé: historia de una ciudad del siglo XV: su repartimiento y privilegios. Ph.D. dissertation, University of Granada.

Le Flem, Jean-Paul. 1965. Les Morisques du Nord-Ouest de l'Espagne en 1594 d'après un recensement de l'Inquisition de Valladolid. *Mélanges de la Casa de Velázquez,* 1: 223–43

1967. Cáceres, Plasencia y Trujillo en la segunda mitad del siglo XVI. *Cuadernos de Historia de España* (Buenos Aires), pp. 248–99

1973. Miguel Caxa de Lleruela, un défenseur de la Mesta? *Mélanges de la Casa de Velázquez,* 9: 373–415

López Gómez, Antonio. 1954. Valdelaguna: colectivismo agrario en las montañas burgalesas. *Estudios geográficos,* 15, no. 57: 551–67

López Martínez, Nicolás. 1962. La desamortización de bienes eclesiásticas en 1574: carta-memorial de Fr. Hernando del Castillo, P. P., a Felipe II. *Hispania* (Madrid), 22, no. 86: 230–50

Malefakis, Edward E. 1970. *Agrarian Reform and Peasant Revolution in Spain; Origins of the Civil War.* New Haven, Conn.: Yale University Press

Maravall, José-Antonio. 1973. La imagen de la sociedad expensiva en la conciencia castellana del siglo XVI. In *Mélanges en l'honneur de Fernand Braudel.* 2 vols. Toulouse: Privat, pp. 369–88

Martín Galindo, José Luis. 1958. Actividades agrícolas y ganaderas en Maragatería. *Estudios geográficos,* 19, no. 70: 55–85

n.d. (mid- or late 1950s). *Artículos geográficos sobre la provincia de León.* Valladolid: Miñón

1961. Arcaísmo y modernidad en la explotación agraria de Valdeburón (León). *Estudios geográficos,* 22, no. 83: 167–222

Martín Gil, Tomás. 1938. De la vida del campo extremeño en el siglo XVI. *Revista del Centro de Estudios Extremeños,* 12, no. 1: 27–44; no. 2: 187–202; no. 3: 309–23

Mauro, Frédéric. 1969. *Europa en el siglo XVI; aspectos económicos.* Trans. Alberto González Troyano. Barcelona: Labor

Méndez Plaza, Santiago. 1900. *Costumbres comunales de Aliste.* Madrid: Imprenta del Asilo de Huérfanos del Sagrado Corazón de Jesús

Merino Alvarez, Abelardo. 1915. *Geografía histórica del territorio de la actual provincia de Murcia desde la Reconquista por D. Jaime I de Aragón hasta la época presente.* Madrid: Imprenta del Patronato de Huérfanos de Intendencia e Intervención Militares

1926. *La sociedad abulense durante el siglo XVI; la Nobleza. Discursos leídos ante la Real Academia de la Historia en la recepción pública del Señor Don Abelardo Merino Alvarez el día 11 de abril de 1926.* Madrid: Imprenta del Patronato de Huérfanos de los Cuerpos de Intendencia e Intervención Militares

Morell Terry, Luis. 1888. *Estudio sobre las causas de la decadencia de la agricultura en la provincia de Granada y medios para remediarla.* Granada: Indalecio Ventura

Nader, Helen. 1977. Noble income in sixteenth-century Castile: the case of the marquises of Mondéjar, 1480–1580. *Economic History Review,* 2nd series, 30: 412–28

1979. *The Mendoza Family in the Spanish Renaissance, 1350 to 1550.* New Brunswick, NJ: Rutgers University Press

1981. Rural credit in early modern Estremera. A paper presented at the Twelfth Annual Conference of the Society for Spanish and Portuguese Historical Studies. Toronto, 24–5 April 1981

Naranjo Alonso, Clodoaldo. 1922–3. *Trujillo y su tierra; historia; monumentos e hijos ilustres*. 2 vols. Trujillo: Sobrino de B. Peña

1929. *Solar de conquistadores; Trujillo, sus hijos y monumentos*. 2nd ed. Serradilla [Cáceres]: Sánchez Rodrigo

Nieto, Alejandro. 1964. *Bienes comunales*. Serie J, Monografías Prácticas de Derecho Español, vol. XL. Madrid: Revista de Derecho Privado

Núñez Noguerol, Gregorio. 1969. La población y las formas de aprovechamiento de la Alpujarra oriental. *Estudios geográficos*, 30, no. 115: 241–305

Oriol Catena, José. 1935–7. La repoblación del Reyno de Granada después de la expulsión de los moriscos. *Boletín de la Universidad de Granada*, 7 (1935): 305–31, 499–528; 8 (1936): 139–57, 417–44; 9 (1937): 81–117

Ortega Alba, Francisco. 1973. Evolución de la utilización del suelo en el Subbético de Córdoba. *Estudios geográficos*, 34, no. 132–3: 595–662

Ortega Valcárcel, José. 1966. *La Bureba; estudio geográfico*. Valladolid: Universidad de Valladolid

Orti Belmonte, Miguel Angel. 1954. Cáceres bajo la Reina Católica y su Camarero Sancho Paredes Golfín. *Revista de estudios extremeños*, 10: 193–328

Palomeque Torres, Antonio. 1947. Pueblas y gobierno del señorío de Valdepusa durante los siglos XV, XVI y XVII. *Cuadernos de historia de España* (Buenos Aires), 8: 72–139

Pérez-Crespo, Maria Teresa. 1969. Vicálvaro: contribución al conocimiento de los contornos de Madrid. *Estudios geográficos*, 30, no. 116: 455–87

Pérez Díaz, Victor. 1969. *Emigración y sociedad en la Tierra de Campos; estudio de un proceso migratorio y un proceso de cambio social*. Madrid: Estudios del Instituto de Desarrollo Económico

Pérez de Urbel, Fr[ay] Justo. 1951. Reconquista y repoblación de Castilla y León durante los siglos IX y X. In *La reconquista español y la repoblación del país*, pp. 127–62. Zaragoza: CSIC

Phillips, Carla Rahn. 1979. *Ciudad Real, 1500–1750; Growth, Crisis and Readjustment in the Spanish Economy*. Cambridge, Mass.: Harvard University Press

Planchuelo Portalés, Gregorio. 1954. *Estudio del Alto Guadiana y de la Altiplanicie del Campo de Montiel*. Madrid: CSIC

Polaino Ortega, Lorenzo. 1967. *Estudios históricos sobre el Adelantamiento de Cazorla*. Seville: published by the author

Ponsot, Pierre. 1969. En Andalousie occidentale: les fluctuations de la production du blé sous l'Ancien Régime. *Etudes rurales*, no. 34: 97–112

Quirós, Francisco. 1965. Sobre geografía agraria del Campo de Calatrava y Valle de Alcudia. *Estudios geográficos*, 26, no. 99: 207–30

Quisenberry, K. S., ed. 1967. *Wheat and Wheat Improvement*. No. 13 in the series *Agronomy*. Madison, Wisconsin: American Society of Agronomy

Represa, Amando. 1979. Las comunidades de villa y tierra castellanas: Soria. *Celtiberia*, no. 57 (Soria: Centro de Estudios Sorianos), 7–17

Rodríguez Amaya, Esteban. 1951. La tierra en Badajoz desde 1230 a 1500. *Revista de estudios extremeños* 7, nos. 3–4: 395–497

Rodríguez Arzua, Joaquín. 1963. Geografía urbana de Ciudad Rodrigo. *Estudios geográficos* 24, no. 92: 369–435

Rodríguez y Fernández, Ildefonso. 1903–4. *Historia de la muy noble, muy leal y coronada villa de Medina del Campo, conforme a varios documentos y notas a ella pertinentes*. Madrid: San Francisco de Sales

Ruiz Martín, Felipe. 1967. La población española al comienzo de los tiempos modernos. *Cuadernos de historia; Anexos de la revista Hispania*, 1: 189–202

Ruiz Martínez, Alfredo. 1972. Las variaciones del paisaje geográfico en un municipio de la Hoya de Guadix: Darro. Memoria de Licenciatura, University of Granada

Sáenz Lorite, Manuel. 1974. El Valle del Andarax y Campo de Níjar: estudio geográfico. Ph.D. thesis, University of Granada

Salinero Portero, José. 1970. *Diezmo rural agrícola; Avila, 1557–1840*. Madrid: Universidad Central

Salmerón, Fray Pasqual. 1777. *La antigua Carteia, o Carcesa, hoy Cieza, villa del Reyno de Murcia*. Madrid: Joachín Ibarra

Salomon, Noël. 1964. *La campagne de Nouvelle Castille à la fin du XVIe siècle d'après les 'Relaciones topográficas'*. Paris: SEVPEN

1965. *Recherches sur le thème paysan dans la 'comedia' au temps de Lope de Vega*. Bordeaux: Feret & Fils

Sánchez-Albornoz, Claudio. 1963. The Frontier and Castilian Liberties. In *The New World Looks at its History*, ed. Archibald R. Lewis and Thomas F. McGann, pp. 27–46. Austin: The University of Texas

Sermet, Jean. 1943. La costa mediterránea andaluza de Málaga y Almería. *Estudios geográficos*, 4, no. 10: 15–29

Silva, José Gentil da. 1967. *Desarrollo económico, subsistencia y decadencia en España*. Trans. Valentina Fernández Vargas. Madrid: Ciencia Nueva

Slicher van Bath, B. H. 1963. *The Agrarian History of Western Europe, AD 500–1850*. Trans. Olive Ordish. London: Edward Arnold

Smith, Robert S. 1966. Medieval agrarian society in its prime. In *Agrarian Life of the Middle Ages*, 2nd edn, pp. 432–48. Vol. 1 of *Cambridge Economic History*. Cambridge: Cambridge University Press

Terrasse, Michel. 1968. La région de Madrid d'après les «Relaciones topográficas» (Peuplement, voies de communication). *Mélanges de la Casa de Velázquez*, 4: 143–72

Toro, Mariano José de. 1849. *Memorial de las vicisitudes de Almería y pueblos de su río, con relación a su estado agrícola, desde la reconquista en 1490 hasta la presente época*. Almería: D. Vicente Duimovich

Torre, José de la. 1931a. De otros tiempos: cómo se solucionaba una huelga de campesinos en el siglo XVI. *Boletín de la Academia de Ciencias, Bellas Letras y Nobles Artes de Córdoba*, 10, no. 31: 103–4

1931b. Fernando de las Infantas, músico y teólogo. *Boletín de la Academia de Ciencias, Bellas Letras y Nobles Artes de Córdoba*, 10, no. 32: 159–211

Ulloa, Modesto. 1963. *La Hacienda Real de Castilla en el reinado de Felipe II*. Rome: Librería Sforzini

Valdeavellano (see G[arcía] de Valdeavellano)

Vassberg, David E. 1974. The *tierras baldías*: community property and public lands in 16th century Castile. *Agricultural History*, 48, no. 3: 383–401

1975. The sale of *tierras baldías* in sixteenth-century Castile. *Journal of Modern History*, 47, no. 4: 629–54

1977. Studies of rural life in early modern Castile: History and the other disciplines. *Newsletter of the Society for Spanish & Portuguese Historical Studies*, 3, nos. 8–9: 247–52

1978. Concerning pigs, the Pizarros, and the agro-pastoral background of the conquerors of Peru. *Latin American Research Review*, 13, no. 3: 47–61

1980. Peasant communalism and anti-communal tendencies in early modern Castile. *The Journal of Peasant Studies*, 7, no. 4: 477–91. Spanish version pub-

lished as 'El campesino castellano frente al sistema comunitario: usurpaciones
de tierras concejiles y baldías durante el siglo XVI'. Trans. Manuel S. Miranda.
Boletín de la Real Academia de la Historia, 175, no. 1 (1978): 145–67

    1983. *La venta de tierras baldías; el dominio público y la corona en Castilla durante el
siglo XVI*. Trans. David Pradales Ciprés, Julio Gómez Santa Cruz, Gilbert B.
Heartfield, and Gloria Garza-Swan. Madrid: Servicio de Publicaciones,
Ministerio de Agricultura

Vela Santamaría, F. Javier, and Marcos Martín, Alberto. 1978. Las grandes
ciudades campesinas de Andalucía occidental en el siglo XVI: el caso de
Jerez de la Frontera. In *Actas del I Congreso de Historia de Andalucía (diciembre de
1976); Andalucía Moderna (Siglos XVI–XVII)*, pp. 403–7. Córdoba: Monte de
Piedad y Caja de Ahorros de Córdoba

Villegas Molina, Francisco. 1972. *El Valle de Lecrín; estudio geográfico*. Granada:
CSIC

Vincent, Bernard. 1970. L'expulsion des Morisques du Royaume de Grenade et
leur répartition en Castille (1570–1571). *Mélanges de la Casa de Velázquez*, 6:
211–46

Viñas y Mey, Carmelo. 1941. *El problema de la tierra en la España de los siglos XVI–
XVII*. Madrid: CSIC

Weisser, Michael R. 1971. Les marchands de Tolède dans l'économie castillane,
1565–1635. Trans. Joëlle Mathieu. *Mélanges de la Casa de Velázquez*, 7: 223–36

    1976. *The Peasants of the Montes; the Roots of Rural Rebellion in Spain*. Chicago:
University of Chicago Press

White, Lynn, Jr. 1964. *Medieval Technology and Social Change*. Oxford: Oxford
University Press

Yun Casalilla, Bartolomé. 1980. *Crisis de subsistencias y conflictividad social en Córdoba
a principios del siglo XVI*, no. 19 of the Colección de Estudios Cordobeses.
Córdoba. Excma. Diputación Provincial de Córdoba

Index

absentee landlords: and *presura*, 11, 13; and estate management, 104–5; and alleged obstruction of arable agriculture, 106–7; refuse to permit new plantings, 157; noble from Córdoba, 103; urban investors as, 147; peasants as, 141; in Plasenzuela, 139; *see also* rentals, *complant* contracts

acorns, 36–8, 43, 62, 70, 88, 118

acotamientos, see enclosures

Adobe, 75

Adobezo, 127 n. 3, 169

Aguilafuerte, 35

Ajalvir, 30

Alaejos, 49, 50, 53

Albánchez de Ubeda, 28

alcabala, 32, 221–3

Alcalá de Henares (city), 44, 109, 111

Alcalá de Henares, Tierra of, 46

Alcalá, duke of, 66, 126

Alcántara, Order of, 59, 114, 118

Alcázar de San Juan, 61

Alcuéscar, 168

Alexander VI, Pope, 221

Alfonso X, 29, 30

Alfonso XI, 67, 127

Alhama, 123

alhóndigas, 194; *see also pósitos*

Aliaguilla, 29, 30, 31, 82

alijar, 9

Almaraz, 87

Almazul, 50

Almería (city), 21, 99, 123

Almería (province), 87

Alpera, 196, 226

Alpujarras: First Rebellion of (1499–1500), 176; Second Rebellion of (1568–70), 124–5, 178; Christian resettlement of, 124–5

Altamira, Rafael, 19

Alvala, 69

Andalucía: dominated by noble estates, 103; bourgeois investment in, 149; and medieval ranching, 152; inflation and agricultural boom in, 164; proportion of *labradores* and *jornaleros* in, 144; increase in latifundism in, 164; percentage of *abadengo* villages in, 110; migrant workers in, 196–7; *baldío* sales in, 174; and export market, 185; plague in, 198; locust plagues in, 199; severe weather and famine in, 198–9; proverbial famine of, 227

Andarax, 178

Andarax River, 9

Andújar: ordinances of, 11, 39–40, 72; and *derrota de mieses*, 16; commons of, 26–7, 30; *montes* of, 72; *fueros* of, 126; immigration to, because of communal attractions, 234 n. 7

Anés Alvarez, Gonzalo, 163–5

Antequera, 123

año y vez, see rotation

aparcería sharecropping, *see* rentals

arable: common, 40–52, 84–9; in Lorca, 45; intermunicipal, 60–1; conflict with pastoralism, 152–8; expansion of, 151–8, 160–1, 172, 180–1, 203; converted to viticulture, 164; *see also* vineyards and orchards, *huertas*

Aragon, kingdom of, 74

arbitristas, 161–3, 192, 205, 209, 228; *see also* Barbón y Castañeda, Guillén; Caxa de Leruela, Miguel; Deza, Lope de; Escribano, Juan; Fernández Navarrete, Pedro; González de Cellorigo, Martín; Gutiérrez de Salinas, Diego; Moncada, Sancho de; Soria y Vera, Melchor; Valverde de Arrieta, Juan de

Arconda, 137

Arcos de la Frontera, 22, 130

Arévalo, 16, 186

Arjona, 16, 71–3, 74, 170, 190

Arnedo, 82

Arquillos, 149

arrieros, 159, 182, 196–7

INDEX

censos al quitar, 118, 205–6, 208, 210
censos enfitéuticos, 22, 94–5, 105, 113, 118, 120, 206–7, 211, 212
censos perpetuos, 22, 109, 125, 127, 205–6
cercas, 129, 171; *see also huertas*
Cerezo de Mohernando, 60
cerramientos, see enclosures
Cervantes, Miguel de, 145
Cervariza, 237 n. 3
Chancillerías: and suits over community property, 16, 38, 57, 65, 69–70, 78, 82; and the Law of Toledo, 78; and the Mesta, 80–3, 154; and suits between new and old towns, 167; of Granada, 171, 172, 190; of Valladolid, 225
Charles V: and *propios*, 23; and commons, 67; and the Mesta, 80; and the *encabezamiento* system, 221; and *villazgos*, 166; financial straits of, 169; and *servicios*, 223–4; pro-pasture decrees of, 154; and the Fuggers, 153; and military order pastures, 153; and new plowings, 153; and the wool industry, 153; and the *tasa*, 191; sells patents of nobility, 91; sells jurisdictions, 93, 98, 111; and regrating of pasture rentals, 216; sells military order property, 117; and municipal property, 127
Chinchilla [de Monte Aragón], 29, 75
Christian agriculture clashes with Moslem agriculture, 176–83
church, 109, 209, 220–1; *see also* land-ownership, tithe, monasteries, clergy
Ciempozuelos, 57
Cieza, 23, 29, 189
Cifuentes, 195
Ciudad Real, 92, 101, 115–16, 132, 141, 148, 207
Ciudad Rodrigo, 100, 215
Clement VII, Pope, 117
clergy: 57, 114, 192–3, 205, 222, 224–5
climate, 38, 161, 179, 181, 197–200
Cobos, Francisco de los, 111
Coca, Tierra de, 174–5
Código de las Partidas, see Siete Partidas
colonies (overseas), 80, 85–6, 163–5, 219, 225
Columella, Lucio Junio Moderato, 151, 158
Comares, 177
commons: types of, 26–64; inequality in use of, 34, 47; payment of fee for use of, 9, 33–4, 38, 52–3; personal service for use of, 153; eligibility for use, 33–6, 48–9; parcelization of, 51–2; expansion of, 35; succession and tenure for use of, 44–6, 50–3; registration of arable, 45–7; periodic allotments of, 47–52, 84–5, 88;

arable, 84–9; and Mesta, 79–83; fences and buildings on, 47, 69; and the seigneurial system, 63–4, 83–4; importance of free use of, 85; intermunicipal, 57–64, 126–7; international, 64; protected against local officials, 69–70; defended by municipalities, 107; usurpations of, 26, 53, 67, 101–2, 107, 169–70, 224–5, 234 n. 8; become private property, 66, 127; attacked, because of population growth, 157, 172; seigneurs restrict use of, 93; *see also montes, dehesas boyales, ejidos, baldíos*, community property
community property: devices to protect, 25–42, 70–9; usurpations of, 64–79, 89, 101, 105–6, 107; importance of, in Golden Age, 83–6; institutions transported to colonies, 85–6; in eighteenth–twentieth-century Spain, 86–9; in the rest of Europe, 89; and the nobility, 108–9; laws to protect, 64–79, 127; eroded by *baldío* sales, 172–5; eroded after *villazgos*, 167–9; attracts immigrants, 234 n. 7; *see also* commons, *propios, baldíos, montes*
complant contracts, 132–4
conquistadores, 103, 147
convents, *see* churches, monasteries and convents, names of specific convents
conversos, 148
Córdoba (city): and litigation over reciprocal pasture rights, 16; *montes* of, 40, 22, 43; estates of nobles from, 103; anti-plowing laws of, 106–7; wealthy *hidalgo labrador* of, 108–9; *pósito* of, 208; fruit orchards around, 129; *baldíos* of, plowed, 155; labor unrest in, 196–7
Córdoba (province), 92, 101, 208, 224
corregidores, 76–7, 100, 154–5, 169, 182–3
Cortes of Castile: and shortage of horses, 31; and intercommunalism with Portugal, 64; and boundary inspections, 77; and the Mesta, 80–1; and the sale of municipal offices, 67; and the despoliation of community property, 67; and the Law of Toledo, 77; and the *montes*, 40; and enclosures, 169–70; wants no new vineyards, 164; wants grain exports banned, 164; and the crisis in the kingdom of Granada, 178; on priests and commons, 114; and ecclesiastical land-ownership, 112–13; and the *tasa*, 191–2; and peasant indebtedness, 205, 207, 208–9; and interest rates, 206; and rental rates, 212; and the poverty of *labradores* in the 1590s, 228; and the ox–mule debate, 162–3; and Arrieta's work, 162; and anti-mule laws, 163; and

253

industry, deforestation caused by, 158; *see also* manufacturing, domestic
inflation, *see* price inflation
infurción, 97
inheritance, 5, 41, 44–5, 104, 211
Inquisition, 178
insect plagues, 199
inter-arboreal planting, 43
intercropping, 132
interest rates, *see* debt
intermunicipal commons, *see* commons, intermunicipal
intermunicipal ordinances, 35
inter-planting, 43, 132
investment: and growth of private land-ownership, 88; in land by nobles, 102–4, 148; by *conquistadores*, 103; in livestock preferable to land, during Reconquest, 152; by bourgeoisie in agriculture, 137, 147–50, 164, 171–2; profitability of land, 218
irrigation: and water rights, 10, 54–5; ditch conveys property rights, 12; of *baldío* lands, 12; of *prados*, 32–3; of common arable, 45; project foiled in Lorca, 106; of lands apportioned to Christians in kingdom of Granada, 124–5; of *huertas*, 128; by Moriscos, 177; and annual cropping, 200; *see also* water, wells
Isabella, Queen, 21–2; *see also* Ferdinand and Isabella
Iscar, 26, 234 n. 8
Iznatoraf, 195

Jaén, 26, 199, 210
Jaén, Bishop of, 193
Jerez de la Frontera, 47, 50, 55, 79, 202, 213–14
jornaleros, see laborers
jurisdiction: proverbs about, 98; *señorío* and *realengo* compared, 97–9; and nobility, 92; purchased by bourgeoisie, 164; *realengo* defined, 92; seigneurial, 63, 92–4, 98; causes suits between lords and towns, 98; towns purchase return to *realengo* status, 99, 237 n. 3; of military orders, 115–17; ecclesiastical, 109–13, 166; *see also* seigneurial privileges, *villazgos*
juros, 111, 117, 147

Klein, Julius, 79, 236 n. 28

La Alberca, 37
La Aldea del Puente, 87–8
La Armuña district, 86, 88, 136
La Axarquia district, 177

La Baneza, 187
laborers: hired by *labradores*, 107, 142, 245; youth as, 108; in vineyards, 113; and work levies, 113; hired by priests, 114; and *complant* contracts, 132–4; and ownership of vines and *huertas*, 133–4; poor peasants forced to become, 138; owning land, 143; proportion of, 143–4; from rural areas work in cities, 148; Moriscos as, 182; rise in wages of, 194–5; migrant, 165, 195–7; strike in Córdoba, 196–7; and *pegujalero* and *senarero* contracts, 216–17; salaries and the tithe, 220; and excessive taxation, 223
La Bóveda, 58
labradores: defined, 142; of Quesada, 85; noble, 107–9; as part-time laborers, 143; proportion of, 143–4; wealthy, 145; poor, 145–7; draft animals owned by, 142–7; bankrupted in economic crisis, 149; harassed by Mesta, 154–5; destroyed by *baldío* sales, 175; Moriscos as, 177; and the *tasa*, 192; forced to become migrant workers, 196; indebtedness of, 205, 207–10; destroyed by *censos al quitar*, 210; billeting troops, 225–7; food and dress of, 228; poverty of, in 1590s, 228–9; profit from economic crisis, 228; *see also* peasants; landownership, peasant
La Bureba district: landownership in, 103, 111, 135, 137–8, 140, 149; *labradores* and *jornaleros* of, 142–4; poverty of, 146; *arrieros* from 159; oxen and mules in, 160; crop yields in, 203; rent payments in, 214–18
La Campana, 66
La Iruela, 60
La Jara district, 217
La Mancha region, 141, 152, 186, 189, 195, 199
land grants: royal (to colonists), 8, (to towns), 19–21, 99–100, (to church), 109, (to nobility), 99–100, 122, 124, (to nobility usurped),102–3,(to commoners), 99–100, 127–8, (to military orders), 114; by military orders, 115–16; by nobility, 19, 93, 125–6, 128; by municipalities, 126–31; by individuals to church, 110–11; to peasants, 120–34
landlords, absentee, *see* absentee landlords
landownership: classification of, 2; distribution among estates, 90; as investment, 88, 102–4, 137, 147–50, 164, 171–2, 218; social prestige of, 147, 149–50; forbidden to outsiders, 149; changes in, during economic crises, 148; increasing privatization of, 64–83, 86–9, 126–7, 169–76; and *baldío* sales, 173–5; bourgeois,

rentals: of arable in Tejeda de Tiétar, 10; of common lands, 49, 53; of draft animals, 48–9; discourage colonization, 94; of pasture, 105, 215–16; and absentee landlords, 106; and latifundios, 105–6; of monastery lands, 113–14; for payment in kind, 118; for cash, 118; of military order lands, 118, 210; in Moslem Spain, 124, 212; of vineyards, 133; to complement land owned, 139; of bourgeois property, 148; and use of the *baldíos*, 155; burden of payments, 164–5, 207, 217–18, 229; and the *derrota de mieses*, 172; advantages and disadvantages of, 211; short-term leases preferred by landowners, 211–12; long-term leases and peasant prosperity, 136–7; fixed-payment leases, 213–16; sharecropping, 212–14; 216, and soil quality, 214; contracts specifying rotational practices, 214; *pegujalero* contracts, 216; *see also censos enfitéuticos*

Repariegos, 16
repartimientos, 20 121–6, 129
Repoblación, 6, 12, 109–10, 115, 178–81
Represa, Amando, 58, 62
Retuerto, 111
Ribas de Jarama, 148
Rio Gordo, 177
Rioja district, 213
Robledillo de Mohernando, 60
Rodríguez Arzua, Joaquín, 100
Romans, 6, 54, 100, 109, 158, 204
rotation: biennial, 14, 200; annual cropping, 43–4, 50; of common arable, 50, 67; and compulsory planting districts, 73, 88; of private property supervised by municipal government, 127; system encourages extreme parcelization of land, 140; system encourages use of mules, 159; systems of northern Europe and the Mediterranean compared, 161; system of Castile transplanted to kingdom of Granada, 180; triennial, 200–1, 215; longer fallow periods on poor soils, 201; practices required in certain lease contracts, 214; *see also derrota de mieses*, fallow
rozas, 39–40, 54, 93, 152
Ruanes, 139–40, 142
Rubiales, 111, 136, 218
Rublacedo de Yuso, 137
Rus, 126–7, 148–9

Sabiote, 127
Sahagún, monastery of, 212
Salamanca, 43, 186
Salduero, 86
Salomon, Noël: on community property, 19–20; on feudal service, 96; on noble landownership, 103; on military orders, 115; defines *labrador*, 142; on ecclesiastical jurisdiction, 110, 111; on peasant landownership, 135; on proportion of *labradores*, 143–4; on *villazgos*, 168; on peasant debts and emerging capitalism, 205; on the tithe, 217, 220; on land rents, 217; on peasant taxpayers, 219, 229
Salvaleón, 9, 69
San Millán de la Cogolla, monastery of, 112
San Román de Hornija, 45, 46
San Sebastián, 37
Santa Clara, convent of, 110
Santa Cruz de la Sierra, 33
Santa Cruz de Mudela, 171
Santa Fe, 35, 122
Santa Inés, 107
Santamaría del Rey (?), 186
Santiago, Order of: founded, 114; and *Repoblación*, 12; and intermunicipal commons, 59, 61; special privileges of *comendador* of, 189; lands of, sold as *baldíos*, 118; land of, rented, 118, 215; charges fee for use of acorns, 119; *tierras cadañeras* in lands of, 232 n. 38
Santisteban, 58
Santo Domingo de Silos, Merindad de, 62
secano of Lorca, 45
Segovia, 34–5, 136, 158, 182, 187, 189
Segovia, Tierra of: intermunicipal commons of, 58; *censos enfitéuticos* in, 95; mule-use in, 160; requires walled *huertas*, 171; tax-free market of, 187; regulates workday and wages, 195; declining crop yields in, 203; *pegujalero* contracts in, 216
Segura de la Sierra, 9, 126
seigneurial privilege: and communal rights, 15, 63–4; in *dehesas boyales*, 34; reduced by Ferdinand and Isabella, 92; restricts common rights, 93, 97; and tribute, 93, 94, 96–7, 110, 128, 174; and personal service, 110, 113; *see also* jurisdiction, seigneurial; nobility
senarero agreements, 217
señorío, see jurisdiction, seigneurial
Sepúlveda, Tierra de, 222–3
Serradilla, 75
servicio y montazgo, 225
servicios, see taxes
Seville: *derrota de mieses* in, 17; *propios* of, 21; ecclesiastical property in, 111; Order of Santiago lands near, 118; *vecinos* of, invest in agriculture, 171–2; and the export market, 185; severe weather and poor crops in, 198–9
Sierra Morena, 36–7, 39
Siete Partidas, or *Código de las Partidas*, 7, 22, 121